The Tenth Muse

Illustrations by William McLaren
Cover illustration: Botticelli's *The Wedding Feast* (The Bridgeman Art Library)

H.C.L.
dedicated
The Tenth Muse
to
Angie Laycock
The Editors
dedicate
this new Edition
to
the grandchildren
and
great-grandchildren of the Author

The Tenth Muse

A GOURMET'S COMPENDIUM

HARRY LUKE

Edited by Peter and Michael Luke

The Rubicon Press

The Rubicon Press
57 Cornwall Gardens
London SW7 4BE

Third, revised edition

© Peter and Michael Luke, 1992

A catalogue record for this book is available from the British Library.

All rights reserved. No part of this publication may be reproduced, stored in a retrieval system, or transmitted, in any form or by any means, electronic, mechanical, photocopying or otherwise, without the prior written permission of the copyright owner.

Printed and bound in Great Britain by Biddles Limited of Guildford and King's Lynn

CONTENTS

PREFACE TO THE THIRD EDITION		vii
INTRODUCTORY CHAPTER		1
GLOSSARY OF CULINARY TERMS		33
RECIPES:		
I	Hors d'Oeuvres; Egg, Rice and other Entrees; and Savouries	37
II	Soups	65
III	Fish	87
IV	Poultry, Game and Meat	107
V	Vegetables	141
VI	Sauces, Salad Dressings, Salads and Herbs	171
VII	Sweets	199
VIII	Drinks	225
CONCLUDING CHAPTER: DON'TS		243
APPENDIX: A NOTE ON SAINT ZITA, PATRON OF COOKS		247
INDEX:		249

    A. *Recipes and Ingredients*

    B. *Places of Origin*

THE MUSES

The nine beautiful daughters of Zeus and Mnemosyne according to myth were the inspiring goddesses of learning and the arts. Their names:

CLIO (The Muse of History)

THALIA (Comedy)

MELPOMENE (Tragedy)

EUTERPE (Music)

TERPISCHORE (Dancing)

URANIA (Astronomy)

CALLIOPE (Poetry)

POLYMNIA (Hymn)

ERATO (Erotic Poetry and Mime)

The tenth, but unacknowledged Muse is, according to the author of this book, NECTAMBROSIA, inspiration for the wine and food of the Gods.

PREFACE

In the year 1905 three young men, two of them just down from Oxford, were lying in the heather on the sunny brow of one of the Brecon Beacons. The two graduates were Harry Pirie-Gordon,[1] whose parents lived at nearby Crickhowell, and his friend Harry Luke. The third was an older man of somewhat sinister aspect called Frederick William Rolfe, also known as Baron Corvo.

Resting from the exertion of climbing the hill this - probably hungry - triumvirate were amusing themselves by inventing imaginary savouries.

"On a slice of Bath Chap", declaimed the orotund Pirie-Gordon, "trimmed to fit a disc of fried bread of the size of half a crown, lay a mushroom baked in milk as a base for a piece of cold grouse as large as a thumbnail and a quarter of an inch thick."

"But", objected Corvo, with his penchant for recondite words, "the mushroom must be isomegethic[2] with the disc and five drops of lemon-juice should be squeezed upon the grouse just before serving." Now it was Luke's turn to add his twopenn'orth.

"No", he said, "that would be too sharp. Let us add, rather, half a mulberry."

Luke also claimed that while still up at Oxford he quelled an affray between members of his college, Trinity, and their neighbours, Balliol, by offering the antagonists hot sausages spiked with Worcestershire sauce which he happened to be cooking at the time. So it is easy to see from an early age in which direction he was going, both as a diplomat and as the author of a book about food.

The Tenth Muse, first published in 1954, has since passed into three editions and has come to be regarded as a minor classic, which is to say that it is still being quoted and written about in the 90s. In fact the late Cyril Ray, that food and wine man for all seasons, included 'Harry Luke' items in the last two issues of his long-running classic, *The Compleat Imbiber*. Further, Mr. Patrick Reyntiens writing in *Harpers & Queen* (1986) describes *The Tenth Muse* as, ". . . the most entertaining book ever written on cuisine."

Mrs. Elizabeth David, rightly designated by Cyril Ray as the *grande dame* in her day of English writers on food, had for many years been an admirer of *The Tenth Muse* - and, indeed, of its author. In her delightful book, *An Omelette and a Glass of Wine*

---

[1] The late Mr. Harry Pirie-Gordon, OBE, DSC
[2] Not to be found in the Shorter Oxford Dictionary.

(1984), she wrote at some length about them both. "Sir Harry," she says, "has collected recipes from British Residencies and Government Houses, from their chatelaines, their cooks - cooks Goanese and Polynesian, cooks in South American capitals, cooks of French princes and Brazilian countesses, of Turkish Grand Viziers and Patriarchs of the Syrian Orthodox Church - and in setting down his recipes Sir Harry has acknowledged the source of each and every one . . . Few authors . . . provide the stimulus, the improbable information, the traveller's tales, the new visions which to me makes this book a true collectors' piece."

So what sort of a man was this Harry Luke, scholar, traveller, author and gourmet, such as he is known to have been? Referring to his autobiography, *Cities and Men*, that wit and scholar, Sir Ronald Storrs, said of his friend, "Harry Luke's parents lavished upon their only son the education almost of an eighteenth-century nobleman: not only Eton and Oxford but such long and continual spells of continental and transatlantic travel that he entered the public service with altogether exceptional qualifications."

Lawrence Durrell, the novelist and poet, knew him in Cyprus and described their friendship in his famous work of non-fiction, *Bitter Lemons*. "Sir Harry Luke," he wrote, "whose gentleness and magnanimity of soul were married to a mind far reaching and acute, who was fantastically erudite without being bookish, and whose life had been one of travel and adventure. . ."

Perhaps, with regard to the man, the *Dictionary of National Biography* may be permitted the final word: "Luke," it says, "was one of the great line of British proconsuls who regarded themselves as entrusted with a mission which sprang less from Whitehall than from conscience and culture. . . combined with a prismatic cosmopolitanism." It is this very cosmopolitanism that provides the lard with which these gastronomic memoirs are so richly laced.

And since it is held that we are what we eat, it has been thought meet to give 'Nectambrosia', the tenth Muse, a third unveiling - and in new raiment.

The Editors would like to thank Anthea Page and Juanita Homan of The Rubicon Press for making this possible; and June Tobin and Elizabeth Godfrey for contributing their culinary expertise.

PL and ML

INTRODUCTORY CHAPTER

1

Exotic as some of this collection of dishes are, in so far as their provenance is concerned, they will be found to demand few ingredients not readily procurable in Great Britain. I, therefore, offer no recipe for an omelette of ostrich eggs, although I have seen one, by the chef of a former Bey of Tunis. I shall not prescribe

> 'the heads of parrots, tongues of nightingales,
> the brains of peacocks and of ostriches';

I shall not preface any of them (as I might feel it my duty to do if writing for Venezuelans or for Salvadoreans in Lent) with the injunction 'take an iguana', or 'shell two armadillos'. Sir Osbert Sitwell gives somewhere a description of a roast saddle of iguana served to him in a circle of its own eggs, which he says he found 'good, *very* good', to eat. He goes on, indeed, to admit that the iguana's appearance is repellent to many; and, as I am definitely ranged among the many, I feel myself absolved from competing. Yet it is not really more repellent than the baskets of dried *cuero reventado* (pork crackling) you may buy at Ecuadorean food stalls, and it is certainly less so than the chunks of pachydermatous sun-dried and salted alligator meat I have seen offered for sale in the markets of the Guatemalan Highlands. For similar reasons I refrain from quoting from my *South Seas Diary* the manner in which to prepare a dish of water-snakes for a 'chiefly' banquet on the island of Taveuni in Fiji, although they tin rattle-snakes in the United States, so snakes must have their fanciers. They probably taste much like eels.

'Alas,' exclaimed Hilaire Belloc in an unforgettable poem -

> *'Alas! What various tastes in food*
> *Divide the human brotherhood!*
> *Birds in their little nests agree*
> *With Chinamen but not with me . . .'*

To what even more immortal lines might Belloc have been inspired could he have foreseen a banquet, held in Hong Kong in 1957, for twenty visiting Chinese *aficionados* of the classical Manchu school of gastronomy!

This banquet - so it was claimed and we may well believe it - was recognized to be the most lavish display of the traditional *cuisine* of China since the fall of the Manchu dynasty in 1912. The repast, consisting of thirty-two main courses, began with a dish of subtle piquancy to whose principal ingredient two hundred ducks contributed their tongues. One hundred large frogs were needed merely for the flavouring of the next. There followed - served in silver tureens - a delicacy known as 'Magnificent Evergreen': the kidneys of chickens enveloped in the lining of hand-picked bamboo shoots. Sucking-pig and Sharks' Fin Soup, even though the soup took a fortnight to prepare, were mere banalities beside the 'Dragon Crystals' (composed of the internal organs of a dried rare Siberian fish marinated until they gleamed like precious stones) and the culminating *pièce de résistance* in the form of Bears' Paws. The Paws had previously to be soaked for ten days in cold water so that the hairs could be pulled out one by one and the skin peeled off in such a manner as to avoid the slightest bruising of the flesh. Hot water might have acted more quickly, but would, it appeared, have impaired the flavour.

Such compositions of highly particularized appeal I must leave to others; nor, conversely, do I prescribe the T-bone steaks of the *tavernas* of Buenos Aires, which have the same sort of relation to a *filet mignon* as the grilled sturgeon steaks I have nibbled at in Baku have to a filleted sardine. Even their Baby Beef (pronounced 'bebbibif') steaks attain what a European would regard today as formidable dimensions. No; I observe, I hope, in these 'gastronomic sorties' of mine (as one reviewer has called them) a proper sense of proportion. My daring stops short of including items such as the one - derived from the more generous era of William IV - beginning with the simple words: 'take an ordinary sized cow, cut it up in joints'.[1] It is not surprising that from the same source comes a recipe for Beef à la mode directing the cook to 'choose a piece of thick flank of a fine heifer or ox'.

2

One of the essential aspects of eating intelligently is the pursuit and achievement of variety to the extent that our environment allows. Not to all, of course, is it given to be able to vary the daily bill of fare: not, for example, to the Eskimo in the extreme north of the American Continent, whose medium of cooking, when he cooks at all, is blubber; not to the wretched Alakaluf in the extreme south of it, who has to subsist on the raw sea-urchins and mussels for which his women plunge naked into the icy Patagonian fjords; not to the inhabitants of the Gilbert and Ellice Islands in that remote part of the Pacific where the International Date Line crosses the equator, whose low and narrow coral atolls produce only the coconut and the pandanus palms; not to some West African bush-men, whose digestive organs are exclusively attuned to rice, and to one kind of rice at that.

Now those of us who live in more bountiful and sophisticated regions have no excuse for such monotony. We need not, to be

---

[1] I owe this gem to a Cookery Book of 1836 in the possession of my cousin by marriage, Mrs. John Sterndale-Bennett. The Recipe is for a mart, that is to say, a fattened cow or ox killed about Martinmas and pickled, in the words of the Recipe, 'for winter store, much used in the Highlands and other lone parts of Scotland'.

sure, emulate the fabulous recipe for olive into ortolan into lark into thrush into quail into partridge into capon into duck into goose into turkey into peacock, each one stuffed inside the next. But a dull dog, missing so much, is he who refuses to vary his breakfast eggs and bacon, perfect dish though this is, with an occasional Dover sole or even the modest fresh or kippered herring, or now and again to combine with his bacon a home-made sausage, a grilled kidney, a mushroom or two.

When as a youth I paid my first visit to the United States, I had the good fortune to be the guest for some months of an elderly couple who were as wealthy as they were generous and hospitable. That is to say that they were very, very rich. But they had never learned the beauty of variety. When they liked a thing, whether a dish or a play or whatever it might be, they liked it. On the evening of my arrival in New York I was introduced to Lobster Newburg and thought it the most perfect synthesis of ambrosial flavours I had ever tasted. But, after eating it for sixty nights in succession, I could scarcely look any lobster in the face, and it took me years of abstinence to enjoy Lobster Newburg again. Then, with the change of season, there followed a six weeks' unrelieved course of another marine delicacy, Planked Shad, resulting (on my part) in that same deplorable satiety which ever dogs, as we are told by those who claim to know, the heels of pleasure. Not thus are the good foods of this world to be enjoyed.

Still less the not so good foods. I was to experience a different form of culinary monotony early in the First World War when serving in H.M. cruiser *Doris* off the coasts of Asiatic Turkey. In January 1915 my Captain had occasion to send me from one part of the theatre of operations to another, for which purpose I was given passage in that ancient sloop, H.M.S. *Proserpine*. The *Proserpine's* Commanding Officer was determined to do his passenger as well as his circumstances permitted, but supplies were short just then in the Eastern Mediterranean and salt pork was all he had to offer. Undeterred, he laid on a five-course dinner and we worked our way through a meal of clear soup, croquettes, roast, *mousse* and mince on toast, composed exclusively of a substance that became progressively more thirst-making and repellent.

Naturally it is in the Imperial and Royal Courts of pre-austerity Europe that one would expect to find the most complete achievement of variety, in the confection of individual dishes as in the composition of the menu. As regards the former, no other recipe I have seen competes in width of range combined with subtlety of blending with the famous State soup of the Habsburgs. From the time of the Empress Maria Theresa's father Charles VI to that of her great-great-grandson Francis Joseph this masterpiece was offered at the Court Balls of the Hofburg in Vienna and the Royal Castle of Buda, served in the delicate white and gold cups of the Vienna porcelain factory. I append its description as an item of historic no less than gastronomic interest:

'The first stocks were made from three kilograms (about 6½ lb.) of veal or ham, three kilos of mutton, five or six kilos of venison and other game, roast in butter and then boiled; others were made from eight calves' feet and two cowheels converted into jelly, four white cabbages stewed with three and a half kilos of smoked and fresh pork, two kilos of maize seeds, two kilos of chestnuts, three quarts of lentils, one kilo of pearl barley, and a few French carrots baked with sugar.

'When ready, these stocks were laid on ice for four hours, so that every fraction of grease could be removed.

'A bouillon was then made from beef and veal bones, mushrooms and other vegetables, and this liquid of a hundred quarts was cleared by the addition of five kilos of hashed beef, two kilos of hashed ox liver, and five litres of white of egg. While the bouillon was boiling it was strengthened by the addition of three cooked fowls (specifically mentioned as "old"), two ducks, one turkey, four pigeons, five partridges, two pheasants, one goose, and two wild duck.

'The concocting of the soup took two days and two nights. The personnel was directed by a first-class Court chef, and consisted of three second-class chefs, three kitchen-maids and three scullions, all chosen for their endurance and conscientiousness since the creation of the various stocks lasted for thirty-two hours without a pause.

'The bouillon itself was boiled on a slow fire from eight to ten hours, the stocks and salt being added just before it was ready. When the finished product had been drained through muslin bags it was poured into small cauldrons. These were carried into the ballrooms and transferred to porcelain jugs, from which the soup was poured into china cups for the guests, serving from 1,000 to 2,500 persons.'

Two world-shattering wars in the first half of this century have put an end to splendour on a scale such as this; but let me also quote the menu of the banquet offered by President Lebrun in the Galerie des Glaces at Versailles to Their Majesties King George VI and Queen Elizabeth during their State visit to France in July 1938 as evidence of what could still be done up to the eve of the second catastrophe (see p. 7).

Not only is this the perfectly composed *dîner de circonstance* both in food and drink, since the order of the meats should be from the more substantial to the lighter, while the wines should be served in the reverse order. It also illustrates the fact that no temporary reverses of fortune can destroy French supremacy in the art of living. Not wrongly are the words *'fluctuat nec mergitur - she may rock but she will not sink'* - the motto of the armorial barque of the city of Paris. This is not to say that in time of war culinary planning must not make way for that of the soldiers. 'The Marshal of Soubise,' jeered Frederick the Great, 'is always followed by a hundred cooks. I am always preceded by a hundred spies.' But no country other than France could have produced a character such as the late Monsieur Maurice Sailland, *soi-disant* 'Curnonsky, Prince des Gastronomes'. The Prince of Gastronomers ate his way through goodness knows how many wars and died in 1956 of a fall from his balcony at the age of 83. His works include a book on the erotic side of cookery, as do those of Norman Douglas, who also died at 83.

No less ample than the French President's banquet but, as one might expect, less subtle in composition is the menu which I copied and translated from an obscure exhibit in the King Ludwig II Museum in Ludwig's island Palace of Herrenchiemsee, the Bavarian Versailles. It was the menu for one of the ceremonial banquets[2] which the romantic and in the end demented monarch - the friend and patron of Wagner - was in the habit of setting before his Knights of S. George on the high days of his senior Order of Chivalry (see p. 8).

---

[2]The preference for sparkling red burgundy (very non-U) and the other sweet cups, wines and liqueurs which he drank seem to reflect yet another dimension of this monarch's personality. *Eds.*

MENU

Les Perles Fraiches de Sterlet
Le Melon Frappé
Le Xérès Mackenzie 'Amontillado Grande Reserve'

Les Délices du lac d'Annecy à la Nantua
Le Chevalier Montrachet 1926

Les Mignonnettes d'agneau Trianon
Le Magnum du Château La Mission Haut Brion 1920

La Timbale de Cailles Farcies à la Talleyrand
Hospices de Beaune 'Cuvée Charlotte Dumay' 1915

Les Aiguillettes de Caneton Rouennais à la Montmorency
Salade Gauloise

Le Cortons Grancey 1910
Magnum du Château Mouton Rothschild 1918
Le Granité au Lanson 1921

Le Suprême de la Poularde de Bresse au Beurre Noisette
avec les Pointes d'Asperges à l'Etuvée
Le Château d'Yquem 1921

Les Truffes à la Mode de Périgord
Le Magnum du Château Latour 1914
La Mousse Glacée Singapour
Les Pêches de Montreuil Princesse
Les Frivolités

Le Magnum de Champagne Pol Roger 1911
Le Magnum de Champagne G.H. Mumm 1911
Le Champagne Louis Roederer 1914

Le Champagne Veuve Cliquot 1900
Le Champagne Pommery 1895

MUNICH
24 April, 1877

*

Turtle Soup
Plovers' eggs - Caviare - Radishes
S. George's *Spiesse* (a Mixed Spit, so to speak)
Salmon, Sauce Hollandaise
Turkey with new vegetables
Lendenbraten (Sirloin of Beef) with stuffed mushrooms
Saucissons à la Richelieu, haricots verts
Calves' ears with truffles
River Crayfish, Herb Sauce
Maiwein[3]
Roast Snipe and Capons
Asparagus, Melted Butter
Pineapple au Riz
Petits Fours
Strawberry, Vanilla and Apricot Ices

*

Wines
Sherry
Château Yquem
Hermitage Mousseux
Champagne
Tokay, Forster Freundstück, Ausbruch 1874
Liqueurs[4]

They must have been good trenchermen, those Knights of S. George; and they certainly look, in the paintings of one or two of these functions in the same Museum, as if they were thoroughly accustomed to doing themselves well, notwithstanding the full dress robes of light blue silk and mantles of heavy velvet in which

[3] *Maiwein* is a Hock Cup flavoured with sweet woodruff (Lat. *Asperula Odorata*, German *Waldmeister*).
[4] King Ludwig's favourite liqueur, as we are told by his cook Theodor Hierneis in *The Monarch Dines* (Werner Laurie, London, 1954), was *sparkling* brandy.

they feasted. In this respect King Ludwig differed from another monarch of modern times, an even greater exponent of the art of living, who preferred to enjoy his meals in comfort.

It was King Edward VII, who simplified private dining in England by causing champagne to be served throughout the meal in the place of a different wine to each course. A very sensible choice for a short, informal dinner, as sensible as his substitution on such occasions of the dinner-jacket for the tail-coat. But for the meal of many courses the Continental fashion of serving a succession of the appropriate wines is surely to be preferred. It may surprise some of those born since the First World War to learn until how recently the dinner of many courses survived in private houses in England, even on merely semi-formal occasions. Here, for example, is the menu, almost unbelievable at the present time, of a man's dinner attended by my father in a private house in London in King Edward's lavish reign:

148 PICCADILLY
Dîner du 22 Juin, 1904

*

Tortue Liée
Consommé de Boeuf froid
Whitebait à la Diable et au Naturel
Pain de Saumon à la Riche
Sauces Genevoise et Hollandaise
Cailles Braisées Printanières Demi-Glace
Côtelettes d'Agneau Rachel
Canetons à la Voisin au Coulis d'Ananas
Salade des Gobelins
Hanche de Venaison à l'Anglaise,
Sauces Porto et Cumberland
Granit au Champagne
Poulardes rôties flanquées d'Ortolans
Asperges d'Argenteuil, sauce Mousseline
Oeufs de Faisan Parmentier
Croûte à l'Ananas
Coupes Petit-Duc
Petites Friandises
Fondants au Chester
Petites Glaces au Café et Pain bis Vanillées
Petites Gaufrettes

I should not think the Emperors Nero and Vitellius could have done much better.

Among my own happiest gastronomical memories of France are those Sunday luncheons at Voisin's, last survivor of the great restaurants of the Second Empire, during my parents' regular winter sojourns in Paris at the turn of the century. Our choice on these occasions was quite simple and generally more or less as follows. It would begin with a *petite marmite* or *croûte au pot*, followed by a Châteaubriand steak grilled as only Voisin's chefs know how - crisp and brown on the outside, juicy and red within - topped by its pyramid of butter and chopped parsley and accompanied by its all-important seasoning of Sauce Béarnaise and by *pommes soufflées*. Then would come a Brie, *coulant* to just the right degree, eaten with toasted *pain de ménage*, and in conclusion a French pear, sometimes in the form of the *Cuisse-madame* whose piquant name may be due to its qualities, defined by the experts as '*micassante, musquée et sucrée*'. The meal would be *arrosé*, as the French say, with a contribution from what was in those days the finest collection of clarets in the world.

How different was the luncheon at which my friends the Dudley Honors and I were entertained by one of the leading Spanish Colonial families of Quito, Ecuador's historic capital on the equator 9,000 feet above sea-level. The menu comprised:

Raw fish (*serviché*) pickled in lemon juice, mixed with raw sliced onion;
tamalés of chicken, eggs and maize, seasoned with *aji* sauce (composed of hot chillies, black pepper-corns and garlic) and steamed in canna leaves;
a yearling pig *(chancho)* with lots of crackling, the pig's head adorned with horns cut out of large chillies;
a Sorbet of Passion Fruit.

Before the wines there was served a refined variety of *chicha*, the maize beer of the Andean Indian. Our host, don Francisco Uribe, confessed that he himself preferred French cooking and that the menu had been designed in deference to my interest in local dishes. He called it an 'atomic bomb lunch.' It was.[5] Perhaps I might mention here the name the Fijians have for those fiercely hot little red peppers so popular in Spanish America. They call them 'goddammits', a highly appropriate appellation. A little unfair, on the other hand, is their name for the harmless mushroom, *vakururu ni Tevoro*, which means 'the Devil's umbrella'.

Another memorable South American meal of my experience was a luncheon at the Buenos Aires Jockey Club, whose cooking was probably as good as that of any other Club in the world. The luncheon began with iced cantaloupe melon accompanied by raw smoked ham, and continued with *Oeufs Pochés Polignac*. The saddle of lamb was served with a *Sauce Périgourdine* compounded of truffles and sour cream; the sweet was *Figues Vendôme*, an ice-cream with peeled fresh figs mixed in with it. This admirable Club was first suppressed by the former Dictator Peron, then burned down by his *descamisados*.

3

The primary object of this book is to make known to those who will buy it some of the dishes which have particularly appealed to me in my sojourns in many parts of the world. In a much-travelled existence I have not merely wandered through but have lived in every continent, and have tasted many foods. This collection is admittedly an entirely individual one and makes no claim to any sort of method or comprehensiveness. Still less does it pretend to be a manual of cookery on even the most modest scale.

I have, as I say, chosen for this collection some of the dishes I have encountered in a long lifetime of (I hope) intelligent eating and drinking which have pleased me the most. But there is another, less agreeable aspect of the practice of eating internationally. Writing as a former member of the Colonial Service, I venture to utter the conviction that the paymasters of British Government officers stationed in foreign parts have little or no realization of the nastinesses we are sometimes called upon to swallow as a part of our

[5] And see Recipe 142.

official duty in order to avoid giving just offence to our hosts. And more particularly is this the case with those who have attained a seniority requiring them at times to be the guest of honour at, say, an Oriental feast.

My years in the South Seas would certainly have been gastronomically pleasanter did I not dislike the taste of the coconut in whatever form it is eaten or drunk. That is a small matter; but a bold man is the Occidental who will swallow without flinching that morsel so honourable in Arab lands, the eye of a sheep or goat, even if he is constrained to do so *ad majorem regis gloriam*. I for one would certainly have preferred the brain of a barbecued squirrel, which is, or used to be, the portion of the guest of honour at picnics in the Deep South of the United States.

Some truly revolting substances have been set before me in the course of my career in the Near East and Far West, although seldom anything worse than the New Caledonian dinner recorded by J.C. Furnas[6] as consisting of roast flying fox (a large bat), white grubs dug out of rotting tree stumps and uncleaned pigeon guts stewed with rice. I can take Kangaroo Soup with pleasure (especially if cold and jellied), and cherish nostalgic recollections of Toheroa from my five visits to New Zealand; but I never really fancied, while serving in the South Pacific, the broth made of the roe of the sea-slug or *bêche-de-mer*. Nor even that most bizarre of all sea foods - as highly appreciated by the local Europeans as it is by Pacific Islanders themselves - the *mbalolo*.

What is a *mbalolo*?

'The *mbalolo* (I quote from my *Islands of the South Pacific*[7]) is an annelid. What is an annelid? An annelid, explains the encyclopaedia, is "a segmented worm constituting a major phylum of coelomate invertebrate animals". In plain language the *mbalolo* is a thin jointed worm about eighteen inches long, which lives several fathoms deep in the fissures of the coral reefs fringing some of the Fijian and Samoan islands. From these reefs it rises twice a year with mathemat-

[6] In *Anatomy of Paradise*, Gollancz, London, 1950.
[7] Harrap, London, 1962.

ical precision to die in the propagation of its species. The late Sir Basil Thomson described it as "a transparent pipe ... mere living vermicelli". What actually rises to the surface, just before dawn on the days fixed by sun and moon, is the spawn of these creatures, the female spawn moss-green, the male reddish-brown. So the fanciers in their boats are ready with their receptacles to scoop up as much of the stuff as they can in the short time available, for within an hour the sacs burst and the fertile milt floats away to provide the next generation of *mbalolo*.'

My own introduction to the processes of eating, so to speak, on duty took place as far back as the winter and spring of 1907-8, in the last months of the reign of Abdul Hamid II as absolute ruler of Turkey. With my Oxford friend Harry Pirie-Gordon and his parents, with whom I was making a prolonged caravan tour in the eastern provinces of the Ottoman Empire, I was staying in the most magnificent of the Crusaders' Syrian castles, the noble Krak des Chevaliers which the Arabs call Qalat al-Hosn.

Our host was the Qaimaqam (Commissioner) of the District, whose capital and residence were within the castle *enceinte*. When the two sheep killed in honour of our arrival had been cooked (which meant boiled for so long that they could be dismembered with the hand, as no eating utensils were then used in those parts), we squatted on the floor round the vast brass dishes on which the animals were served whole. Our host having pulled the best (*i.e.* the fattest) pieces off the carcasses for his guests, and then helped himself, he proceeded to pick out the juiciest morsels of the mutton off his own plate, roll them into gigantic pills with the rice, onion, pine-kernels, cinnamon and garlic with which the sheep were stuffed, consolidate them in the fat and then place the resultant bolus firmly in our mouths. I must admit that when later we entertained the Qaimaqam in our camp we amused ourselves, and apparently pleased the Qaimaqam, by popping suitably kneaded bits of bully-beef, which was all we had to offer, from our plates into his mouth.

Another embarrassing feature of Oriental hospitality is the belief entertained in parts of the East that politeness requires the host to stuff his guests to the verge of suffocation. Politeness similarly requires the guest to absorb what is pressed upon him. The following story used to be told of the Oriental sweetmeat *baqlawa*, a rather sticky confection of pastry and honey highly appreciated in the Levant. In the reign of Queen Victoria an Ottoman Grand Vizier once gave a dinner in Constantinople to the British Ambassador of the day. The dinner was ample, and by the time the sweet had arrived - it was *baqlawa* - the Ambassador could eat no more.

'Supposing,' asked the Grand Vizier with apparent irrelevance, observing that his guest had passed the dish, 'that you were in a very crowded apartment and that your Queen wished to enter, what would you do?'

'I would press against the others,' said the Ambassador, 'and make room for her somehow.'

'That is exactly what you must do,' retorted the Grand Vizier, 'for the *baqlawa*, who is the Queen of Sweets.'

But there is a limit to even the Turk's capacity for politeness. When a Turkish guest has been gorged to the extent that he can chew but no longer swallow, he will gasp a final plea for mercy in the terse and homely saying: *'Yemek sizin, qarn bizim* - the food is yours but the belly is mine.'

Nor is the practice of stuffing the guest wholly unknown farther west. Take Malta, for example. The official residence of the Lieutenant-Governor of that former bastion of the British Empire, I had the honour to occupy for eight years, was the charming early eighteenth-century Palace of Dar il-Lyuni (House of the Lions), built as the country residence of an art-loving Grand Master and situated 3 miles out of Valetta in the parish of Santa Vennera. This parish is served by excellent Capuchin friars, who lead the lives of austerity prescribed by their Founder. But on one day in the year, the feast-day of S. Vennera, their parochial patron saint, they let themselves go and invite their friends and neighbours, among whom they were kindly wont to include me, to a blow-out justly named the *'tremenda'*. Unfortunately the parochial *festa* falls in the hot season of the year at the end of July, a circumstance which throws an additional strain on its participants. On the last occasion on which I attended a *'tremenda'* I broke down, I recall, at the penultimate of the seventeen items on the menu, a dish of winkles; but my A.D.C. stayed the course.

It was my fortune in 1920, when I was British Chief Commissioner in the three Trans-Caucasian Republics of Georgia, Armenia and Azerbaijan, to be entertained at many typical Caucasian banquets, a process that required on the part of the stranger some training and a certain corporal elasticity if it was to be undergone without disaster. How the Georgian officers of those days retained their greyhound figures despite the quantities they ate and drank was a mystery I could explain to myself only by means of the vigorous *pas seuls* they would execute between courses.

These banquets, which never got under way until at least two hours after the time for which one had been bidden, began with cold *zakuski* (hors d'oeuvres), eaten standing and washed down with small glasses of vodka. The *zakuski* were always so appetizing that the uninitiated were apt to leave insufficient accommodation for what was to follow. Fresh caviare straight from Baku, bears' hams, mushrooms steeped in wine, smoked river-trout, salmon and tongues and every other conceivable savoury dish, were an irresistible temptation to the unwary, largely thanks to the fact that good vodka (for there are many grades, ranging from wheat vodka to that made of wood pulp) is the world's perfect apéritif. That is to say that it creates and stimulates an appetite which, even if artificially induced, at least never flags while the process continues and is never known - at all events in my experience - to result in the least suggestion of a hangover provided that only the best vodka is used.

One then passed into another room to sit down to the hot *zakuski*, which were an ample meal in themselves. They consisted first of pheasant[8] or partridge soup in which one soaked large game pasties handed round separately; next of the delicious variety of salmon-trout found only in lovely Lake Gyökché on the borders of Georgia and Armenia and aptly known as *ishkhan*, the Armenian word for 'prince';[9] then (the menu in the hot *zakuski* rooms of Tiflis was nearly always the same) of kidneys stewed in sour cream and a Madeira-type wine from the Crimea. And it was only after this more than adequate preparation, as the Western European might suppose, that one entered the dining-room and sat down to the real meal of the evening.

[8]The word 'pheasant' is derived from the Georgian river Phasis, classical name for the present Rion.
[9]cf. Recipe 121.

At this stage it was the amiable custom of one's Georgian hosts to drink - to the accompaniment of cries of *Allah verdi*, the Turkish and Tatar for 'God has given' - the health of the visitors in a pony-glass of wine, which had to be lowered without heel-taps by both toaster and toastee and demanded quite definite powers of endurance on the part of the visitors if the hosts, as in the case of a military mess, were many. For each host claimed, and exercised, his privilege. My friend Prince Napoleon Murat, great-grandson of Joachim Murat, Napoleon's Marshal and subsequently King of Naples, and grandson on his mother's side of the last Queen of Mingrelia, told me in Tiflis - he was then a General in the Georgian Army - that when he left the French Army to go to Russia as an officer of the Imperial *gardes à cheval*, his new Russian brother-officers welcomed him at a banquet which lasted uninterruptedly for two nights and the intervening day.

Apropos of Russian meals, I was once charged in 1915 - I was then serving on the Naval staff of Admiral Rosslyn Wemyss (afterwards Admiral of the Fleet Lord Wester Wemyss) in the Eastern Mediterranean - with taking some much-needed supplies of flour, sugar and the like as a gift from my Admiral to the great Russian monastery in the monastic Republic of Mt. Athos. Now the Russian monks of Mt. Athos never eat meat, wherein they differ from their Greek, Serb, Bulgar and Rumanian *confrères*, who abstain only during the prescribed seasons of feasting. But the Abbot of the vast Rossikon, which then housed no fewer than 5,000 monks, was determined to do what he could to show his appreciation of the Admiral's timely help. He raised steam and laid on for our party a fourteen-course dinner within the limitations of his monastery's rules. Not all the dishes were exclusively vegetarian in the strictest sense, for several consisted of fish as well as, of course, of caviare, which is permitted even in Lent. But they contained no particle of meat, yet were varied, intriguing and uniformly delicious. At the composition of many of them we could barely guess; but the dinner was a revelation of what could be done by monks - or, indeed, by anyone - on an exclusively fish, vegetable, fruit and flour basis.

I partook of another interesting *maigre* repast in the course of a journey which a party of four of us were making forty years later, in 1955, in Northern Syria and the southernmost province of Turkey, now known as the Hatay.

Our venerable host was an old friend of mine in the person of the Patriarch of that ancient Oriental Christian body, the Syrian Orthodox (sometimes called the Jacobite) Church; I had known him many years earlier in Palestine or Iraq, when he was still a Bishop. His Beatitude was now of considerable age, a noted Oriental scholar gifted with a sense of humour; he was entitled the Mar (Lord) Ignatius Aphram I. This particular tour was, so far as I was concerned, a re-tracing (by more modern means of transport) of a route along which Harry Pirie-Gordon and I had ridden almost half a century earlier with our caravan of horses, pack-mules and tents in the course of the expedition already mentioned. On this occasion I was halting once again in the city of Homs, the classical Emesa, where the Patriarch had his seat and insisted on entertaining our quartet at a formal luncheon although we were in the middle of Lent.

His Beatitude overcame the consequential difficulties as triumphantly as had the Russian Abbot in Mount Athos surmounted those of his monastic discipline. The hors d'oeuvre (appealing, I must admit, to an Eastern rather than to a Western palate), consisted of a cold *purée* of *aubergines* mixed with onion, garlic and sesame oil; the entrée was a pilav of admirably crisp rice garnished with the white truffles abounding at the proper season of the year in these regions at the junction of the Desert and the Sown. The main course was excellent fresh fish from the Lake of Homs a few miles away; dessert took the forms of crystallized shaddock-peel and of the Syrian Orthodox speciality called 'manna', a sort of nougat of pistachio nuts bound together with the resin of an aromatic tree that grows north of Mosul.

His Beatitude himself provided a nice touch not so much with the previous half-century as with an even earlier age: after the coffee he smoked his cigarettes from a *qaliun*, a tiny pipe affixed to the end of a stem more than a yard long. A young deacon with sprouting beardlet applied the matches as required. Painters of the Settecento have sometimes depicted turbaned Pashas lolling luxuriously on their divans in fur-lined pelisses as these pipes are lighted for them by bowing attendants. It was pleasing to see some features of the process surviving into the second half of the twentieth century.

The best cooked meals I have ever, in a fairly wide experience, eaten in the East were those which were served when I was staying, in 1924, with Said Beg, the hereditary Mir (Prince) of the Yezidis or Devil-Worshippers, and his formidable mother the Khatun Meyan, at his castle of Ba Idra north-east of Mosul. All the dishes were Oriental and were served on trays of tinned copper, unaccompanied by knives, forks or spoons; the flat round bread of the country took the place of these. Generally Eastern viands, many of which might otherwise be palatable, are spoiled - for me, at all events - by being cooked in sheep's tail fat or in *samné*, a form of clarified butter resembling the Indian *ghi*. But here, in this fastness of the worshippers of Satan on the marches of Kurdistan, were produced for us meals with which not the most fastidious Western palate could have found a fault. Their merits were enhanced by the circumstance that for picturesque interest the *mise en scène* could not have been bettered. After the dishes were cleared away, the Mir's gloriously apparelled bodyguard, the one a Yezidi, the other an Assyrian, would hand round a *chibuq* filled with pungent Kurdish tobacco, the mouthpiece a singularly noble piece of dark-brown amber.

Thirty-two years later, in the spring of 1956, when I had the good fortune to revisit the Yezidis at Ba Idra, I found to my astonishment that the Khatun was still alive at about ninety and clear in her recollection of the details of my stay in 1924. A sauté of *haricots verts* and whole chicken livers at the luncheon was evidence that the *cuisine* was still up to standard.

Another eastern meal I recall with interest was that set before me by the Chelebi of Konya when I visited that high Islamic dignitary in 1913. Konya, the ancient Iconium, is situated in the heart of Asia Minor, and the Chelebi of Konya was the hereditary head of the Mevlevi Order of Dervishes, popularly known in the West as Dancing Dervishes; together with the other Dervish Orders in Turkey it was suppressed by Kemal Atatürk in 1925. But in the Ottoman Empire it was the privilege and function of the Chelebis, who were the lineal descendants of the Founder of their Order in the thirteenth century, to gird the Sultans of Turkey on their accession with the Sword of Osman, a ceremony which was the Ottoman equivalent of a coronation; so that they were very great Lords indeed.

On the soft turf of the Chelebi's country house, under the shade of poplar-trees, a table was spread; and for nearly two hours a Dervish attendant brought and removed a bewildering number of courses, all contained in tinned copper dishes from which one helped oneself directly with one's fork. Their order was something as follows, meats, vegetables and sweet dishes being interspersed with pleasant inconsequence:

>Grilled pieces of mutton *(kebab)*
>Meat patties *(bürek)*
>A sweet pastry with honey *(baqlawa)*
>Stuffed *aubergines*
>Vegetable marrows stuffed with rice
>Stuffed tomatoes
>A sweet rice pudding with cream
>Stewed okras
>A sauté of mutton and vegetables
>Pilav
>Pears stewed in their skins
>Melons

In addition, there were side-dishes of cheese, salad and *pimientos* (sweet peppers).

But even these feasts pale beside that offered by an hospitable English Consul in Aleppo to the officers of a small English squadron which put into the harbour of Alexandretta in the year 1676. The visit was recorded by a convivial Royalist Chaplain, R.N., the Reverend Henry Teonge; and foremost among the entertainments prepared for the squadron was, he says, 'a treate of our Consull's providinge; but such a one as I never saw before. The perticulars whereof you may see below:

>A DISH OF TURKEYS   A DISH OF TARTS
>A PLATE OF SAUCEAGES
>A DISH OF GELLYS   A DISH OF GAMMONS AND TONGS

19

A BISQE OF EGGS
A DISH OF GEESE   A DISH OF BISCOTTS
A PLATE OF ANCHOVIES
A DISH OF GREEN GEESE
A GREAT DISH WITH A PYRAMID OF MARCHPANE
A DISH OF HENS
A DISH OF HARTICHOCKS
A PASTY   A DISH OF MARCHPANE IN CAKES
A DISH OF SAUCEAGES
A PLATE OF HERRINGS
A DISH OF TURKEYS
A PLATE OF ANCHOVIES

4

I have selected the menu quoted above from countless others I might have chosen to illustrate my argument, because the particular banquet for which it was devised, although held in an eastern setting, was composed of English dishes with the English lavishness of the period, and thus brings me to the second object of this book. And this second object is to plead, if only by implication, for the more *intelligent* preparation of food by British cooks and housewives. Let me hasten to say that I am not one of those who can find no good in British cooking. On the contrary, I contend that some English and Scots dishes are, when well prepared, among the world's better foods. I have already hinted at the delights of an English breakfast, holding as I do that breakfast can be the best meal of the day, especially in the country, where one is the more likely to have the leisure to enjoy it.

I refer, I need hardly add, not to breakfast of the joyless, dyspeptic toast-coffee-and-, it may be, cereal-or-fruit-juice type, nor to the scarcely more satisfying Continental variety. I refer least of all to the so-called breakfasts gulped down by the proppers-up of American drug-store counters, which are about as mechanical a form of refuelling as is filling the tank of one's car at a petrol pump. No, I refer to the honest-to-God English breakfast of tradition. For not only does breakfast follow the longest fast; it is, or it should be, the indispensable preparation for the labours of the day. Is not the octogenarian Lord Palmerston reported to have consumed as his earthly *viaticum* on the morning of his journey to the next world a breakfast of pork chops?[10]

Pork chops may not be everybody's conception of the ideal breakfast; but it is sad to think that few are likely to see again the sideboard laden with that noble array of breakfast dishes sizzling gently on the heater: the grilled fresh herring, the fried whiting swallowing his tail, the finnan haddock, the kedgeree, then the scrambled eggs, the home-made sausages, the kidney and bacon; while in the background loom temptingly the cold bird and the tongue - not one of those compressed and tinned tongues made to be carved sideways in meagre shavings, but a tongue glazed, arched, upright and generous.

Here may I mention parenthetically that the most delicious (if also the richest) tongues I have ever eaten are the smoked tongues of Lapland reindeer to which I was introduced in Finland. Less tempting to me, though not to the citizens of Narvik, are the fresh cods' tongues that flood the fish markets of northern Norway during the cod-catching season in the Lofoten Islands.

The few Civic and City Company dinners I have been privileged to attend have revealed the heights to which the more elaborate English cooking can rise; while Trinity College, Oxford ('my most kindly nurse' as 'Q' with piety described her in the dedication of the 1906 *Oxford Book of English Verse*) long ago taught me how good it is still possible for a College table to be. Just how well composed a Trinity banquet can be may be judged from the menu of the 1959 'Domus Dinner', a springtime annual repast attended by the Fellows and Honorary Fellows:

White Burgundy:　　　　　Huîtres au Naturel
　Corton
　Charlemagne
　1951　　　　　　　　　　　　　　—

　　　　　　　　　Tortue Claire

[10] For a nine-meat-course dinner despatched by Palmerston in his eighty-first year, shortly before his death, cf. vol. IV of G.E. Buckle's *The Life of Benjamin Disraeli*, p. 422.

Moselle:
   Zeltinger
   Himmelreich
   1949

                Truite Saumonée à la Colbert

                —

                Poulet Sauté Hongroise

Claret:
   Ch. Cheval
   Blanc 1947

                Petits Pois au Beurre
                Pommes de Terre Duchesse

                —

Champagne
   Pommery &
   Greno 1949

                Jambon de York Braisé
                Salade Trinity[11]

                —

                Ananas Georgette

                —

                Copeaux Favorite[12]

Port:
   Warre 1920

                —

Madeira:
   Bual 1849

                Dessert

Cognac:
   Fine Old
   Demelle's

                —

As regards the sister University I recall with nostalgic satisfaction the occasions when I had the good fortune, as a friend of the regretted Stephen Gaselee, to be bidden to his August Bank Holiday week-end parties at Magdalene. The blend, as composed by Gaselee for these congenial and convivial gatherings, of the eighteenth-century dishes prepared by the Magdalene cook with the host's all but eighteenth-century Madeira, seasoned with the spiced wit of Ronald Storrs, remains with me a happy and characteristic memory of that original (also in the French sense), friendly, versatile, erudite scholar-*bon vivant*.

    [11]Cf. Recipe 305.
    [12]Pieces of Gorgonzola wrapped in thin rashers of bacon and then in cigar-shaped puff pastry, glazed with egg and baked.

It is no wonder that English food *can* be so good, because nowhere else in the world can the raw material be bettered: the butter and cream, the vegetables, the fruit, the birds, the meat, the fish. What more delicious viands than a grilled salmon steak; than a saddle of lamb with fresh marrowfat peas; than the undercut of a sirloin of beef with a lightly made Yorkshire Pudding and horseradish cream sauce; than a green gosling stuffed with *foie gras*, roast, and served in a thick coating of the same paté;[13] than the world's supreme outdoor luncheon, which to my taste is a cold grouse with bread and Cheddar and a bottle of beer?

What more appetizing spectacle than the display on an English fishmonger's marble slab: the silver salmon, the pale amber finnan haddock, the flat white surfaces of turbot and the unjustly despised plaice, the patterned sheen of the homely but delicious mackerel, the slim and tasty smelt? And then the crustacea: the angry-looking lobster, the Dublin Bay prawns now snobbishly preferring to be known as *scampi*, in the interstices the modest but meritorious shrimps? Here let me digress for a moment to recall how Ben Jonson transmutes this noble 'sea-food', as the Americans choose to call it, into the fantastic courses of his rich imagination:

> *'We will eate our mullets*
> *Soused in high-country wines, sup phesants eggs,*
> *And have our cockles boild in silver shells,*
> *Our shrimps to swim againe, as when they liu'd,*
> *In a rare butter made of dolphins milke*[14]
> *Whose creame dos looke like opalls.'*

In view, then, of all this excellence of the raw material, it is the more unpardonable that so often - indeed, so generally - English cooking *is* so bad. I speak now not of the high-priests and temples of the gastronomic art, of good-class restaurants large and small, of the private houses of the more discerning eaters. I speak of the

---

[13] A dish composed by the late Major Leslie Renton, sometime M.P. for Gainsboro'.

[14] Ben Jonson here refers to the true dolphin, the friendly, playful, highly intelligent mammal we generally call porpoise, and not to the fish *Coryphaena hippuris*, which in some parts of the world is also called a dolphin.

ordinary run of places in Great Britain where food is cooked: of hotels, railway trains and station buffets, of ships, of most (but by no means all) country inns, of schools - in short, of the form in cooking of the country at large. It is well that the native genius has evolved a Worcestershire sauce - deservedly famous, and less desirably imitated, throughout the civilized world - to camouflage the dire results of the efforts of these establishments.

Two psychological causes, it seems to me, operate against good cooking in England. First is the apathy in applying intelligence to cooking, the absence of the will necessary to effect a departure from time-dishonoured methods.

The second psychological cause is the fallacy, so tenaciously held, that intelligently cooked food costs more to prepare than bad food. What utter nonsense! Does it cost any more to peel a potato properly than to hack off the skin in chunks so that most of the flavour escapes the pot? (In any case, why not bake your potato, unless a new one, and eat the skin?) Does it cost any less to cut young French beans obliquely into pieces, with the same result, than to cook them whole? Does it cost any more (other than, of course, in labour) to make excellent soups of pea-pods and of lobster shells than to throw pods and shells away? The contrast between luncheon or dinner in the dining-car of a British train and a French *wagon-restaurant* is so fundamental that it defies depiction, yet the cost of the two meals is normally much the same. Who cannot give a host of other examples of the wilful, barbaric ignorance that has given to English cooking a reputation which in part, indeed, it has merited but which it should not and need not have earned?

An indication that it was not always thus is the fact that what was probably the first of all cookery books was written for King Richard II, that luckless Richard of Bordeaux. And how well English people fared in earlier days, whether in manor or cottage, we may infer from the volume entitled *Two Fifteenth-Century Cookery Books*.[15] We may also infer it from this pleasant Elizabethan grace before meat:

---

[15] Edited by Thomas Austin. Published for the Early English Text Society, Trübner & Co., London, 1888.

'For bread and salt, for grapes and malt,
For flesh and fish, and euery dish:
Mutton and beefe, of all meates cheefe:
For cow-heels, chitterlings,[16] *tripes and sowse,*
And other meate thats in the house:
For backs, for brests, for legges, for loines,
For pies with raisons, and with proines:
For fritters, pancakes, and for freyes,
For venison pasties, and minc't pies:
Sheephead and garlick, brawne and mustard,
Wafers, spic'd cakes, tart and custard,
For capons, rabets, pigges and geese,
For apples, carawaies and cheese:
For all these and many moe
Benedicamus Domino.'

How different in its exuberance from this chastened little grace of the Barbadian peasantry:

'I t'ank de Lawd fo' dis li'l mite;
It's scarcely mo' dan I can bite.
But since it has become my lot,
I t'ank de Lawd fo' what I got.'

And from this line of an ancient Hawaiian prayer before food: 'Bless those who bear the hardship of hunger in humility.'

Here may perhaps be recalled the greedy eighteenth-century parson who, when asked to say grace at houses where he was bidden to dine, would first cast a quick but expert eye over the table appointments. If the number of glasses promised well he would joyfully open with 'O most bountiful Jehovah'. But if the lay-out was meagre he would dolefully intone, 'We are not worthy, O Lord, of these the least of Thy mercies.'

In the Elizabethan grace, it will have been noticed, the foods are enumerated in their simplest, indeed, in almost their crudest terms. Such plain language is no doubt appropriate to prayer, of

---

[16] A pig's small intestines, eaten fried.

thanksgiving and otherwise. But in order to attract to the table the more unimaginative type of mortal, something more enticing is required than the blunt designation of the animal or the relevant portions of the carcass. How pleasant a combination of scholarship and gentle humour is this Latin menu to which I sat down in prewar days on the Dalmatian coast, in a little restaurant established by the priest-archaeologist Monsignor Bulič beside his excavations at Salona.

'*Viator habes*', announces the delightful bill of fare of this inn '*ad Bonum Pastorem*':

> *Vinum Salonitanum sive album sive rubrum sive nigrum optimum quod non corrupit malitia hominum*
> *Zythum Bosnense vel Slovenicum*
> *Aquam saluberrimam Iadri fluminis*
> *Pernam Salonitanam vel Croaticam vel Slavonicam*
> *Clupeas Issaeas Salsas*
> *Ova recentia vel sorbilia vel cocta*
> *Butyrum recens*
> *Caseum vel Dalmaticum vel Bosnensem*
> *Panem bis coctum vel domesticum*
> *Lac vaccinum*
> *Cognac Spalatinum*
> *Mel quod apis Tusculana condidit*
> *Potionem ex faba Arabica*
> *Ficus. Uvam. Pira. Melones ex agro Salonitano.*

Could anything be more engaging, more encouraging than this? What if the *potio ex faba arabica* jumps a century or two, the *cognac Spalatinum* even more? Can we doubt that the wine of Salona, white or rosé or red, was not equally proof against the adulterations of rogues in the days of the Roman Empire? Can anyone resist the appeal of the *mel quod apis Tusculana* - industrious insect - *condidit*?

Here, for the benefit of those whose Latin has rusted, is the translation of this simple menu:

> Excellent wine of Salona, white, rosé or red, which the villainy of man has not corrupted

    Beer of Bosnia or Slovenia
    Salubrious water from the river Iadra
    Salona, Croatian or Slavonian ham
    Salted sprats of Lissa
    Fresh eggs, soft or hard boiled
    Fresh butter
    Dalmatian or Bosnian cheese
    Biscuit or bread
    Cow's milk
    Brandy of Spalato
    Honey from the bees of Tusculum
    A potion of the Arabian berry
    Figs - grapes - pears - melons from the gardens of Salona

    English cooks, to revert to the vernacular, have tried to exercise their imagination in such dishes as 'Bubble and Squeak' and 'Toad in the Hole'; in parts of Jamaica a cooked sucking-pig is called, for what reason I have never been able to find out, a 'moses'. Spain has produced that sweet with chocolate sauce amusingly called *'tocinos del cielo* - piglets from heaven', and for its particular light type of *beignet* the charming name 'nuns' sighs - *suspiros de monjas'*. Even more piquantly named are the delicate Portuguese pastries *'papas de freiras* - nuns' nipples' - and 'Cardinal's wet-nurse', a sweet from Evora. Nuns reappear in France as godmothers to the small fritters called *'Pets de nonne'*. For the realization, with typically Gallic *gaillardise*, of the French sweet called *'Peches en chemise'* I refer the interested reader to Recipe 128 of Paul Reboux's *Le Nouveau Savoir Manger*.

    Equally realistic if less romantic is the salad eaten in parts of the Congo, made of the fleshy-leaved plant which the natives of the region call *'matako ya bibi* - my woman's bottom'. And in this connection may be mentioned the Roussillon wine *'Pipi d'Ange'*, now reported to be coming into favour and described in the wine-merchants' lists as 'unique in character and bouquet, light-bodied and dry'. All these are genuine names; but a party of us dining in a Beirut hotel in 1960 could not help feeling, when we saw a sweet described on the menu as 'Religious Tarts', that the management had overrated its command of the English idiom.

Most countries, as a matter of fact, seem to be content with the prosaically descriptive name, with the evocation of some *cordon bleu* or well-known *restaurateur* of the day, with the humdrum *à la mode* that makes sense and grammar only if followed, as in *à la mode de Caen* or *de Tours*, by the geographical provenance. Not so, however, the Turks, who must be rated high in the naming of their dishes. Who, for example, could fail to be intrigued by, who would not want to know more about, a dish which is called *'Imam Bayildi* - the Imam fainted' [17] and its kindred concoction *'Khünkiar Beghendi*[18] - what the Sultan fancied'.

Who will deny that the asparagus becomes more engaging when it proclaims itself as *'qush qonmaz* - no bird can perch here'?

Does it not stand to reason that the Turkish form of doughnut, a delicate confection with a depression in the centre made by a gentle application of the pastry-cook's middle finger, must acquire additional piquancy from being called *'kadin gyöbeyi* - lady's navel', considered a most apt simile by those who have seen the one and the other?

5

Most of the recipes that follow are those of my friends of many races and walks of life, of my friends' cooks, and of my own cooks in Europe, Asia, Africa and Australasia. I have not mined for them in other cookery books, although I have used many such books to advantage in my own house.

[17]*Imam Bayildi* is a stew of egg-plants or *aubergines*, stuffed with tomatoes, onions and a touch of garlic. The name implies that the Imam, on first tasting the dish after leading a long Friday service at the mosque, fainted with joy at its exquisite flavour. But according to another (and I think more probable) derivation, the Imam, who was of a parsimonious nature, fainted with mortification at the amount of oil which his wife had lavished upon the creation.

[18]*Khünkiar Beghendi* is a variant of the dish that either transported the Imam into an ecstasy or mortified him beyond endurance. It consists of a *purée* of *aubergines* with the addition of *kebabs*, small pieces of fat mutton skewered and grilled over a charcoal fire.

The first cookery-book I ever possessed is the admirable regional collection of recipes called *Leaves from our Tuscan Kitchen,* by that famous Victorian lady, Janet Ross, châtelaine of the fifteenth-century Villa of Poggio Gherardo outside Settignano in which some of the tales of the Decameron were originally told while the plague was raging in Florence. I made the acquaintance of this precious little volume in one of the Tuscan holidays of my youth at the same time as I made that of the authoress herself. Mrs. Ross was the daughter of the Lady Duff-Gordon who wrote the once widely read *Letters from Egypt* and the grand-daughter of John Austin, the jurist; she died in 1927 in her eighty-sixth year. When I first met her she was already an elderly lady - formidable, perhaps, to her contemporaries, but approachable by the young. In the sixty-odd years that have elapsed since then I must have earned the gratitude of scores of my friends for introducing them by means of this book to the delights of Italian soups, vegetables, risotto and *pasta asciutta*.[19]   I might add that a more comprehensive work on Italian cookery is the happily named *Talismano della Felicitá.*

Among other regional books for which I have been grateful are Edmond Richardin's classic *L'art du Bien Manger* and the much later, pleasant little *French Dishes for English Tables,* by J. Berjane; among quite recent works I would like to cite with appreciation a book in English, published in New York in 1947, on the best French cooking, *The Cordon Bleu Cook Book,* by Dione Lucas, expert teacher as well as *restauratrice,* if there is such a word.

Then there is the monumental *Wiener Küche,* by Hofrat Hess and his wife, and Evelyn Bach's slighter *Recipes from Vienna.* I mention these from among scores of other admirable and interesting collections for the reason that to my taste, at all events, the best national cooking in the world is the French, particularly in the provinces, and the next best the Austrian. French cooking needs no praise here; its supremacy is unchallenged and unchal-

---

[19] I was once puzzled by the item *nhoqui* on the menu of an up-country Brazilian hotel until I realized that it was *gnocchi* transliterated into Portuguese.

lengeable. As regards the Austrian, it cannot be emphasized too strongly how widely this differs from the heavy and often coarse cooking in Germany. Austrian cooks have the light hand and the delicate touch. They do not cater for gross feeders of the type of the late Reichsmarschall Göring; they look for their inspiration not to the Spree nor to the Elbe, but to the gay, blue Danube.

How delicious a way, for example, of preparing beef, and how simple if you can get the stuff, is the Viennese *garniertes Rindfleisch mit Schnittlauchsauce* - boiled beef of a wide selection of choice cuts with dyed-in-the-wool Viennese names such as *Hüferschwanzel, Hüferscherzel, Beinscherzel* and *Tafelspitz* - garnished around the edge of the dish with little heaps of fried cauliflower, carrots, red cabbage, spinach, croquettes of Duchesse potatoes and so forth, and seasoned with that piquant confection, a sauce of egg and chive.[20] How wonderful - but not quite so simple - a sweet is *Ausgezogener Apfelstrudel*, whose name is apt to puzzle or amuse those whose knowledge of culinary German is limited! And who does not know the *Sachertorte*, most renowned of chocolate cakes - invented in 1832 for his employer by the original Eduard Sacher, then a young assistant cook in the palace of the great Prince Metternich? Distinguished from other chocolate cakes by the thin layer of apricot jam beneath its chocolate icing and served with whipped cream, it laid the foundations of the fame of the House of Sacher and has contributed to the glories of the city of Vienna.

Yet how natural a phenomenon is the excellence of the Viennese cuisine. For many centuries Vienna was the capital, not only political but cultural (and therefore culinary), of the Holy Roman Empire and of the Austro-Hungarian Empire which succeeded it, the latter a microcosm in itself. As nine languages of the Empire's component races figured on the Imperial Austrian banknotes, so did all the peoples of the Danubian basin contribute their part to that synthesis of the best Central European cooking which is enshrined in the *Wiener Küche*.

I can speak only in terms of respectful admiration of the London Wine and Food Society's *Concise Encyclopaedia of Gast-*

---

[20]Cf. Recipe 293.

ronomy, edited by its sage, Monsieur André Simon, which certainly justifies its claim to be both concise and encyclopaedic. The Countess Morphy, too, in her invaluable collection, takes the whole world in her more than competent stride; while a delightful English series is formed by Mrs. Turner's slim *Fifty Ways* volumes, which, beginning with *Fifty Ways of Cooking a Pheasant*, are full of good and unexpected things.

To revert to regional collections, many, like myself, are grateful for Elizabeth David's volumes and articles, as explicit and lucid as they are interesting, on the food and cooking of southern Europe. An enlightening volume, to go farther afield, is the *United States Regional Cook Book*, by Ruth Berolzheimer. For here we see, apart from the more widely known dishes of North America, what happens when the peasant cooking of the Low Countries and Scandinavia is transplanted to the New World. There are some unusual and savoury dishes, little known on the English side of the Atlantic, to be prepared from the recipes of the Pennsylvania, Michigan and Wisconsin Dutch and Minnesota Swedes and their kin, not to mention the Creole dishes that are the speciality of New Orleans. F.P. Stieff's *Eat, Drink and be Merry in Maryland* deals pleasantly, *inter alia*, with the Maryland speciality of curing hams and other meats, and makes bear steak, nay, even a muskrat sound palatable as prepared by a Maryland cook. And there are some surprising forms of nourishment, solid and liquid, with a definite South Seas and Pacific Coast atmosphere, in *Trader Vic's Book of Food and Drink*.

But as the best food in the world is an incomplete thing if unaccompanied by the appropriate wine, so let no cookery-book be consulted without a study of the perfect companion-piece to any such work. I refer to Professor George Saintsbury's *Notes on a Cellar-Book*, a small volume into which its venerable author distilled the fruits of the sound and tested judgment, the mellow *expertise*, of long years of scholarly and intelligent living.

But if I, too, as I like to make myself believe, have some slight appreciation of the art of eating intelligently, I must firmly disclaim to be a cook myself. At best I can do no more than teach cooks, provided that they have the knowledge and receptivity to transmute my impressionistic instructions into the desired effects.

Of such have been my cooks Yanni in Cyprus, who could roast woodcock and the vanishing francolin to perfection and cooked me the only camel's hump I have ever tasted; plump old Zanzu in Malta; and my wonderful old Bala in Fiji. Bala was a Hindu of such strict observance that he would taste not a drop or sup of a sauce or other dish he was preparing if it contained the slightest trace of a non-vegetarian ingredient, yet invariably he produced flawless results.

So without the expert collaboration of Mrs. John Godfrey there would have been, I fear, a most noticeable absence of the accepted forms and phrasing in the wording of these recipes, scribbled down as were many of them at odd times and in odd places - even at my hosts' dinner-tables (for I may claim to be an observant diner-out) - by the veriest amateur. She has given coherence to what before was chaos, apart from her own contributions of unusual Continental savoury and sweet dishes with which she became familiar as the wife of our Military Attaché in several Central European capitals. But for her I would have had to say of this little collection, changing one word of a sentence of Montaigne: *'C'est la matière de la cuisine crue et informe; chacun en peut faire son profit autant qu'il a d'entendement.'*

As for the recipes themselves, their sources are individually acknowledged, with gratitude to the kind hosts and hostesses and other well-wishers from whom they come. Indeed, I like to regard this book as in a sense a symposium of my friends in many lands. If I may here single out one name in particular, it is that of the late Sir John Leche, expert cook no less than *fin gourmet*, who was generous to me not only with his vast culinary lore, but also with the finished products of his skill in two of his Embassies abroad.

H.C.L.

Note: *Where the sources of the Recipes are indicated by the initials H.C.L. and E.G. they refer respectively to the author and his helper Elizabeth Godfrey.*

GLOSSARY OF CULINARY TERMS

Aspic: A savoury jelly, used for coating and garnishing.
Bain-marie: A shallow pan containing boiling water in which small saucepans are stood in order to keep them hot without actually boiling.
Béchamel: One of the basic sauces. See Recipe 252.
Bisque: Shell-fish soup, usually made of lobster, crayfish, prawns or shrimps.
Blanching: Preliminary cooking in cold water, which is then brought to the boil and drained off, as a means of removing any bitter taste.
Bouquet Garni: A bunch of herbs and flavourings usually tied together in a square of muslin and removed before serving. The bouquet should consist of a bay leaf, mace, a teaspoon of peppercorns and parsley, thyme and other herbs as liked, such as tarragon, chervil, marjoram and winter savoury. Sage should not be included, and fennel used with discretion. The herbs should be fresh, not dried.
Braise: To stew very slowly in gravy in a tightly covered pan, with cut-up vegetables and herbs.
Caramel: Sugar boiled with a little water or lemon juice till dark brown, and used either to flavour certain dishes or more often as a means of producing a rich brown colour in stews and cakes.

Casserole: In French Recipes this should be understood as an ordinary stewpan, but in English it has come to mean exclusively a fireproof dish, either of earthenware or oven glass. Sometimes referred to as a cocotte.

Chaudfroid: A creamy aspic sauce, used to coat cold chicken or other meats. See Recipes 274, 275.

Clarify: To clear or clean. Fat is clarified by pouring boiling water over and allowing the fat to solidify on top of the water. The cake of fat can then be lifted and any remaining impurities easily removed from the bottom by scraping. Soups and jellies are usually clarified by whipping egg-whites into the boiling liquor and then straining well.

Court-bouillon: A liquid in which to boil fish and shell-fish, composed of water, white wine, and vinegar in which have been boiled sliced onions and carrots, lemon peel, salt, peppercorns and a bouquet garni.

Croûtons: Bread cut into dice, fried in fat and served with thick soups.

Demi-glace: A thick brown sauce, for which see Recipe 271.

Escalopes: Collops, that is to say, small, round boneless and skinless cuts of meat or fish.

Farce: A forcemeat or stuffing spread on some other meat or game.

Flambé: A dish over which hot rum or brandy has been poured and lit.

Frappé: Iced.

Fumet: Fish stock.

Garnish: Tasty and decorative trimmings surrounding fish or meat on the dish on which it is served.

Glaze: A strong stock of meat, bones, vegetables and herbs reduced by boiling to a stiff jelly. If this is not available, Bovril or Marmite can be substituted.

Gratin, au: Has come to mean fish, vegetables, etc., served in a cheese sauce, baked, with breadcrumbs on top, although originally cheese was not necessarily implied.

Julienne: This term refers to the method of cutting vegetables such as carrots, turnips, onions, French beans, etc. into shreds or fancy shapes and cooking each separately. They are then served with meat in small groups according to colour, or mixed together as a garnish to soup.

Jus Lié: Rich meat stock much reduced by boiling and thickened with arrowroot or cornflour dissolved in Sherry. Should be of a dark, clear colour and brilliancy.

Lard, to: To thread small, even strips of fat bacon through the breasts of poultry, or across meat and hare.

and cream. Cf. the French *lier*, to bind.

Line, to: To line a mould with jelly implies that a little jelly at setting point is run over the sides and base of the mould to form a thin, even film on which garnishings can be arranged.

Marinade: A liquor in which to steep fish, meat or game, made of oil, vinegar, lemon juice, vegetables, wine, herbs and condiments. Cf. Recipe 288.

Mask, to: To cover anything with sauce, icing, farce, etc.

Mijoter: To simmer.

Nouilles: English noodles, German *Nudeln*. A paste (of Chinese origin) similar to macaroni with the addition of eggs, for serving in soup, etc.

Panade: Bread and butter boiled to a pulp.

Panard: An ingredient of various forcemeats, made of flour, water, butter and salt cooked together till thick.

Papillotes: The paper envelopes in which fish, meat, etc. are sometimes wrapped before grilling to conserve the juices.

Pilav (also *Pilau, Pilaf*): Persian, Arab, Turkish, Armenian, Greek and Balkan savoury dishes of rice with meat, shell-fish and/or other ingredients.

Purée: Cooked fruit or vegetables, reduced to a pulp and then sieved.

Quenelles: Small shapes of uncooked fish or white meat pounded with *panard (q.v.)* and poached in soup.

Ragoût: A stew or hash.

Reduce, to: To boil down soups and other liquors in order to concentrate flavour by diminishing the quantity.

Relever: To season.

Roux: Equal parts of flour and butter cooked together as the base of a sauce, and allowed to colour or not according to whether a white or brown sauce is intended.

Salamander: A circular iron plate which is heated and placed over a pudding to brown it.

Salmi: A ragoût of game birds or domestic duck.

Salpicon: Cooked vegetables, fowl and meat chopped small and mixed together, used as a garnish.

Sauter: To cook very quickly in a shallow, buttered pan, tossing the food so that it browns evenly and lightly.

Tammy: A cloth through which sauces and soups are rubbed to make them perfectly smooth. French *étamine*.

Zest: The natural oil found in the rind of oranges and lemons, which is the reason for paring such rinds very thinly as a flavouring.

I

*Hors d'Oeuvres —
Egg, Rice and other Entrées
— Savouries*

1. A Venetian and South American Hors d'Oeuvre

A surprisingly good summer hors d'oeuvre, popular at Venetian and other Mediterranean dinner parties, consists of slices of iced cantaloupe melon served with slices, cut thin and rolled, of smoked raw (Parma, Ardennes, Westphalian, etc.) ham.

In Spain and South America iced fresh figs are sometimes served in the same way.

Mrs. Brian Webb-Carter of Ashton Cottage, Bishop's Waltham, serves slices of cantaloupe melon surmounted by a delicious accessory taking the form of prawns embedded in thick double cream which itself has been lightly flavoured with curry-powder.

2. Avocado Pears

The avocado pear grows on a smallish tree and originates in Mexico and Central America, its name being derived from the Aztec *ahuacatl* and the pear-like shape of certain varieties. Some have ignorantly corrupted 'avocado pear' into 'alligator pear'. The Portuguese word is *abacate*, but in Spanish South America it is called *palta*.

Avocado pears may also be eaten to advantage cut up in a cold consommé. They are normally eaten raw, but in parts of South America they are sometimes lightly baked with their stuffing of prawns or the like.

Source: **H.C.L.**

3. A West African Small Chop

1 tablespoon butter
1 mustardspoon made mustard
a few drops H.P. sauce
a little curry powder
a little cream

Beat all together to a thick cream, thickening if necessary with a little finely crumbled biscuit. Serve piled on dinner biscuits.

The dish can be varied by adding grated cheese instead of curry powder.

Source: H.C.L.'s West African cook, Freetown, Sierra Leone.

4. Winter Salad with Avocado

chapons or croûtons aillés
    (garlic toast pieces)
4 small beetroot or 2 large
1 cauliflower
2 avocado pears
parsley
lemon juice
salt and freshly ground black
    pepper or ground ginger

Put some chapons or croûton aillés (pieces of hard dry toast rubbed on both sides with garlic) in a salad bowl. Follow with chunks of cooked beetroot, florets of a small blanched cauliflower, 2 avocado pears sliced and plenty of parsley. Dress with olive oil, lemon juice, salt and freshly ground black pepper or ground ginger.

Source: Miss June Tobin (Mrs. Peter Luke), Jimena de la Frontera (Cádiz), Spain.

5. Saltsticks (Salzstangel)

½ lb. butter
½ lb. flour
½ lb. cooked potatoes
1 egg yolk
salt

Sieve the cold cooked potatoes, and work all the ingredients into a smooth dough. Roll out, and leave to settle for 15 minutes. Then cut in strips and roll as for cheese-straws; dip a feather in the white of a raw egg and brush it over each stick; and bake in oven slowly with a liberal sprinkling of caraway seeds.

N.B. For Caraway Seeds see Recipe 316.

Source: Baroness Joelson, Alt-Aussee, Austria.

6. Tarragon Butter

A good light tea- or cocktail-sandwich is made with finely chopped tarragon leaves mixed with the butter. A simple and satisfactory example of a *beurre manié*.

Source: The same.

7. The Classic French Omelette

Take 2-3 eggs per person. Break them into a bowl, add salt and pepper, and beat. In an omelette pan heat a piece of butter and when the fat is smoking hot, pour in the beaten eggs. Tilt the pan so that one side only is over the centre of the flame. The mixture will run down and set in a thin film or 'leaf'. As it sets, fold back this leaf without breaking and continue to tilt and fold back until most of the mixture is set, although some is still soft in the middle. Fold the omelette in half, allow it to brown for about 30 seconds, and serve at once on a hot plate.

For *Omelette aux fines herbes* add finely chopped chives, parsley, tarragon or other herbs. *Omelette aux tomates* is made by skinning tomatoes by dipping them for a minute in boiling water, slicing them and heating them in their own juice with a little salt, sugar and black pepper, and serving them in the centre of the omelette. Chopped fried chicken livers, spinach purée or grated cheese are other additions by which the basic mixture can be varied.

Source: E.G.

Note by H.C.L.: A good omelette (like scrambled eggs) should be what the French call *baveuse*, i.e. verging on the sloppy side.

The so-called 'fluffy' omelette - it would be more correct to call it 'the fluffy so-called omelette' - is to my mind a waste of time and good materials.

8. Oeufs Mollets

Soft-boiled eggs, to serve on *fonds d'artichaut* and spinach, in a pastry case or in cheese cream, etc., are prepared by cooking the eggs in boiling water for 4½ minutes. They are then removed, covered with cold water, shelled, and reheated for a few minutes in the oven, care being taken that they are not allowed to become dry during this last process.

9. Creamed Eggs

| ½ pint cream | 2 heaped tablespoons grated Parmesan cheese |
| 2 eggs | salt, pepper |

Mix together well, and cook in deep egg dishes, standing them in a pan of hot water in the oven until set.

Serves 4.

10. Swiss Eggs

Butter a flat fireproof dish rather thickly, and cover with thin slices of cheese. Break neatly as many eggs as you need on to this, sprinkle with pepper and salt, and pour 3-4 tablespoons of cream over the top. Dust with grated cheese and bake in the oven for 10 minutes or until the eggs are set, browning under the grill if necessary.
Source: E.G.

11. Baked Potato Eggs

2 large potatoes   2 oz. butter or margarine
4 eggs   salt, pepper

Bake the potatoes well in their skins, then cut in half lengthways.
   Scoop out some of the potato in the middle of each half while still quite hot, loosen the consistency of the remaining potato inside the skin with a fork, then put butter or margarine, with salt and pepper to taste, in the hollow, break an egg on to it and replace in the oven until the eggs are lightly cooked.
   Serves 4.
   Source: H.C.L.

12. Egg Mousse

6 hard-boiled eggs   ½ oz. gelatine
1 cup cream   salt, pepper
½ pint Mayonnaise

Chop the eggs, whip all the ingredients together and place in a cold mould lined with aspic jelly.
   Source: Lady Laycock, Sant Anton Palace, Malta, G.C.

13. Bee's Toast

Sardines boned, skinned and sieved, mixed with cream, vinegar, chili, red pepper and a pinch of curry powder. Serve cold in a sauce-boat with hot toast handed separately.
Source: A Lincolnshire family recipe.
(See also 'Tap' savoury recipe 35).

14. Chicken Livers with Eggs - I

Fry chicken livers lightly over a low flame, add more butter and rub through a sieve, taking care not to overcook, as chicken livers can easily become hard. Serve on hot toast with poached eggs on top.

15. Chicken Livers with Eggs - II

Put small china soufflé cases in a bain-marie, half fill with boiling cream of chicken livers, and break an egg on top of each. Add a little more cream and cook lightly. Put a whole liver on top and sprinkle with chopped parsley.
Source: Sir John Leche, K.C.M.G., British Embassy, Santiago, Chile.

16. Eggs with Black Butter

Fry the eggs in butter, take them out, and continue to cook the butter until nearly black. Season with salt and pepper, and shake a few drops of tarragon or other vinegar and, if liked, some chopped capers into the boiling butter.
Pour over the eggs and serve immediately.
Source: The same.

17. Egg and Onion Savoury

    2 small onions   2 hard-boiled eggs
    2 oz. butter   salt, pepper
    parsley

Fry chopped onion and chopped parsley in the butter, slice the hard-boiled eggs and fry all together, adding pepper and salt to taste and serving on toast.

    Source: Mrs. Edward Pirie-Gordon, Gwernvale, Crickhowell, South Wales.

18. Tortilla de Sacramonte

This Spanish omelette is a speciality of Sacramonte, the gypsy quarter of Granada.

    6 eggs   1 small onion
    2 sheep's or kid's brains   2 teeth garlic
    a handful of mushrooms   parsley
    2 lamb's kidneys   salt and freshly ground
                                             black pepper

Beat 6 eggs in bowl, season and leave to stand. Wash, trim and devein the brains and boil them gently until tender (4/5 mins.). Fine-chop the kidneys, onion, garlic and mushrooms and lightly fry together with the brains (2/3 mins.). Now stir the fried mixture in with the eggs adding some chopped parsley. Grease your omelette pan with a little olive oil, heat the pan and when really hot pour in the egg, brain and kidney mixture, gently tipping the pan backwards and forwards until the eggs begin to set and leave the sides of the pan. While the omelette mixture is still moist in the middle take a flat saucepan lid the size of your pan, place it on top of the pan and turn upside-down so that the half-cooked tortilla falls into the lid. Slide the tortilla back into the pan the other side up and cook in the same way. Finally repeat the process but this time turning the tortilla on to a warmed plate on which it will be served. Garnish with parsley.

Source: Eds.

19. Eggs Benedict

Butter and toast the half of a split muffin. Cover exactly with a round of grilled (or chopped) ham or bacon. On this place a lightly poached egg, and cover the whole liberally with either Hollandaise or Béarnaise sauce (*qq.v.*).

Source: Captain and Mrs. H. Harrower, First Acre, Tobago, West Indies.

20. Tomatoes, Eggs and Cheese

2 lb. tomatoes	1½ oz. butter
6 hard-boiled eggs	1½ oz. flour
6 oz. Parmesan cheese	½ pint milk

Brown the tomatoes in a little butter, boil the eggs hard and sieve them. Make a Béchamel of the butter, flour and milk, add the grated cheese and season with salt and pepper. Arrange layers of tomato, eggs and Béchamel in a fireproof dish, finishing with a layer of the sauce and a sprinkling of the cheese. Bake in a slow oven for an hour.

Source: Mrs. J.H. Luke's cook Josephine, Alt-Aussee, Austria.

21. Moussaká

>   1 lb. lean tender beefsteak
>   4 large ripe tomatoes
>   6 egg-plants (aubergines)
>   2 tablespoons finely chopped onion
>   1 tablespoon finely chopped parsley
>   salt, pepper, lard for frying
>   2 tablespoons butter
>   1½ tablespoons flour
>   1 pint milk or milk and stock
>   5 tablespoons grated cheese

Mince the meat. Heat 2 tablespoons lard in a frying-pan, add meat and onion, and fry till all the meat liquid is absorbed. Add tomatoes which have been skinned and cut up coarsely, and a little water or stock. Season with salt and pepper and cover, simmering till the meat is quite tender and the tomato juice absorbed. Add the parsley.

Make a sauce with the butter, flour, milk and cheese. Wash but do not peel the egg-plants. Cut them lengthways in thin slices and fry in hot fat until a light golden colour, and drain on brown paper to remove all greasiness. Arrange layers of fried egg-plant and cooked meat alternately in a fireproof dish, finishing with egg-plant. Pour over the sauce, sprinkle with grated cheese and breadcrumbs, and brown in the oven.

Source: Lady Blackall, Kyrenia, Cyprus.

22. Egg-Plant or Aubergine Soufflé

>   1 egg-plant
>   1 cup breadcrumbs
>   ¾ cup milk
>   2 oz. grated Parmesan or other cheese
>   1 tablespoon butter
>   2 eggs
>   1 onion

Peel and slice the egg-plant, boil in salted water till tender, and chop finely. Similarly chop the onion and beat the eggs well. Mix all these with the milk and butter and put in a well-greased baking-dish. Cover with the cheese and buttered breadcrumbs and bake in a moderate oven for 30-40 minutes.

Source: Mrs. Livingstone of Bachuil.

23. Cold Cheese Soufflé

*4 oz. grated cheddar or
  similar cheese
2 egg yolks
whites of 3 eggs*

*1 gill milk
1 gill whipped cream
1 teaspoon gelatine
1½ dessertspoons baking powder*

Whisk the egg yolks and the grated cheese over the bain-marie; add the milk and cook until the mixture thickens, stirring continuously.

Dissolve the gelatine in a little water and add to the mixture. When cold, add the whipped cream and the stiffly beaten egg whites, and pour into a soufflé dish.

Source: Mrs. John Maxse, Catercross, Fittleworth, Sussex.

24. Small Cheese Soufflés

*6 oz. butter
10 eggs
7 oz. Parmesan cheese*

*7 oz. Gruyère cheese
pepper
sugar*

Melt and heat the butter in a pan. Beat the yolks of the eggs in a basin, and blend them with the butter, mixing together for a few seconds over a moderate fire. Add the two kinds of grated cheese, season with pepper and a pinch of sugar, and stir over the fire until smooth, without boiling. Remove from the fire, add the stiffly whipped whites of two eggs, and set aside.

25 minutes before serving, fold in the remaining 8 stiffly whipped whites, and fill 15 small china or paper soufflé cases with the mixture, placing them on a baking-sheet. Cook in a moderate oven, and serve at once.

This mixture does not rise very much, but neither does it fall flat.

Source: Hotel d'Angleterre, Geneva, where these soufflés were enjoyed by H.C.L. when an Accredited Representative to the Permanent Mandates Commission of the League of Nations in 1930.

25. Arroz Blanco

3 cups rice (round)
4½ cups chicken stock

6 teeth garlic
2 tablespoons olive oil
fistful of parsley

Chop parsley and garlic into deep saucepan and stir-fry. Add rice and mix. When rice becomes translucent add the stock which must be cold, clear and very tasty. The accent here is 'white' rice. Bring to boil, turn down flame to minimum and lid. Cook for about 20 minutes. Half-way through cooking give it a stir to keep from sticking. When the rice is almost cooked and the liquid absorbed turn off flame and leave lid on for about 5 minutes. On a large round or oval plate arrange the rice in a mound, smoothing it into shape with a knife. When a well shaped mound is achieved garnish it with strips of red peppers and sprigs of parsley. Should cut like a cake.

Source: Sra. Antonia Cortes Fernandez. One time cook to Mr. and Mrs. Peter Luke in El Chorro, Málaga.

26. Risotto

1 large onion
2 oz. butter
5 oz. washed rice
1 pint stock

saffron to taste
2 oz. clarified butter
2 tablespoons grated Parmesan
marrow (the fat, not the vegetable)

Fry the sliced onion in butter for 10-15 minutes without colouring, add the rice, saffron and stock, bring to the boil, cover with a buttered paper and simmer for ½ hour with the clarified butter. Add the cheese, mix well, and serve with a lump of cooked marrow (the fat, not the vegetable) placed on top of the risotto. Chicken livers and/or peas may be added with advantage; the saffron is essential.

Source: H.C.L. This is but one of many examples of an Italian risotto. For others cf. Janet Ross's *Leaves from our Tuscan Kit-*

chen referred to in the Introductory Chapter. See also the Lobster and other Pilavs in the Fish Section herein and the following Recipe.

27. Pilav Stambul

2 oz. butter	½ teaspoon pepper
1 tablespoon oil	1 dessertspoon sugar
2 chopped onions	2 tablespoons tomato purée
1 cup washed rice	2 cups stock
1 teaspoon salt	

Melt the butter and oil, fry the onions, add the rice and seasonings and stir constantly for about 5 minutes, until the fats have been absorbed. Add the tomato purée and the stock, cover the pan with a lid and cook slowly until the liquid has been absorbed, that is, for about 20 minutes. Remove the pan from the fire and cover with a cloth for 20 minutes, serve with fried giblets and mushrooms or any kind of game or poultry.

Source: Mrs. S.F. Newcombe.

28. Paella Valenciana

1 jointed or deboned & chopped chicken	green & red peppers as desired
2 doz. mussels	garlic
1 lb. prawns	tomatoes
1 lb. squid	bay leaves
4-6 soft Spanish chorizo sausages	saffron
	white wine
1 cup of round rice per 2 people	onions
	stock

Brown the chicken pieces and put aside. Clean, chop and lightly fry the squid and put with chicken. Sweat onion, garlic and the other vegetables in olive oil with bay leaves and reserve. Before doing so put aside some raw finely chopped green and red peppers for garnish. Now get out your paella (which is the name of the round flat metal dish traditionally used). In it fry the rice in olive oil stirring it around till the grains are translucent. Add saffron and flood with stock and white wine in ratio of approximately 2/3 cups of liquid to 1 cup of rice. From this moment the contents of the paella must be kept constantly on the move to avoid sticking, bearing in mind that more liquid can be added if required. When the rice is nearly cooked but there is still liquid to be absorbed, add the other ingredients starting with the chicken followed by the chopped chorizo. It is useful here to have an assistant who can keep stirring while the cook opens the mussels by sweating them for a moment in about a glass of white wine. Mussels, squid and prawns are ruined by over-cooking, so should be added at the last moment. The prawns will cook in the paella liquid but some (cooked) should be kept aside for decoration. Ditto a few mussels in the half shell. When the rice is finally cooked, garnish with the above plus the green and red diced peppers and anything else that takes the cook's fancy. (Nasturtium flowers have been used.) Edge the dish round with quartered lemons and place on table. You may even get a round of applause.

Source: Mr. Peter Luke, M.C., Jimena de la Frontera (Cádiz), Spain.

29. Bobotie

½ lb. beef (raw or cooked)
1 large slice white bread
1 onion (finely chopped)
8 fried almonds or equivalent quantity of peanuts
1 tablespoon seedless raisins
3 eggs

2 oz. butter
1½ cups milk
1 tablespoon vinegar or lemon juice
1 tablespoon curry powder
1 teaspoon brown sugar
salt, pepper

Mince the meat and soak the bread in half the milk. Fry the onion in the butter. In a bowl mix the vinegar, curry powder, sugar, salt and pepper and add to the mince, subsequently adding the soaked bread and the fried onions with 1 of the eggs. Mix well all together and put in a greased Pyrex dish.

Now whisk the 2 remaining eggs with the rest of the milk and pour on to the mixture. Surmount with the nuts and raisins and with dabs of butter and bake for ½ hour at 350º F. Serve with fried or boiled rice and chutney.

Source: Mrs. Jean Marshall Campbell. A South African speciality.

30. Dolma

If you have access to a vine (if you have not, there are substitutes), try as an entrée one of the many forms of this popular Turkish savoury dish:

1 lb. fat mutton	*juice of 1 lemon*
1 cup rice	*1 chopped clove of garlic*
1 lb. tomatoes	*1 tablespoon chopped parsley*
½ lb. pimientos	*1 teaspoon chopped mint*
12 vine leaves	*salt, peppercorns*

Blanch the vine leaves till tender. Chop (but do not mince) the meat, and cut up the tomatoes and sweet peppers. Mix with the rice and other ingredients except the lemon juice, and roll up in the vine leaves. Put in a pan and boil for ½ hour; then add the lemon juice and leave on a slow fire for another ½ hour.

Makes 12 *dolmas* to serve 4 people.

Failing vine leaves, you may use the leaves of spinach beet with the hard stalks removed. More romantic is the leaf of the wild cyclamen *Persica*, which the Dowager Lady Loch uses for the same purpose in her lovely house Dramia below the mediaeval castle of Buffavento in the Kyrenia Mountains of Cyprus. It is as romantic an ingredient of food or drink as the gardenia petals which some Pacific Islanders add to their tea leaves.

In another form of *dolma* the containers are egg-plants (aubergines) with the tops sliced off and replaced after the mixture has been inserted in the place of the pulp of the vegetable.

In *Yalanji Dolma* ('the liar *dolma*') chopped onions and walnuts take the place of the meat.

A pinch of pounded coriander seed adds, literally as well as metaphorically, a spice of the East to all the above.

Source: H.C.L.

31. Wild Rice (Mah-no-Min)

> 'Then Nokomis the old woman
> Spake and said to Minnehaha:
> "'Tis the moon when leaves are falling,
> All the wild rice has been gathered."'

Wild rice, according to the botanist Roxburgh the parent of all cultivated rice, is indigenous to parts of India and Australia and of the State of Minnesota, U.S.A., where it is harvested by the Amerindians from their hand-propelled canoes. In the north of that State the banks of the numerous lakes between Winnebigosh and Mille Lacs, the region where the Mississippi has its source, are the home of the wild rice, a natural food for whose stands Algonquin and Sioux Indians battled continuously for two hundred and fifty years. The Algonquins called it *mah-no-min*, 'the good berry'; the seventeenth-century French Jesuit missionary Père Marquette refers to it as *'la folle avoine'*. The Indians at the gathering of the crop would make a savoury stew of it with game and dried whortleberries. And it is a good food not only for man but also for birds: for the wood-duck, who feeds on its flowers and stems when they begin to appear above the water; for the mallard, who dives down into the muddy bottoms of these shallow lakes for its seed, his favourite form of nourishment.

Today the Indians of the region still gather the wild rice harvest as their ancestors did before them.

'In this traditional method (say Messrs. Gokey of Saint Paul, Minn., the marketers of this rare product) two weeks before the rice matures, squaws paddle their canoes through the rice field, tying standing rice stalks into bunches with twine which they have made from the green inner bark of basswood trees. This typing protects the seeds to a certain degree from the wind and rain, which might otherwise loosen ripened rice from its stalk. The manner of stalk-tying is individual and indicates who owns the crop. When the grain is ready to harvest, the canoes again go through the field while squaws pull the fruiting stalks over the canoe's side and, using a curved sickle-hook, knock the ripened seeds into a blanket spread over their canoe-bottom.'

In taste the wild rice compares with its cultivated descendant somewhat as a very delicate sweet corn bred for the table compares with a coarse mealie. Thus it is the converse of most fruits and vegetables, which are normally an improvement on the wild stocks from which they spring. Cultivated rice, good as it can be, lacks the subtle, elusive flavour of its wild progenitor, an unusual delicacy even in the United States, still more so in Europe. But the two following dishes may be prepared with ordinary rice in the absence of the wild variety.

Source: H.C.L., who was introduced to wild rice by Mr. and Mrs. Randall Kirk, formerly of Minnesota.

32. Minnesota Recipes for Wild Rice, Chicken & Mushrooms

1 boiling fowl
3 cups wild rice
½ lb. mushrooms stewed in milk
butter

3 stalks celery
1 small onion
1 small sweet pepper (pimiento)
salt, pepper

Stew the chicken and cut the meat off the bones. Butter a casserole dish. Sauter a mixture of the celery, onion and pimiento in 1 tablespoon of butter. Put alternate layers of the chicken, wild rice and the sauté mixture in the casserole; season the stewed mushrooms with salt and freshly ground black pepper and pour them with their milk over the whole. Bake covered in a slow oven for 40 minutes at 325º F.

Source: Mrs. Randall Kirk. Mrs. W. Uihlein of Milwaukee, Wisconsin recommends wild rice cooked with field mushrooms in water with an infusion of wine. And cf. Recipe 146.

33. *Albondigas*

1 lb. minced raw pork
breadcrumbs
1 medium onion
4 cloves garlic
parsley
thyme
brandy

1 teaspoon cinnamon
½ teaspoon cumin
pinch each nutmeg & mace
1 egg yolk
cooking oil
salt & pepper

Mix together mince and the inside of a day old brown or white loaf crumbled up, onion and garlic, parsley and thyme chopped finely, the spices, salt and freshly ground black pepper. Add a little brandy and bind all together with the egg yolk. Roll into little balls and fry in deep smoking hot sunflower oil. To be eaten with Sauce Espagnole (Recipe 270) with the addition of pounded up fried garlic and almonds.

Source: Miss June Tobin, Jimena de la Frontera (Cádiz), Spain.

34. Timpana of Macaroni

1 lb. macaroni	5 eggs
½ lb. minced meat, bacon, brain, etc.	4 tomatoes
	1 small onion
½ lb. chicken livers	grated cheese
¼ lb. fat	1 tablespoon olive oil
short pastry to line and cover cake tin	

Chop the onion finely and fry in fat and oil. Add the minced meat, etc., and the livers, finely chopped. Peel the tomatoes, slice, and fry with the above.

Boil the macaroni, strain and dry over a sieve. Add to it 3 beaten eggs, the sauce and the grated cheese. Line a fairly deep sandwich or shallow cake tin with short pastry and insert the macaroni mixture. Place 2 thinly sliced hard-boiled eggs on top and cover with pastry.

Leave the dish in a moderately hot oven for 10 minutes, then turn the oven down to moderate heat and leave for another 20 minutes.

Source: A popular traditional Maltese dish.

35. 'Tap' Savoury

Drain the oil from 2 tins of sardines and pound the contents up with the yoke of 1 egg, a good teaspoonful of chutney and several shakes of Worcestershire sauce. Spread on toast and put briefly under grill. A dash of Tabasco can be added for those who like it hot. This is an approximation of a savoury served at 'Tap' at Eton in the 1930s.

Source: Eds.

36. Schinkenfleckerl

1 lb. flour
4 eggs
1 pint water

½ lb. butter, margarine or lard
¼ lb. finely minced ham
2-3 tablespoons sour cream

Work the flour and one egg smooth, add the water, roll out until the dough is thin, and allow to dry. When dry, cut into ½-inch squares and cook in boiling water with a little salt for 10 minutes, then drain. Mix the butter, ham, cream and 3 egg yolks together thoroughly, add the whipped whites of egg and the squares of dough, and bake 10-15 minutes in a well-buttered pie-dish.

For 5-6 people.

Source: Mrs. J.H. Luke. An Austrian recipe for a light entrée.

37. Nockerln

½ lb. flour
1 egg

½ pint water
salt

Beat together thoroughly with a wooden spoon. Then drop small spoonfuls into boiling water to which salt has been added, until cooked (about 10 minutes). Then fry in butter for a few minutes only, and serve hot.

Source: The same.

38. Quiches Lorraine

4 oz. Gruyère cheese
4 oz. Parmesan
1 egg
1 gill cream

a little milk
bacon or ham
½ teaspoon paprika
cayenne pepper

Grate the cheese, add the egg and the cream, the paprika, a dash of cayenne and small pieces of crisp bacon or ham, with a little milk if necessary. Pour into a flan lined with short-crust pastry that has been partly baked, put in the oven for 15 minutes or until the mixture has set, and serve warm.

Source: A favourite dish in Nancy, the capital of Lorraine, whose eighteenth-century Place Stanislas is one of the noblest squares in Europe.

39. *Colombines de Foie Gras ou de Volaille*

3½ oz. semolina
1 quart milk
2 egg yolks

spinach or sorrel purée
foie gras or chicken livers

Cook the semolina in the boiling milk which has been well seasoned with salt and pepper. When the semolina is cooked, remove from the fire and add the 2 yolks, mixing well. Fill small buttered oval moulds with this mixture, making a hole in the centre of each. This is filled with a little sieved sorrel or spinach, in the centre of which is inserted a little foie gras purée, or *salpicon* of chicken, or sieved chicken liver. Cover each mould with a lid of the semolina paste, and steam the moulds for 10 minutes in the bain-marie.

When cold, turn out of the moulds, dip in beaten egg and breadcrumbs, and fry in butter until golden. Serve without sauce.

Source: Madame Daguet, La Capilla, Colombia, a Frenchwoman, widow of an artist, exponent of the French *haute cuisine* and châtelaine of one of the most idyllic hotels in the New World.

La Capilla, where H.C.L. once stayed as the guest of Group Captain and Mrs. Dudley Honor, lies 5,000 feet above sea-level in the Cordilleras of the Republic of Colombia. But it also lies 3,700 feet below the Colombian capital of Santa Fé de Bogotá. So when Bogotanos come here for a change of air, they talk in all seriousness of going *down* to the mountains.

40. Fish Pudin

½ pint raw prawns
4 or 5 small cooked potatoes
meat of a good-sized crab or crab-sticks
1 lb. good steaky white fish, cod or monk-fish
3 hard-boiled eggs
5/6 teeth garlic
1 glass white wine
1 pint water
1 small tin red peppers
2 pkts. aspic powder
½ tspn. fennel seeds
black pepper
aïoli
2 tbspns. paprika pepper

Plunge prawns into the boiling liquor that the white fish was cooked in. Lift them out as soon as they have turned colour. Peel them and put back heads and shells plus the bones and head of the white fish, if any, and the garlic and fennel. Bring to boil and simmer until you have a tasty *fumet*. Mash and grind up the shells during the simmering to get the maximum flavour. Strain the liquor and add paprika and black pepper and wine. Bring to the boil again, stir in the 2 packets of aspic powder and take off flame. Allow to cool. Meanwhile in bottom of bowl arrange a few prawns, slices of hard-boiled eggs with little pieces of the red pepper and a few sprigs of parsley with some of the cooled gelatine mixture to cover. Now put in layers of white fish, strips of red pepper, slices of hard-boiled egg, potatoes, crab meat or sticks until the bowl is almost full. Pour in rest of gelatine mixture and place in refrigerator until set. Spread a stiff *aïoli* (mayonnaise with garlic) over the fish pudding or serve separately.

This dish was first encountered in The Plaza Mayor, Madrid and billed as above.

Source: Eds.

41. Haddock Fingers

Make some very thin, small pancakes. Flake cooked smoked haddock finely, add seasoning and a little grated cheese, and mix to a smooth paste with cream, heating in a thick pan. Fill each pancake with the mixture and roll up to make fingers, serving very hot.

If this dish is used as a savoury, it is advisable to make two separate dishes full, as guests never refuse a second helping.
Source: E.G.

42. Smoked Salmon

An excellent and unusual cold savoury, easy to prepare, is an éclair filled with chopped-up smoked salmon (eaten by H.C.L. at a banquet in the Painted Hall, Greenwich).

Another good way of serving smoked salmon is in the Norwegian fashion, surrounded with scrambled egg.

43. Marrow Bones

Cut the bones into lengths of 3-4 inches, bring to the boil, then simmer for 2 hours, covering the ends beforehand with a paste of flour and water to contain the marrow.

When ready, remove the paste and serve, in the bone and piping hot, in a dish lined with a table napkin. Hot toast should be handed round separately, likewise salt and the pepper-mill.

With this excellent and easily prepared savoury should be drunk a liqueur glass of Cognac or Armagnac to correct the richness of the marrow.
Source: H.C.L.

44. Devilled Chicken Livers

1½ chicken livers to each person
1 teaspoon Worcestershire sauce
1 teaspoon tomato sauce

1 large teaspoon Madras curry powder
1 tablespoon butter

Warm the butter in a pan, add the Worcestershire and tomato sauces with the curry powder. Simmer and stir for ¼ hour, chop the livers very fine and add to the mixture, cooking slowly for another 15 minutes. Serve on toast, very hot. This should be cooked at the last moment.

Large-size sardines, free from skin and bones, can be used with the above devil mixture, and kidneys are also good.

Source: Mrs. John Stone, Malta.

45. *Chicken Livers with Apple and Onion*

5 chicken livers
1 apple
1 moderate-sized onion
1 cup cream
butter

Slice the apple, chop up the onion, and fry together lightly in butter over a low flame. Cut the livers in two, taking care not to salt them, as this makes them hard. Add them to the apple and onion, fry or steam quickly, and cover with the cream.

Source: Mrs. R.T. Smallbones, São Paulo, Brazil.

46. *Cheese Wafers*

6 oz. flour
¼ oz. butter
a little milk
salt, pepper
1 egg yolk
½ oz. grated cheese, preferably Parmesan

Season the sifted flour with salt and pepper, melt the butter, beat up the egg in a little milk, and add to the butter; then stir into the flour with the grated cheese. Mix into a stiff paste, adding more milk if necessary. Knead well, roll out, sprinkle with grated cheese, fold in three and then leave the pastry for 30 minutes. Roll out paper-thin, stamp into rounds and leave on a sieve or wire tray for 2-3 hours. Fry in butter in a shallow frying-pan until golden brown, drain, sprinkle with grated cheese and serve hot.

47. Welsh Rarebit à la Green Jacket

1 oz. butter
½ oz. flour
½ pint milk
½ pint ale

1 egg yolk
½ lb. finely grated cheese
pepper, salt, mustard
rounds of toast

To make the mixture: Melt half the quantity of butter in a saucepan, stir in the flour and cook for a few minutes. Add the milk gradually, bring to the boil and cook for at least 5 minutes. Stir in the grated cheese and the egg yolk and place in a bain-marie until required.

To serve: Prepare some rounds of freshly made toast. Melt the remainder of the butter or margarine. Bring the ale to boiling point. Then serve each - the cheese mixture, the hot ale and the melted butter - in separate sauce-boats and let the diners pour them on to their toast in this order: the hot ale, the melted butter and lastly the cheese mixture.

Serves 4.

Source: 2nd Battalion, The Rifle Brigade, Malta 1933-37.

48. A Hot Cheese Titbit

1 cup mayonnaise
¾ cup grated Parmesan and
   Romano cheese

1 medium-sized onion thinly
   sliced rounds of bread

Mix the Mayonnaise with the blended and grated cheese and spread the rounds of bread lightly and evenly with some of the resultant mixture. Then cover with a thin slice of the onion and top with a more generous dollop of the Mayonnaise and cheese. Bake in a hot oven for approximately 12 minutes, until puffed up and well browned.

Source: Mrs. Ray Hare, U.S. Embassy, Ankara.

49. *Potted Cheese*

  1 lb. Cheddar cheese cayenne pepper or chili wine
  1-2 glasses Sherry mustard

Sieve the cheese, add the Sherry, the cayenne pepper or a few drops of chili wine, and some freshly made mustard, and mix thoroughly to a thick paste.

  Place in a glass dish with a sprig of parsley, and serve at luncheon as an alternative to ordinary cheese.

  Source: Mr. F.H. Jarvis, R.N., Chief Steward to Admiral of the Fleet Sir John de Robeck, H.M.S. *Iron Duke* (in which H.C.L. served in World War I).

50. *Liptauer Cheese*

  2 lb. fresh cottage cheese 1 tablespoon castor sugar
  1 onion finely chopped 2 oz. paprika
  1 sprig parsley finely chopped cayenne pepper, black pepper
  juice of 1 small lemon   and salt to taste

Mix thoroughly and allow to stand for 1 to 2 days. Then beat again to the required consistency, if necessary with a little milk.

  Serve with dry biscuits or toast Melba as an *amuse gueule* or savoury.

  Source: Mr. Michael Luke, Sawmill House, West Wycombe Park, Bucks.

51. An Epicure's Cheese

Pound equal quantities of ripe Gorgonzola, Camembert and butter with the admixture of a few drops of brandy.

Spread on a cheese biscuit, oatmeal biscuit, ordinary brown bread or Pumpernickel.

Source: Miss Norah Penhaligon's adaptation of a Belgian Recipe.

Note by H.C.L.: The cheese-loving reader may here be conveniently directed to what must be the world's most comprehensive cheese-shop, at 17 Place de la Madeleine in Paris, and to the *Calendrier des Fromages* there offered to its clientèle. This lists over 200 cheeses of France and Corsica (some with amusing names such as *Vache Sérieuse* and *Vache Qui Rit*) and some 60 from other Western European countries.

52. Small Cheese Cakes

4 oz. Parmesan or Gruyère cheese	2 egg yolks
	blanched almonds
8 oz. butter	salt, pepper, paprika
8 oz. flour	

Mix the above ingredients other than the almonds, roll the resulting paste on a floured board and cut into rounds not more than 2 inches in diameter. Top the rounds with an almond each and bake till they begin to brown. Serve with cocktails as an *amuse gueule*.

But if intended as a savoury course, then make a filling composed as follows:

2 oz. Parmesan	1 egg yolk
½ oz. butter	1½ gills milk

Heat the milk, add the cheese and yolk, season to taste, then stir in the butter over the fire without allowing the mixture to come to the boil. When it begins to thicken, spread on the biscuits (the lower ones having no almonds) and top each with a biscuit with almond.

The above quantities should serve 8 people.

Source: Princess Chlodwig Hohenlohe-Schillingsfürst, Alt-Aussee, Austria.

II

Soups

'Neither food nor drink, soup partakes of an is above both.'
A Fourth Leader in *The Times*.

53. Bouillabaisse and the Like

3 onions
a few cloves of garlic
3 medium tomatoes
1 strip orange peel

a bouquet of parsley, thyme,
bay leaf and fennel
saffron, nutmeg
1 gill olive oil

Make a layer in the bottom of a pan of chopped onions, peeled and pipless tomatoes, and the bouquet. On this place fish with a firm flesh such as conger eel, turbot, lobster; the olive oil and enough water to cover the fish. Season with salt, pepper, grated nutmeg, and a good sprinkling of saffron. Bring to the boil and boil fast for 5 minutes.

Then add pieces of smaller, softer fish such as red mullet, whiting, smelts and cook for 5-6 minutes more on a quick fire. Remove the bouquet and peel, dispose the pieces of fish sprinkled with chopped parsley in one dish, and in another have ready slices of bread that have been fried in oil and rubbed with garlic, over which the soup is poured through a strainer. Serve in soup plates and provide both fork and spoon.

The quick boiling is the secret of this dish, in order that the oil and stock may be blended well.

This is a typical Bouillabaisse of Marseilles. But H.C.L. was once given a lighter, more delicate Nordic version at Scott's Restaurant in the Graabrødre-torv, Copenhagen, and preferred it. It is called *Cannes Casserolle*, and is composed of filleted plaice, salmon, shrimps, mushrooms, tomatoes, button onions and quenelles, cooked in a rich cream and white wine sauce.

54. Cream of Prawns

2 oz. carrot
2 oz. onion
a bouquet garni
30 large prawns
½ pint white wine

1 dessertspoon brandy
1½ pints white stock
4 oz. washed rice
cream and cayenne to taste

Brown the carrots, onion, and a bouquet garni. Add raw, unshelled prawns and sauter until they are red. Add the white wine and brandy. Let it reduce a little and add ½ pint white stock. Cook a few minutes, peel the prawns and cut the meat into small pieces. Mash up the prawns' heads and the vegetables with their juice, add 4 oz. cooked rice and pass through a sieve.

Add to this 1 pint of stock, put all in a bain-marie, cook for 10 minutes more, and complete with a little cream and cayenne to taste.

Before serving, put in the meat of the prawns and serve with fried croûtons apart.

Source: Sir John Leche.

55. *A Simple Bisque of Prawns*

1 lb. large raw prawns
1 small wineglass white wine
1 small wineglass Sherry
1 large cup milk
3 tablespoons cream

1 tablespoon flour
1 tablespoon butter
1 tablespoon tomato purée
salt, garlic salt, pepper

Cook the prawns in just over ½ pint water, the white wine, salt and pepper for 10-15 minutes, according to size.

Drain, and use the stock to make the Bisque, together with the milk. Thicken with the flour and butter. Then add the Sherry, the cream, the tomato *purée* and a dash of garlic salt.

The Bisque should be fairly highly seasoned with salt and pepper. Garnish each serving with a little chopped prawn.

Serves 4.

Source: Mrs. F.J. d'Almeida, São Paulo, Brazil.

56. Birds' Nest Soup

The 'birds in their little nests' which disagreed with Mr. Hilaire Belloc are swiftlets of the genus *Collocalia* and inhabit certain caves in Sarawak and British North Borneo, living on a diet of beetles and other flying insects. The soup is made of their nests, the most highly prized of which are small half-cups of a gelatinous, colourless matter that is exuded from the salivary glands in the birds' beaks and then coagulates. It is this same substance that enables the nests to adhere to the rock surfaces of the caves. Commoner and cheaper are the 'black nests', containing feathers which have to be extracted before the nests can be converted into soup. Mr. Tom Harrison, D.S.O., Curator of the Sarawak Museum and expert on this as on most other subjects, estimates the number of these swiftlets nesting in the Niah caves of Sarawak alone at a million, and Borneo is known to have exported the nests to China at least as far back as the Ming era (A.D. 1368-1644). I ate my first Birds' Nest Soup while spending the early spring of 1956 with Mr. and Mrs. Eric Bevington in Brunei.

Even in Sarawak itself Birds' Nest Soup is an expensive delicacy (costing £1 a *kati* of c. 21 oz.) for the reason that the men who collect the nests from the roofs of these lofty, mile-long caverns have often to climb to heights of over 200 feet on connecting series of bamboo poles pegged together, and along their flimsy, perilously swaying, lateral cat-walk extensions.

The 'soup' is glutinous, colourless like 'white' of egg, intrinsically flavourless; what taste it acquires is wholly provided by the sauces for which it is the vehicle. I can only suppose that its Chinese fanciers induce men to endanger their safety to secure this negative form of food, and in so doing impoverish themselves, in the belief that it possesses other potencies. This belief, or hope, probably underlies quite a number of the culinary preferences of the Chinese otherwise difficult to understand, such as their addiction to the sea-slug known commercially as trepang or *bêche-de-mer*.

Birds' Nest Soup is perhaps the only dish included in this collection because of its bizarre interest rather than because I really like it.

Source: H.C.L.

57. Thick Turtle Soup

  1 lb. turtle meat and fat
  1 lb. rump steak (to remove
      fishiness)
  2 onions
  1 orange
  quenelles of eggs (below)
  1½ pints of beef or chicken stock

  a stick of cinnamon
  cloves
  tomatoes
  1 glass Port
  1 lemon
  a bouquet garni

Boil the turtle, to clean. Fry the rump steak, pieces of turtle, orange and lemon peel, cinnamon, herbs, cloves and onions, and pour on tomato juice or tomato sauce. Add beef or chicken stock, sieve and thicken. Prepare quenelles as under. Before serving add the glass of Port, shreds of turtle, turtle fat and the quenelles.

Enough for 5-6 people.

Quenelles: 5 oz. raw chicken, meat or cooked fish, 1 tablespoon thick Béchamel sauce, ½ oz. butter and 1 egg; mix together, sieve, add 1 tablespoon cream, and make into small oblong dumplings by shaping in two spoons.

Source: The same, Government House, Fiji.

58. Consommé

The world's supreme consommé of all time, that of the Habsburg Court, is described in the Introductory Chapter.

Today this masterpiece could be attempted in its entirety only by millionaires anxious to rid themselves of their capital. But to others it may be as full of helpful ideas as it is full of ingredients.

59. Stock

Take bones, soup meat and, if wanted to jellify, calf's or pig's feet. Crush the bones. If brown stock is required, brown them in a hot oven.

Put meat, bones, calf's feet, etc., in cold salted water, boil up and skim carefully. Add onion, carrot, turnip, herbs, plenty of celery and parsnip. Cook slowly for 7 or 8 hours. Let it cool, removing all grease. To clarify, take a little minced raw meat, finely

chopped carrot and celery, and the shell and white of an egg. Mix together, put into the cold stock, boil up, skim carefully, and pass through a cloth.
Source: Sir John Leche.

60. *Madrilène Saint Antoine*

Take the requisite quantity of chicken stock, add 1 tablespoon of tomato ketchup for each pint of stock, and clarify.
If desired to be served *en gelée*, add isinglass and leave to set in the refrigerator.
Source: Lady Laycock, Sant Anton Palace, Malta.

61. *Beef and Liver Bouillon - I*

Chop finely 2 lb. beef and 1 lb. liver. Place all together in a large glass jar and cover with cold water. Put lid on jar and steam for about 1 hour. Strain well and flavour with salt, pepper, Worcestershire sauce and half a cocktail glass of Sherry per cup.
Source: See following Recipe.

62. *Beef and Liver Bouillon - II*

Make a good ordinary broth of meat and bones; strain and add 2 lb. beef, chopped finely and sauté in oil and butter. Boil for 2 hours, seasoning well with parsley, celery, etc. Add 1 lb. chopped liver and continue boiling for another hour. Strain well and add Sherry to taste, with salt, pepper and Worcestershire sauce. Serve very hot.
A farther refinement of this super-excellent bouillon is achieved by the addition of some chopped kidney.
Source: Circulo de la Union, La Paz, Bolivia, where it was given to H.C.L. by Mr. T. Ifor Rees, first British Ambassador to Bolivia, and Mr. Anthony Ashton of the Embassy.

63. Chicken Liver Soup

Mix 2 quarts of stock with 3 oz. of roux. Fry very lightly ½ lb. chicken livers, add to the mixture and cook ¼ hour. Pound the livers and put back, pass through a sieve and boil up; add some Sherry and a few sliced sauté livers.
Source: Sir John Leche.

64. Kidney Soup

Brown 1 lb. kidneys in small pieces with chopped onion and a bouquet garni. Add 3 pints stock. Cook for 3 hours and strain. Make a purée of the kidneys, return to the soup with roux to thicken and add a little Sherry.
Source: The same.

65. Hare Soup

1 hare	herbs
1 carrot	12 peppercorns
1 onion	salt
1 turnip	3 quarts stock
1 strip celery	1 glass Port or Sherry

Cut hare in joints. Fry until brown with onion, carrot, turnip, celery, all chopped, and herbs. Add crushed peppercorns, salt and stock. Cook for 3 hours, pound and sieve the meat. Boil up, add roux and a glass of Port or Sherry; heat up, and serve.
Source: The same.

66. Jugo Doble

Mince, or chop very finely, ¾ lb. rump steak; place the minced meat in a bowl with 2 cups cold water and allow to stand for an hour, pressing down occasionally with a metal spoon. Cover bowl with a lid, place in bain-marie with water half-way up bowl and steam for 2 hours, adding more hot water as necessary. Then strain and serve after poaching in it 1 egg for each person.

Source: Mrs. George Blackburn, Lake Panguipulli, Southern Chile.

N.B.: Mrs. Blackburn puts a touch of powdered nutmeg in the following soups: potato, onion, cauliflower.

67. Crème d'Artichauts

Wash globe artichokes and take them to pieces, discarding the tough outer leaves. Cook the tender leaves with 2-3 potatoes and sieve them, meanwhile cooking the *fonds d'artichaut* in the same liquor. Make a thickening base with 1 oz. flour, about a gill of milk, and two yolks of eggs, and add the artichoke stock. Shred the *fonds* finely and add with the purée to the soup.

Croûtons may be served with this soup if desired.

Source: Madame Daguet, La Capilla, Colombia.

68. Potage Dorich

Make of either smoked ham, smoked gammon, bacon rind, smoked sausages or the like a stock sufficiently strong to 'jelly' when cold, and flavour it with dried rosemary, bayleaf, turmeric and dill herb (or seeds) and with a touch of cinnamon, cardamon and mace. Cook for several hours until it 'jellies'.

Take milk and water in equal parts, some brown sugar and a little more cinnamon, and boil up with some Jerusalem artichokes, stirring until the mixture becomes a *purée*.

Add this *purée* to the stock and boil together for ½ hour. At the end squeeze the juice of a clove of garlic into the boiling soup and serve.

Source: The Hon. Mrs. Richard Hare (Dora Gordine), of Dorich House, Kingston Vale, where H.C.L. was privileged to partake of this original, rich and exciting concoction as invented and prepared by his hostess. It proved her to be as brilliant a composer of dishes and cook as she is a sculptress.

69. Cheese Cream Soup

2 oz. butter
2 oz. flour
1½ pints cauliflower stock
1 gill cream

6 oz. grated cheese
pepper, salt
a little cooked macaroni

Make a roux with the flour and butter, add the cauliflower water by degrees, then the grated cheese, and stir till smooth and boiling. Add the cream, season well with freshly ground pepper, and serve with small pieces of cooked macaroni in it. (The cauliflower can, of course, be used for another dish.)
Source: E.G.

70. Gazpachuelo

1 cup rice (round)
6 large potatoes
lemon juice

Mayonnaise
6-8 pints chicken stock
fresh mint or parsley

Into a very tasty boiling chicken stock slice the potatoes quite thickly and after 5 minutes throw in a cupful of rice and the juice of ½ a lemon. Have ready a freshly made mayonnaise with the egg-whites reserved. When the rice and potatoes are done pour in the whites which will set almost at once. Turn off the flame and when the soup has been off the boil for about 10 minutes, in order to prevent the possibility of the mayonnaise curdling, make a liaison before adding it to the *Gazpachuelo*. Garnish with fresh chopped parsley or mint.

A very delicious, creamy, traditional Andaluz soup.
Source: Eds.

71. Pot-au-Feu

>4 lb. brisket beef
>½ a cabbage
>2 leeks
>1 large onion
>2 carrots
>6 quarts cold water
>
>a bouquet garni
>1 dessertspoon chopped parsley
>4 cloves
>12 peppercorns
>1 tablespoon salt
>½ lb. French bread

Put the meat and water into a stock-pot, let it come gently to boiling point, and skim well. Wash and clean the vegetables, stick the cloves in the onion, tie up the cabbage and leeks, and put all in with the meat. Add the carrots cut into large pieces, the herbs, salt and pepper, and simmer gently for 4 hours. Just before serving cut the bread in thin slices, place them in a soup tureen and add some of the carrots, leeks and onion cut in small pieces. Remove the meat from the pot, season the broth to taste and strain into the tureen, sprinkle with chopped parsley and serve.

The meat and remaining vegetables may either be served as a separate course or be used up in some other form.

72. Petite Marmite

Cook together 2 lb. beef, 1 marrow bone, 1 chicken cut in joints, and 4 chicken's giblets; 3 quarts stock, 4 leeks, ½ lb. carrots, ½ lb. turnip, both in very large pieces, 2 or 3 sticks of celery, and some herbs.

Boil, and at the last moment put in half a small cabbage already lightly fried, remove grease without straining, and serve in the pot in which it was cooked with bits of toast and grated Parmesan.

Serves 10.

N.B.: The above recipe may be varied by substituting the hind legs of a hare for the chicken.

Source: Sir John Leche.

73. A Dieting Potage de Légumes

3 good-sized carrots, not peeled
4 large green leeks or a bunch of green spring onions
1 large sweet pepper, with seeds removed
1 root, with its green tops, of celery
3-4 outside leaves of cabbage
a handful of parsley
1-2 unpeeled tomatoes, with core and seeds removed
a large pinch of thyme
1 bay leaf
Marmite

Chop all the vegetables and herbs together moderately fine and place in pan. Pour over them 1 quart of boiling water, and allow to continue to boil with the cover off for ¾ hour.

Pass into a colander, place an inverted saucer on top with a weight super-imposed to express all the vegetable juices. Allow to remain until well drained, then add a teaspoon of Marmite and serve.

Source: Mrs. James Martin White, Monte Carlo, Principality of Monaco.

74. Bortsh - I

Boil a few beetroots and keep them and the water in which they were boiled. Cut ½ lb. lean beef into large dice and blanch. Half roast a small duck, cut into very fine strips 10 oz. of beetroot, 2 leeks, a medium-sized onion, 6 oz. of cabbage, a stick of celery and the root of a parsley (or put in a good-sized sprig of parsley). Cook for 5 minutes in butter, add 2 quarts of stock and 5 or 6 tablespoons beetroot juice. Add a sprig of fennel and sprig of marjoram, the beef, and the duck.

Cook until all is tender, remove all grease, take out the duck, fillet the breast, and put back into the soup. Add a spoonful of chopped parsley and fennel, mixed, and a few grilled cocktail sausages.

Heat up and serve with sour cream and beetroot juice apart.

N.B.: For the beetroot juice, boil a beet until soft and squeeze out the juice.

Source: Sir John Leche.

75. Bortsh - II

4½ pints of water	1¼ lb. raw tomatoes
2¼ lb. raw meat	1 bay leaf
10 raw beetroots	1 large onion
6 peppercorns	¾ lb. raw carrots
salt	1 small head white cabbage

Chop the vegetables finely and place all the ingredients in a pan together with some meat bones. Simmer gently for 3 hours, strain, add olives or small sausages, and serve with sour cream.
    For 7 people.
    Source: Lady Durlacher, Green Walls, Liss.

76. Barscz

1 quart good stock	vinegar
2 lb. round beetroots	seasoning

Prepare a good stock of meat and vegetables, cool and skim thoroughly to remove all fat. Boil the scrubbed whole beets until the skin can be moved when touched, strain, skin and grate or chop finely. Place the grated beet in a large stewpan and sprinkle well with tarragon vinegar; add the stock, boil up for 2 minutes, strain, and serve with sour cream: 1 tablespoon to each plate.
    Source: E.G. A Polish recipe.

77. Soupe aux Choux

Wash a cabbage thoroughly and cook for a few minutes in fast-boiling water. Drain carefully, pick off the broken outside leaves, put in a pan of cold, slightly salted water, and boil until tender. The cabbage is then removed, and can be eaten separately.
    Skim and reduce the liquor in the pan, colour it to the tint of a good consommé with a few drops of burnt sugar, then add a little very fine tapioca, sprinkling in and stirring continuously until quite cooked. Serve with toasted slices of French roll.

78. Russian Cabbage Soup

1 cup minced cooked beetroot
½ cup minced raw carrot
1 cup minced onion
4 cups hot meat stock
½ cup heavy sour cream

1 cup shredded cabbage
4 cloves
1 sprig marjoram
1 teaspoon salt
1 tablespoon lemon juice

Cover beetroot, carrots and onion with stock, and simmer for 30 minutes. Add cabbage and seasonings and simmer for 20 minutes more. Add lemon juice and garnish each serving with a tablespoon sour cream.

79. Beetroot Soup

2 large beetroot (raw)
2 medium carrots
1 medium onion
2 or 3 teeth garlic
1 cup shredded white cabbage
1 cup diced smoked ham or bacon
red wine vinegar

1 tbspn. sliced ginger root
1 tbspn. thinly sliced lemon peel
6-8 pints chicken and/or bacon stock
caraway seed
sour cream
dill

Finely chop the beetroot, carrot, garlic and onion and with the ginger, lemon peel and cabbage sweat in butter and olive oil. Add the diced ham or bacon, and the stock, stir and bring to the boil. Let simmer for about an hour and half-way through throw in a teaspoon or more of caraway. Add vinegar to taste. Spoon sour cream on to each plate of soup and garnish with fresh dill.

Source: Miss June Tobin, Jimena de la Frontera (Cádiz), Spain.

80. Botvinka

2 bunches or handfuls of baby beetroots, complete with leaves
lemon juice
salt, pepper, sugar
1½ pints beef or chicken stock

2 tablespoons cream, sour for choice
1 teaspoon flour
fennel

Scrub the beets clean and remove outer leaves; cut into tiny shreds, including the leaves, and cook in water till tender with lemon, salt and a little sugar to keep the colour. Add the stock, bring to the boil, blend flour and cream and use to thicken, re-boil the soup, and serve with chopped fennel, lemon and sugar to taste, and cochineal to colour if necessary.

To serve cold, add small pieces of cucumber and thin slivers of cooked veal or chicken and the chopped fennel, which is essential.

Serves 4-6.
Source: E.G.

81. *Potage Bonne Femme*

1 good-sized lettuce
half that quantity of sorrel leaves
1 medium-sized cucumber
1 onion
12 sprigs tarragon
chervil

1 quart stock
1 gill cream
2 egg yolks
1 oz. butter
salt, sugar

Chop up the onion and shred the other vegetables finely. Add the butter and stir all together over a slow fire for 10 minutes. Then put into the boiling stock, together with the herbs and seasoning, and cook for 15 minutes.

Beat up the egg yolks with the cream; and, when the soup has cooled, stir into it until it thickens.

Serve with croûtons if liked.

Source: H.C.L.'s cook Zanzu, Dar il-Lyuni, Malta.

82. *Onion Soup - I*

6 large onions
3 sticks celery
1 small tomato
a bouquet garni
1 oz. flour

1 oz. butter
a little cream
peppercorns, salt, sugar
bacon rind, stewed ox-tail or
  kidney (optional)

Slice 2 onions and brown slowly in a little butter. Mince the celery and the remaining onions finely and cook to a purée in water. Add the browned onion and, if liked, a small quantity of separately stewed oxtail or kidney provided the vegetables predominate. Boil up again, making up the liquid to 1½ pints; add a bouquet garni, a little sugar, peppercorns, the cut-up tomato, salt and bacon rind. Cook till all are tender and sieve.

Make a fawn roux with the butter and flour, add the sieved soup and bring to boiling point, adding at the last moment, without boiling, a little cream.

Serves 6.

Source: The Misses Warren, Mdina, Malta.

83. *Onion Soup - II*

> 4 good-sized onions
> 1¼ quarts meat bouillon
> butter
>
> salt
> grated Parmesan

Cut the onions in rings and sauter in butter to a golden brown. Add the bouillon and salt to taste (but no pepper), and cook till the onions are soft.

Before serving, add fingers of well-browned toast to the soup and sprinkle the whole well with grated Parmesan. Serve piping hot.

Source: Mrs. Arthur Haxtun, Kent, Connecticut, U.S.A.

84. *Onion Soup - III (A Variant of the Above)*

For each person you require:

> 1 large onion
> 1 oz. grated Parmesan
>
> 1 large cup milk
> 1 oz. butter

and for every four people:

> 1 egg yolk

Chop the onions very fine and fry in the butter until they are soft but not too brown. Add the milk and heat until about to boil. Then add the grated cheese and stir well until this has melted. Just before serving, stir in the beaten egg yolk or yolks.

Source: Mrs. Alan Morton, British Council, Beirut.

85. *Springfield Soup*

    4 large onions
    2 tablespoons butter
    3 pints water
    1 teaspoon salt
    ½ teaspoon pepper
    2 pints good beef stock
    2 dessertspoons cornflour
    1 gill cream
    2 egg yolks
    parsley

Chop the onions very fine and cook in the butter without browning. Add the water, salt and pepper, and a bunch of parsley; boil 1 hour. Strain, and rub the onions through a sieve into the liquid. Blend the cornflour with a little cold milk and add to the onion purée with the stock. Bring to the boil, stirring all the time, cook for another 15 minutes and thicken with the yolks and cream just before serving.

    For 4-5 people.

Source: Lady Harford, formerly of Government House, Springfield, St. Kitts, Leeward Islands.

86. *Dormers Soup*

    calves' head or chicken stock,
      unstrained
    ½ pint milk
    1 oz. butter
    1 egg
    ½ lb. mushrooms
    1 medium-sized onion
    1 small carrot
    1 stick celery

Cook the mushrooms and vegetables for a few minutes in the melted butter, shaking occasionally. Add the stock and simmer for 2 hours. Then remove the onion, carrot and celery.

    Beat the egg into the milk and add when the soup has cooked a little. To serve, make hot but do not boil.

Source: Mrs. Herbert Wolseley-Lewis, Dormers, Wimborne.

87. Sorrel Soup à la Marguery

    10 oz. sorrel, roughly chopped   *1 quart milk*
    2 oz. butter   *1 quart water*
    salt, sugar, chervil   *3 eggs*
    a little potato flour, or flour   *8 tablespoons fresh cream*

Cook the washed sorrel gently in the butter, sprinkle with flour, mix together, and cook over a slow fire till the flour is lightly browned. Bring the milk and water together to the boil, add salt and a little sugar; pour over the sorrel and cook for 15 minutes.

Beat the eggs as for an omelette, pour them over croûtons of bread and place in tureen. Pour the soup into the tureen, sprinkle with chervil, and add the cream.

Serves 8 people.

Source: Madame Daguet, La Capilla, Colombia. Monsieur Marguery owned a restaurant famous at the end of the nineteenth and beginning of the twentieth century near the Théatre Gymnase in Paris.

88. Polish Sorrel Soup

    1 lb. sorrel leaves   *1 tablespoon cream*
    1½ pints stock   *1 teaspoon cornflour or*
    salt, pepper   *arrowroot*
    fennel   *2 hard-boiled eggs, chopped*

Wash and pick over the sorrel leaves and cook as for spinach. When tender, rub through a sieve, add the stock, bring to the boil, and thicken with the cornflour blended with cream, and season well. Serve with the chopped eggs sprinkled on top and also finely chopped fennel.

This soup is delicious cold.

Serves 4-6.

Source: E.G.

N.B. For a Sorrel Sauce cf. Recipe 269.

89. Potage Germiny

Cook in butter until soft ½ lb. mixed spinach and sorrel or watercress. Pass through a fine sieve, add 1½ quarts stock and finish cooking. Complete with 10 egg yolks and ½ pint of cream or milk.

At the last minute add 5 oz. of butter and stir it in with a little chopped chervil and parsley.

90. French Pea-pod Soup

pods from 2 lb. peas
1 onion
2 potatoes
1 sprig mint
salt, pepper

½ oz. margarine
½ pint milk
1 pint stock or water
1 dessertspoon cornflour

String the pods and peel off the inner shiny skin. Put these in a saucepan with the peeled and sliced potatoes and onion, and sauter in the margarine. Add water or stock, season, and simmer gently for ½ hour. Sieve the soup and return to the pan. Add the blended cornflour and milk and reheat till the soup boils and is thickened by the cornflour.

Serve with sippets of fried bread.
Source: H.C.L.

91. Cream of Spinach

To a good chicken stock add the juice of some minced spinach just before serving, and serve with a spoonful of cream in each plate or cup.

Source: Mrs. Stanton, Sam Lord's Castle, Barbados, now a period-piece hotel on the Barbadian windward coast, but originally the lordly mansion, built with his ill-gotten gains, of the notorious and successful Regency wrecker, Sam Lord.

92. Creole Soup

Chicken stock with cut-up okras stewed in the soup, fresh or tinned tomatoes being added at the last minute.

The okra (*Hibiscus esculentus*) is a vegetable of West Indian origin also cultivated in Turkey and farther East, and sometimes known as Ladies' Fingers.

Source: The same.

93. Groundnut Soup (Ful Sudani)

    10 oz. groundnuts   1 oz. butter
    ½ pint milk   1 oz. flour
    ½ pint light stock   1 onion

Roast the nuts in a moderate oven until the skins can be rubbed off easily and the nuts are a light golden brown. Remove the skins, and grind to a smooth paste. Simmer 4 dessertspoons of this paste with the milk and onion for an hour. Make a thin sauce with the butter, flour and stock, add the simmered groundnuts, strain and serve very hot with the addition of Sherry to taste.

Although somewhat rich for a tropical climate, this dish, laced not only with Sherry but liberally with pepper wine, used to be popular in West African military messes, where it sometimes went by the macabre name of Promotion Soup.

Source: H.C.L.

94. Tomato and Egg Soup

    2 lb. tomatoes   1 teaspoon sugar
    1 quart white stock   olive oil, butter
    2 hard-boiled eggs   chopped parsley
    1 large onion   salt, pepper

Slice (without peeling) the tomatoes, and slice the onion. Place them in the pan with butter or oil and cook for 10 minutes, mashing the tomatoes to release the juice. Add the stock and parsley. Cover and simmer for 1 hour, then sieve, add the condiments and stir in a pat of butter.

When ready to serve, pour into a hot tureen in which have been placed the sliced hard-boiled eggs.

Serves 6.

Source: Lady Laycock, Sant Anton Palace, Malta.

95. *Gazpacho Andaluz*

tomatoes
onions
green peppers
cucumber

olive oil
white wine vinegar
salt/pepper

Crumb half a loaf of stale country bread (*pan integral*) into a soup tureen and pour onto it a good wineglass of olive oil (the tastier and greener the better). Fine chop equal quantities of onion, cucumber and green pepper *(pimiento)* and add half the quantity to the tureen. Keep the rest (separately) for garnish. Pulp as many juicy red tomatoes as will make the liquid contents of the tureen. Using an electric hand-mixer (if available) stir all the ingredients together until a homogenized thick soup is achieved (this can be done by hand if necessary). Finally, add spoonful by spoonful as much wine vinegar as may be required to sharpen the soup. Season with salt and pepper and serve with the remaining chopped onion, cucumber and *pimiento* in separate bowls. The *Gazpacho* should be served cold, either from the refrigerator or, if the soup needs thinning, by the addition of ice-cubes. *Gazpacho* originated, without the aid of refrigeration of course, as a midday meal for field workers in the heat of an Andalusian summer.

Source: Mr. Peter Luke, Jimena de la Frontera (Cádiz), Spain.

96. Ajo Blanco

2 cups blanched and peeled almonds
5 or 6 teeth garlic
1 tabspn. sherry vinegar
1 pound grapes

2 cups olive oil
1-2 cups water
salt, pepper
ice cubes

In a blender put the almonds, garlic, olive oil and water and blend until white and creamy in texture. Add salt and freshly ground white pepper and pour into suitable bowl over the grapes (de-pipped and de-skinned if thought necessary). Add sherry vinegar to taste or a mixture of white wine vinegar and Oloroso sherry, ice-cubes and serve.

Very substantial and nourishing. One plateful is enough for a first course. The ice helps to thin this rich soup and chills it, obviously, if the day is hot.

A traditional Andaluz soup but not many recipes are as good as this.

Source: Eds.

97. Potage Glacé Xanadu

2 cups cooked peas
4 cups milk

3 tablespoons chopped mint
1 tablespoon Sherry, brandy or rum

Mix the above ingredients thoroughly, preferably in the electric mixer, and serve iced.

Source: Mrs. A. Embiricos, Barbados.

III

Fish

98. On the Words 'Lobster' and 'Crayfish'

As Nova Scotia and Maine and Robinson Crusoe's island of Juan Fernandez (where they are the only industry) are the homes of some of the best lobsters and crayfish of the New World, so is the Dalmatian coast a breeding ground of the better specimens of the Old. The English word 'lobster' (French *homard*) is derived from the same source as the word 'locust', namely the Latin *locusta*; and it is an odd coincidence that the Dalmatian island of Lágosta, lying almost half-way between Split (Spálato) and Dubrovnik (Ragusa) and owing its name to the same origin, should have as its characteristic but so divergent products both the lobster and the locust- or carob-bean.

As regards 'crayfish', there are those who hold that this form of the word should be applied only to the fresh-water miniature lobster *Astacus fluviatilis*, or *Potamobius pallipes* (French *écrevisse*), and that 'crawfish' should be used to denote the spiny lobster *Palinurus vulgaris* (French *langouste*). This is, however, not correct English usage, according to which the two forms are varieties of the same word, and interchangeable. It is in the United States that 'crawfish' is generally used to denote the *langouste*.

The word crayfish, like *écrevisse*, is derived from the Old French *crevice* and has nothing to do with 'fish'.

Source: H.C.L.

99. Lobster à l'Américaine

Opinions differ as to the most humane way of killing lobster and crayfish. The theory of boiling them is that the animals are suffocated in the steam before touching the water, wherefore they should always be put in head first. Some kill by driving the point of a sharp knife into the head. H.C.L.'s cook Zanzu in Malta affirmed that the swiftest way was to put salt in their eyes.

>   2 lobsters - medium size   ½ pint tomato purée
>   shallots   cayenne pepper
>   1 glass white wine   1 tomato

Take the white flesh of two lobsters and cut in pieces ½ inch thick. Cook some chopped shallots in a saucepan with butter for 2 minutes, add a glassful of white wine. Let the mixture cook, add a little more white wine and about ½ pint tomato purée with 1 saltspoon of cayenne pepper. Add the lobster and let the whole mixture reduce for 10 minutes. Cut a small peeled tomato into dice, removing pips, let it simmer over the fire a few minutes, add, and serve in a deep dish.

Source: Mrs. Leonard Boys, Deben House, Aldeburgh, Suffolk.

100. Homard à l'Armoricaine

2 lobsters about 2 lb. each
12 oz. butter
1½ teacups olive oil
4 tablespoons chopped shallots
3 tablespoons tomato sauce
chopped tarragon
1 teacup good brandy
2 cups white wine

Kill the lobsters, which must be fresh, by driving a sharp knife into the centre of the head. The legs and claws should then be removed and cracked, the coral and lobster butter set aside in a bowl, and the stomach thrown away.

Heat half the butter and the oil in a large pan, add the lobster (including head and claws) with shallots, tomato sauce, a sprinkling of pepper and a pinch of chopped tarragon. Fry on a quick fire 5 minutes. Add the brandy, set it alight and allow the contents of the pan to flame for a few seconds. Then add the white wine, put the lid on firmly and cook for 25 minutes.

While the lobster is cooking, beat the remaining 6 oz. butter with the coral and lobster butter till smooth and creamy. When the lobster is cooked, arrange the solid pieces and claws on a hot dish, leaving the liquor in which it has cooked in the pan. Add to this the creamed butter by degrees to make a sauce, which is then strained over the lobster before serving.

A 2-lb. lobster should serve 6.

Source: A Breton dish.

101. Lobster en Casserole

1 medium-sized lobster
1 glass brandy
1 glass Sherry
black mushrooms or
   champignons
lobster stock prepared from the shell
3 egg yolks
4 fresh tomatoes
cayenne, salt and pepper
1 carton cream
lemon juice

Cook the lobster. When perfectly cold, open and put the flesh into a casserole, together with the other ingredients, and cook in the oven for about 20 minutes.

An exceedingly succulent and not too complicated lobster dish.

Source: Union Club, Malta.

102. Lobster Newburg - I

1 small lobster
1 wineglass Sherry
1½ gills thick cream
2 egg yolks

Remove tail and claws from a cooked lobster and shell carefully. Cut the tail in slices slantwise, place in a well-buttered fireproof dish with the claws on top. Sprinkle with a little Sherry, cover the dish and put in oven to heat. Make a sauce with the cream, Sherry, yolks and a pinch of cayenne and salt, whisking over a pan of boiling water till creamy; then pour over the lobster and serve with a pilav of rice.

This is sufficient for three people; and South African chilled crayfish tails may be used instead. If lobster is used, save the shell to make a Bisque.

103. Lobster Newburg - II

2 cups boiled lobster meat
½ pint cream
2 tablespoons butter
2 egg yolks
1 wineglass Sherry
salt and cayenne

Melt the butter in a saucepan or chafing dish, add the cream, boil gently for 30 seconds, and add lobster meat cut into good-sized pieces. When the cream has again reached the boil, add the well-beaten egg yolks, to which the Sherry has been added. Season to taste with salt and cayenne, and allow to thicken for 2-3 minutes, stirring constantly. Replace in shell before serving.

104. Lobster Newburg - III

1 oz. butter
1 oz. flour
½ pint milk
½ pint cream

2 egg yolks
1 small glass Sherry
2-3 cups boiled lobster meat
salt and pepper

Make a sauce with the butter, flour and milk, adding the cream and eggs and stirring till smooth. Then add the sherry, season as required, heat the lobster in the sauce and serve on toast.

A richer sauce can be made by omitting the milk and flour and using instead a pint of cream.

Serves 5.

Source: A recipe from the United States.

105. Grilled Lobster

1 lobster per person, each of about 1¼-1½ lb.
butter

3 tablespoons cream
Worcestershire sauce

Split the lobsters lengthways, crack the claws and place the shell down in the grill pan, with small dabs of butter over the exposed flesh. The lobster coral and the liver should be left in. Grill from 20 to 25 minutes, taking care not to overcook, as this toughens the lobster.

Make a sauce with 1 oz. butter, the cream, a dash of Worcestershire sauce and the juice from the bottom of the grill pan, and serve poured over the lobster, with lobster picks or small forks beside each half-shell.

Source: The same.

106. Lobster Thermidor

3 1-lb. live lobsters
1 cup cream
2 oz. butter
a few mushrooms
½ cup milk

4 teaspoons grated Parmesan cheese
1 dessertspoon Sherry
mustard, pepper, salt
a pinch of paprika
onion juice

Plunge the lobsters into boiling water for 5 minutes, then simmer for 20 minutes. Lay them out to drain and, when cold, split them in two lengthways. Clean out the shells completely, but retain only the meat from the tail and claws, and cut it up roughly.

Heat the butter in another pan, add the condiments, including 2 drops of onion juice, then the milk and Sherry and the mushrooms which have been simmered in butter and cut up; stir until smooth and bring to the boil.

Add the lobster meat to the mixture and fill the empty shells with it. Then sprinkle the entire surface with the grated Parmesan and place in hot oven or under the grill until the cheese is browned.

Serves 6.

107. Lobster Cocktail - I

Make a Hollandaise sauce with three eggs mixed with 1 tablespoon tomato sauce, 1 tablespoon Worcestershire sauce, 1 glass brandy, Tabasco pepper. Mix small pieces of cold boiled lobster with the sauce and serve cold in champagne glasses.

Source: General Sir John du Cane's Polish cook, Sant Anton Palace, Malta.

108. Lobster Cocktail - II

Mrs. R.D. Blandy, at the British Residency, Vila, New Hebrides, had the interesting combination of *fonds d'artichaut* cut up in a lobster cocktail.

109. Lobster Cocktail - III

Cut cold boiled lobster or crayfish into chunks and serve in a glass in a sauce composed of a mixture, in quantities to taste, of:

Worcestershire sauce *Curaçao*
tomato sauce *horseradish*
Tabasco sauce *cream*
whisky

A very smooth composition, rich, subtle and delicate.
Source: Cogen (U.S. Army Officers') Club, Kronberg, Bad Homburg, Germany, where H.C.L. enjoyed it in 1951 as the guest of Mr. and Mrs. Randall Kirk.

110. Langouste à la Crème Truffée

Make a court-bouillon by boiling together for 20 minutes 1 quart water, salt, peppercorns, a bouquet garni, 1 tablespoon white wine or vinegar and 1 tablespoon lemon juice. Cook the crayfish (or lobster) in this liquid, remove the meat from the tail and cut in neat slices.

Arrange the slices on a well-buttered sauté pan, season well and heat on both sides to increase the colour; then add Madeira or Port practically to cover the slices, and allow this to reduce almost entirely. Make a sauce from cream, egg yolk, truffles, paprika, cayenne and freshly ground peppercorns, arrange the crayfish on the serving dish and cover with the sauce.

Source: Vice-Admiral Dubois, French Navy. A delicious dish at a luncheon (attended by H.C.L.) given by the Admiral on board his flagship during his Squadron's official visit to Malta in November 1930.

111. Suprême Surprise de Ste. Lucie

This is a delicious and admittedly somewhat exotic dish, especially if the heart of palm (called 'palm cabbage' in West Africa) can be adhered to. It is this heart of palm which is also the principal ingredient of the aptly named 'Millionaires' Salad', for it can be prepared only in a country of edible palms and someone must be prepared to sacrifice an entire palm tree, since the removal of the head naturally kills the palm. But *fonds d'artichaut* will provide an adequate, more accessible and less ruinous substitute.

>   *12 river crayfish (écrevisses)*
>   *½ pint cream*
>   *1 wineglass Sherry*
>   *heart of palm, or, if unobtainable, fonds d'artichaut*

Boil the crayfish until cooked and shell them. Leave the flesh of 4 crayfish and all the shells in the water used to boil them, and reduce to stock.

Cut the heart of palm into steaks about ¾ inch thick and bring slowly to the boil. When tender, remove the palm and reduce liquor to stock. Add the palm stock to the crayfish stock, make a roux of flour and butter, add the cream, the stocks, the glass of Sherry and season to taste. Serve very hot with the flesh of two crayfish to each person on a steak of palm (or one in the case of a *fond d'artichaut*) and pour the sauce over.

Serves 4 persons.

Source: Lord Twining, G.C.M.G., as served to H.C.L. at Government House, St. Lucia, Windward Islands.

112. Langouste Sergeant's Cay

Remove the tails of cooked crayfish or lobster, cut in two lengthwise and fry with bacon until slightly brown.

Remove from pan and place on dish surrounded by crisply fried rice, baked beans, grilled tomatoes and sucking-pigs' tails. (The latter can be omitted if difficult to obtain.)

Source: Lady Hunter, Government House, British Honduras.

113. Risotto of Scampi

Scampi are the small salt-water crayfish, about the size of Dublin Bay prawns, found in the Adriatic. For this dish Dublin Bay prawns will do equally well, or even large ordinary prawns.

12 scampi
1 cup washed rice
2-3 onions
oil

4 oz. grated Parmesan cheese
3 tomatoes
salt, pepper

Cook and shell the *scampi*. Chop and fry the onions lightly, add the rice and fry for 3 minutes without colouring in enough oil to cover. Add seasoning, tomatoes and water to cover. Just before the rice is ready add the *scampi* and dust with the Parmesan. The tomatoes should flavour but not overwhelm the dish.

Source: Mr. and Mrs. R.T. Smallbones, Island of Koludarz, Dalmatia.

114. Écrevisses à la Nage

Cook the unshelled crayfish for 10 minutes in the following court-bouillon already cooked: 2 oz. very thin slices of carrot, 4 oz. very thin slices of onion, a bouquet garni, rather less than ½ pint of white wine, 1 gill fish stock and salt.

Serve all together, highly seasoned with cayenne.
Source: Sir John Leche.

115. Écrevisses Bohémiennes

Boil the unshelled crayfish in a mixture of 3 parts beer to 1 part water, to which has been added 1 dessertspoon caraway seeds.

According to the recipe, the beer would be Bohemian, that is to say, Budweiser or Pilsner. A Lager should therefore be used if neither of the above is available.

Source: Prince Charles Victor de Rohan.

116. Prawns Flambées

Fry the prawns whole, *complete with shell*, for about 15 minutes in good oil. Flamber them in brandy in the dining-room and eat hot with the fingers, not forgetting finger-bowls.

Source: Dinner given to H.C.L. in 1947 by Mr. and Mrs. R.T. Smallbones at La Popote Restaurant, São Paulo, Brazil.

In 1953 H.C.L. ate something similar - *langostinas* (half-way between prawns and *langoustes*) well oiled and then grilled over an open fire - when dining with Mr. and Mrs. F.J. d'Almeida at that amusing little tavern, El Pulpito, off the Plaza Mayor in Madrid.

117. Pilav of Prawns

Boil and shell the prawns. Chop one onion finely and brown in a little butter, add the prawns, cayenne pepper, salt and a teaspoonful of curry powder, add a little boiling water, and cook until the mixture thickens. A little flour and water may be added as thickening if necessary.

Cook rice for a pilav until a good brownish colour, and serve the prawns in a circle of rice.

Source: H.C.L.'s Hindu cook Bala, Government House, Fiji.

118. Prawns with Sweet Corn

Boil and shell the prawns. Boil separately the required quantity of sweet corn.

Lay, in small fireproof dishes, the prawns on a bed of the sweet-corn kernels, cover with melted cheese, place under the grill and serve piping hot.

Alternatively, hand round the melted cheese separately in a sauce-boat for pouring over the dish.

Source: Countess Matarazzo, São Paulo, Brazil.

119. Crab Gratiné

1 medium-sized crab	nutmeg
½ oz. butter	a little cream
½ oz. flour	a pinch of grated Parmesan
½ pint boiling milk	

Remove the flesh from the crab and flake it. Make a cream sauce with the flour, butter and milk, adding seasoning, Parmesan, nutmeg and cream. Heat the crab meat gently in the sauce, using enough sauce to make the substance thick. Pour the whole back into the crab shell, sprinkle with white breadcrumbs and melted butter, and brown in the oven or under the grill. Serve with brown bread and butter.

As the flavour of crab is a very delicate one, the Parmesan must be used sparingly. For the same reason crab should never be submerged by such high-powered flavourings as curry powder, onion, Worcestershire sauce or red peppers, which often find their way into it.

120. *The Scallop*

The scallop (Latin *pecten, chlamys*), the mobile bivalve whose decorative shell became the emblem of mediaeval pilgrims to Santiago de Compostela as the 'Coquille de Saint Jacques' and of the mediaeval beggars consequently known as *coquillards*, is a sea food of considerable delicacy and resource. It lends itself to the same sorts of treament as lobster and crayfish and is particularly good à l'Américaine, Thermidor and Newburg (*qq.v.*). Indeed, Monsieur Paul Gaultier, President of the French 'Academie des Gastronomes', who deals eloquently with 'The Scallop at the Table' in the sumptuous volume *The Scallop* published by the Shell Transport and Trading Company in 1957, goes so far as to recommend a dinner of five courses, in each of which the scallop provides the principal ingredient. H.C.L.'s one experience of a five-course dinner composed of a single substance has made him chary of such experiments, however attractive the material; but he is always glad to welcome the return of the scallop season. Under its Manx name *tanrogan* the scallop is very popular in the Isle of Man.

The English word 'scalloping' as used in needlework is, of course, of the same origin, referring as it does to an edging with small semicircular lobes which imitates that of the scallop shell. But the word scallop is not connected with collop (French *escalope*).

Source: H.C.L.

121. On Caviare

Caviare as commonly understood is the roe - of different qualities and preserved for the table in different ways - of various members of the *Acipenser* (sturgeon) family, of which the beluga is the largest. The best caviare is considered to be that of the Caspian, where it is produced not only at Astrakhan and Baku but also - and of an excellent quality - on the Persian shores at the southern end of that sea. In Turkey it is obtained from the Black Sea coast.

The term caviare - now generally adopted into the languages of the West - must, I think, be derived from the Persian (but not, as suggested in some dictionaries, Turkish) word *khaviar*. The word was already known in England in Tudor times: Shakespeare describes a thing unpalatable to the masses as 'caviare to the general', spelling the word *caviary*. Cervantes, in one of the last chapters of Part II of *Don Quixote*, refers to it as *cobiar*. But if you ask a Russian ignorant of foreign languages for caviare he will not know what you are talking about; the Russian word is *ekra*. The Japanese have followed the Russians and call it *ikura*.

Caviare is at its best flavoured only with a squeeze of lemon and eaten with toast Melba and butter to the accompaniment of a glass of good vodka or Kümmel. It cannot be sufficiently emphasized that it is a major gastronomic crime to allow an onion anywhere near it.

The yellowy-pink roe of some of the *Salmonidae* also makes very good eating. In the autumn of 1919 I attended an Armenian banquet given in Novo Bayazid near the southern shore of Lake Sevan or Gyökché, at which we were served with *ishkhan* (a super-excellent form of salmon-trout peculiar to that Lake) surrounded by its own amber-coloured caviare and accompanied by a sauce made of the cream of water-buffalo's milk, mixed with crushed, *fresh* peeled walnuts. A touch of horseradish provided, intentionally or otherwise, a piquant corrective to the sauce's richness. The dish was subtly and incredibly delicious.

In the Levant the roe of tunny, mullet and other fish is popular, when pickled and pressed, under the names *botargo* and *tarama*. On the Mediterranean coast of Asia Minor such roes, pressed and smoked, are produced by the Turks as *baliq yumurta* (fish eggs).

Source: The same.

122. Mussels Gratinées

Carefully scrape the mussels and wash in several waters, then cook in a saucepan with a small piece of butter, a drop of dry white wine and a *bouquet garni*. In 5 minutes they will have opened, and be ready.

Remove the empty half-shell of each, and place the others flat in a fireproof dish. Put on each a pinch of grated cheese and a tiny piece of butter. Pour over all the strained liquid from the cooking mixed with a little cream, glaze in a hot oven or under the grill and serve.

Source: Hotel La Fontaine, Ostend.

123. Lotte Kiriki

2 lb. lote or other fish
1 glass olive oil
½ glass brandy
1 bottle white wine
1 bouquet garni
1 sliced onion
1 clove of garlic

1 tablespoon tomato paste
1 lemon and 1 orange thinly peeled and shredded
2 teaspoons Bovril
salt, pepper, cayenne
4 cloves, nutmeg

Cut the lote into steaks and dip in flour.

Then cook it in the hot oil, place on a plate and flamber with brandy. Drain well, adding this liquor to the remainder of the oil. Put in a pan with the white wine and other ingredients, and cook for at least 30 minutes. Strain, replace in the pan, add the fish and reheat for 15 minutes before serving surrounded with croûtons fried in butter.

Lote, also called burbot and eel-pout (French *lotte*), is a freshwater fish; but cod, rock salmon, angelfish, monkfish and fresh haddock can be prepared in the same way.

124. Dentice Froid aux Rubis

Take a good-sized *dentice* (around 5 lb.) and boil in a court-bouillon *(cf.* Glossary) for 6 minutes to each lb., wrapping the fish in muslin to keep it together.

Then simmer for ½ hour and, when cold, skin and bone the fish and re-form on a napkin, the head and tail being retained in place.

Now cover the fish with chopped red aspic made from the court-bouillon as in Recipe 297, and garnish the dish with stuffed eggs, prawns and diced cucumber and tomatoes. Serve with a Mayonnaise, Remoulade or Green Sauce (*qq.v.*).

To make the stuffed eggs for the garnish, hard-boil them, scoop out the yolks, mix them with Mayonnaise and sieve before replacing.

Source: Lady Laycock, Sant Anton Palace, Malta.

A favourite Maltese dish for a spring and summer luncheon-party.

Note by H.C.L.: The English names of *dentice* (Latin *Dentex vulgaris*; Italian *dentice comune*; French *denté* or *spare denté*) are, so Elizabeth David kindly informs me, dentex, sparus and toothed gilthead. 'The fact,' says Mrs. David, 'that the *orata* or *daurade* (sea-bream) has been translated into English as "gilt-head" has caused confusion in the minds of some English writers, leading them to translate *dentice* as sea-bream.' *cf.* Alan Davidson (1972), Latin *Dentex dentex* (Linnaeus) is of the family *Sparidae* i.e. Sea Bream. Eds.

125. Bacalao

Salt cod	butter
garlic	lemon juice
parsley	dill
new potatoes	

Choose a thick piece of fillet of *bacalao* (salt cod). After soaking it for 12 hours with at least three changes of water, bring to the boil in cold water - cooking gently until tender. Drain and remove skin and bones. Arrange on dish in thick glossy flakes and pour over plenty of hot melted parsley-and-garlic butter. Squeeze lemon-juice liberally over all. Garnish with lemon quarters and black pepper. Serve with boiled potatoes garnished with fresh dill.

Source: Miss June Tobin, Jimena de la Frontera (Cádiz), Spain.

126. Salmon Pilav

Cook a small quantity of salmon, flake it up and add an equal quantity of crisply fried rice (*cf.* Recipe 25). Mix well, put in a deep fireproof dish with a well-seasoned Béchamel and cover with breadcrumbs. Put dabs of butter on top and stand in a tin of water in the oven until browned.

127. Smelts, Pejerreyes and Fresh Sardines

The smelt (French *éperlan*) is a delicately flavoured fish no longer as popular in Great Britain as he has been and deserves to be.

Brillat-Savarin said of the smelt in *Meditation VII*: 'Treat in exactly the same way (*sc.* small trout fried in the finest salad oil) the smelt, of which adepts think so highly. The smelt is among fish what the beccafico is among birds.' (For the beccafico see Recipe 155.)

Fried in fine breadcrumbs and served with a Sauce Bruxelloise (*q.v.*), or even with the juice of half a lemon, he is difficult to beat.

A fish similar in flavour to the smelt is found in a well-grown and succulent form off the coasts of South America under the name *pejerrey*. A popular dish in those countries is to remove heads, tails and bones of the *pejerreyes*, split them otherwise like kippers, and then press them together two and two with a thin layer between them of butter, chopped parsley and, if liked, a few chopped capers. Dip lightly in breadcrumbs and fry.

This method proves as successful with Atlantic smelts as with Pacific *pejerreyes*.

As a postscript to the above I would add a word in praise of the *fresh* sardine, that is to say a small pilchard (provided he really is fresh), a fish as unfamiliar in that state as he has become a universal household accessory when tinned. I have never forgotten a breakfast I once ate between the wars at Cefalù on the north coast of Sicily (a town strangely neglected by travellers despite its superb Norman cathedral and mosaics), which consisted of these delicious little creatures, transferred straight from the Mediterranean into the pan and served lightly fried in olive oil with a squeeze of lemon. That humble dish embodied the true tang of the sea.

Source: H.C.L.

128. Sole Jeannine

Sole is best eaten on the bone, and a good, well-grilled Dover sole needs no bush other than a squeeze of lemon. Filleting tends to dissipate, elaborate sauces to smother flavour; but here is a simple and agreeable French dish for those who think otherwise:

> fillets of sole
> ½ pint milk
> 1 tablespoon flour
>
> butter
> chopped parsley and tarragon

Dip the fillets in flour and fry lightly in butter. Put them unfolded on a flat dish, keep hot and make a sauce with the milk, flour and the butter in which the fish was cooked. Stir well to make a creamy sauce, adding chopped parsley and tarragon, and serve around the fish.

129. A Good Recipe for Turbot

> 2 lb. turbot or other large white fish in one piece
> 1 lemon
> 1 tablespoon anchovy sauce
> 1 tablespoon olive oil
> 1 tablespoon wine vinegar
> 1 bunch parsley (chopped)
>
> flour
> 2 oz. butter
> 2 oz. lard
> 1 heaped teaspoon each of salt, black pepper and red pepper or paprika

Mix in a plate the anchovy sauce, oil, vinegar and condiments. Place the fish in this and allow it to marinate for a ¼-hour. Heat a large frying-pan and, when very hot, put in it the butter and lard. When the fat is brown, sprinkle one side of the fish liberally with flour and place it in the frying-pan floured side down. Move it about in the pan, then sprinkle the other side with flour.

Allow the fish to cook in the fat for about 5 minutes on each side. Add a little hot water from the kettle to the mixture in the plate and pour all the contents over the fish in the frying-pan. Place the pan in a hot oven for about a ¼-hour, basting at least twice.

Slice the lemon very finely and then, having removed the fish from the oven, cover it closely with the slices of lemon and sprinkle freely with the chopped parsley. Replace in the oven and leave for another ¼ hour until done, again basting twice.

Source: Lady Burrows's Goanese cook at the Residency, Bahrain, Persian Gulf, where the fish used is known locally as *hamur* and is not unlike a grouper or rock-cod.

130. Trout or Char au Bleu

Boil up a good court-bouillon, knock a live trout or char on the head and boil for 7-10 minutes in the court-bouillon.

It is noteworthy that Isaac Walton recommends putting into the water, together with 'hard stale beer' and other ingredients, 'a handful of sliced horseradish root, with a handsome little faggot of rosemary, thyme and winter savoury'.

Serve with boiled, round, small (but not new) potatoes and with black butter, browned slowly and very hot, with which the potatoes should also be well doused. Garnish with thin slices of lemon.

The pink-fleshed char (French *umble*, German *Saibling*), found in the English, Savoyard and Alpine lakes, and even as far north as Spitzbergen, is a far tastier fish than its relative, the white-fleshed trout.

Source: H.C.L.

131. Trout in Aspic

Boil the trout in salted water with a good dash of vinegar for 10 minutes. Then cover over and allow to stand all night. Set the trout in aspic jelly and serve with Sauce Tartare.

For the aspic jelly, take 1 pint stock free from grease, a few herbs, carrots, turnip and onion, peppercorns and 1 tablespoon vinegar, salt to taste. (When using for trout, add a little of the liquor in which the fish has been cooked.)

While these ingredients are cold, whip in 1 white of egg, then stir until the liquid comes to the boil. Just before boiling add 1 heaped tablespoon powdered gelatine which has been soaked in cold water, allow to boil gently for 1 minute, strain through a fine cloth and use when cold.

This recipe is particularly suitable for the New Zealand rainbow and brown trout, which run to a considerable size. Good in England for salmon-trout.

Source: The Dowager Viscountess Galway, formerly of Government House, Wellington, New Zealand.

132. Trout Soufflé

1 fair-sized trout	2 level tablespoons flour
4 whole eggs and one extra white of egg	1½ oz. butter
½ pint milk	salt, freshly milled pepper

Poach the trout in a court-bouillon and shred free from skin and bone.

Simmer the sauce made of the butter, flour and milk for 10 minutes, then off the fire stir in the 4 beaten egg yolks and mix into the fish.

When cool, add the stiffly whipped 5 whites of egg, and pour into a soufflé dish. Place this in a preheated over for 35 minutes at 330° F.

Source: The Hon. Mrs. Clarissa Luke, Sawmill House, West Wycombe Park, Bucks.

133. Smoked Fish au Gratin

Bone and skin any good smoked fish and cut into small pieces. Cook slowly in a little milk, and drain off the liquor. Make a sauce with butter, flour, the milk in which the fish was cooked, grated cheese, salt and pepper. Place the fish in a buttered fireproof dish, cover with the sauce, sprinkle with grated cheese and cook for 10 minutes in an oven to brown slightly.
Source: H.C.L.'s cook Bala, Government House, Fiji.

134. Bacalhao Pudding

1 pint milk	½ lb. bacalhao (dried cod) or
2 tablespoons butter	other white fish
2 dessertspoons flour	2 oz. raisins
6 eggs	2 oz. grated cheese

Make a Béchamel of the milk, butter and flour. Then stir the fish, which has been minced, together with the yolks of the 6 eggs, the raisins and the cheese, into the Béchamel, lastly adding the whipped whites of the eggs.

Butter a mould well and line with breadcrumbs. Fill with the mixture and cook in a bain-marie or bake in the oven.

Serve with melted butter or, preferably, cream horseradish sauce.
Source: Mrs. R.T. Smallbones, São Paulo, Brazil. A Portuguese and Brazilian dish.

135. Raw Fish à la Viti

2 lb. white fish	limes or lemons
4 cloves garlic	2 tablespoons olive oil
1 onion	2 tablespoons vinegar
2 hard-boiled eggs	2 tomatoes
6 gherkins	1 lettuce
6 olives	

Wash and skin the fish (any large, white, firm-fleshed fish will do). Cut fish in small squares, place in a pie-dish with the chopped onion, 3 teaspoons salt and a little pepper. Mix with a spoon, then cover fish with fresh lime (or lemon) juice. Place in refrigerator for 4 hours.

Then strain off all juice, chop garlic finely and olives and gherkins in small pieces, mix in the pickled fish and pour over it the vinegar and oil. Serve in a bowl with lettuce leaves, and garnish with tomatoes and slices of egg.

Source: Fiji.

136. Raw Fish a la R.L.S.

Cut fish in dice, soak ½ hour in juice of fresh limes, then wash in fresh water. Soak for ½ hour in tarragon vinegar, serve with Sauce Tartare.

Source: H.C.L.'s improvement (as he thinks) on the dish much enjoyed at Vailima in Samoa as an invalid food towards the close of his life by Robert Louis Stevenson, who had the fish soaked in coconut milk instead of vinegar and used no sauce.

IV

Poultry, Game and Meat

137. Circassian Chicken (Cherkess Tawughu)

    1 boiling chicken   1 medium onion
    2 slices stale bread   1 onion stuck with cloves
    1 lb. dried shelled walnuts   1 dessertspoon paprika
    2 cloves garlic   1 teaspoon cayenne pepper

Boil the chicken and the onion stuck with cloves until sufficiently tender for the flesh to come away. While it cools, mince very fine the walnuts, raw onion, garlic and the bread, slightly moistened.

    Remove all fat from the chicken stock and shred the chicken into the walnut mixture, adding the paprika and the cayenne pepper. Then add the chicken stock until the mixture is like a firm cream. Serve cold with a salad of lettuce and sliced green *pimientos*.
    Source: Mrs. John Brewis's Assyrian cook, Baghdad.

138. Chicken à la King

    1 4-lb. chicken   1 4-oz. jarred pimientos, diced
    5 tablespoons butter   1 teaspoon salt
    5 tablespoons flour   1 green pepper, thinly sliced
    1½ cups milk   1 lb. fresh mushrooms, finely cut but
    ½ cup cream   not shredded

Place chicken (cut up) in saucepan. Add one slice of onion and one piece of celery for flavour and salt to taste. Cover with water and cook slowly until done. Drain and retain soup for other purposes. Separate meat from bones and skin, and cut meat with scissors in pieces as long as possible and ½ inch wide.

    Melt butter in pan without browning. Sauter the green pepper and mushrooms for about 10 minutes over a low flame. Then sift flour over same and toss lightly in pan in order to distribute flour evenly. Add milk, cream and salt, and cook until it bubbles. Add chicken and cook for 10 minutes. Just before serving add the *pimientos* and reheat.

The goodness of this dish depends much upon the quality of the chicken and mushrooms used.

Source: Miss Welden, sometime cook to Mr. and Mrs. Leander McCormick-Goodhart, Bellapaïs, Alexandria, Virginia, U.S.A.

The name derives its origin from Mr. Foxhall Keane, the well-known polo player, who three or four decades ago suggested this manner of preparing and serving chicken to the chef of Delmonico's in New York City. The original name 'Chicken à la Keane' has therefore been regally corrupted.

139. Poulet à la Crème

1 good-sized chicken
a few mushrooms
a few tomatoes
1 rasher streaky bacon
2 egg yolks

a bouquet of parsley, thyme, bay leaf and tarragon, and one clove
a few button onions, if liked
1 tumbler Chablis or Graves
Cream

Joint the chicken, and cook it in butter in a cocotte with the bouquet and the bacon cut in dice, shaking the pan occasionally. Do not let the chicken get brown - only stiff and 'seized'. Then add the wine and cook slowly for ½ hour with the lid on. When cooked, remove bouquet and keep the chicken hot in a serving dish. Mix the two yolks well with a little cream and use it to thicken the liquor in which the bird was cooked, but do not let this sauce boil. Season, and pour over the chicken.

Source: The Misses Warren, Mdina, Malta.

140. Pollo Ajillo

2 small chickens
3-4 heads garlic
1 wine glass brandy
saffron

1 bottle dry white wine
1 cup olive oil
salt

In a heavy iron casserole fry the garlic teeth in the olive oil, remove and set aside. Next brown the jointed chickens in the garlicky oil and season with saffron and salt. Take off heat, add glass of brandy and set alight. Put back over fast heat till flames have gone out. Add the bottle of white wine which will instantly emulsify with the oil. Place lid over casserole and simmer over low heat for approximately 30 minutes or until chicken is cooked through. Before serving, return garlic to casserole and dish up with the chicken. Garnish with parsley and lemon quarters. Arroz Blanco (rec. 25) goes very well with this dish.

Source: Doña Francisca Hidalgo, Alora (Málaga).

141. *Carbery Pie (Cold)*

1 chicken, rabbit or 1½ lb. veal
½ teaspoon mignonette pepper
2 tablespoons chopped parsley
12 white peppercorns
1 small onion
a little salt
½ pint cream

Place the chicken (or alternative) in a stewpan with 1 quart water, the onion, peppercorns and salt, and boil slowly for 1 hour. Remove the chicken and reduce the stock to about ¾ pint. Cut up, skin and bone the chicken and place meat in a fireproof dish with cover (in which it will be served). Remove all grease from the stock, and add the parsley and mignonette pepper. Add the boiling cream and then pour over the chicken, which should be covered entirely. Put in a cool oven for 1 hour. Serve when cold with chopped jelly on top.

The pie should 'jelly'; and in cold weather, or with ice, can be made the same day as required. The cream and mignonette pepper are indispensable.

Source: Madge, Lady Bonham-Carter.

142. A Bolivian 'Picante de Gallina'

Just in case any readers of this book unlikely to visit the High Andes would like to try for themselves one of the corrosively hot dishes favoured by the inhabitants of those lofty regions (whose climatic rigours demand internal compensations), here is their opportunity by means of this favourite Bolivian recipe. The meat is a large boiling fowl (a chicken would disintegrate under the treatment); but, the purer the Bolivian's Indian blood, whether Quechua or Aymará, the more likely he will be to replace the bird with a guinea-pig or even, if really hard pressed, with an unwanted cat.

>   *1 large boiling fowl*
>   *3 large (about 3 inches) red or yellow chillies (ají), sun-dried, preferably stone-ground and with the pips retained*
>   *2 large Spanish onions*
>   *4 tomatoes*
>   *2 slices stale bread*
>   *3 eggs*
>   *olive (which failing, sesame) oil*

Simmer the fowl for 1½ hours in the minimum of water.

Chop the onions and fry in the oil to a golden brown. Peel the tomatoes, mix them with the crumbled bread and the ground chillies and add this pulp to the onions in the frying-pan with more oil and a pinch of salt. Fry to a chocolate colour.

The ensuing thick paste is then thinned out to a thin gruel consistency with the water in which the fowl has been par-boiled.

Now carve the bird into 7 portions and fry these in the same frying-pan, using more oil as may be required. Note that the pan must not be cleaned after the removal of the sauce, since the heat is believed to be helpful in impregnating the meat thoroughly with the sauce.

Place the pieces of bird in a large dish, surround with boiled peeled potatoes and cover the whole with the thinned sauce, garnishing with parsley and hard-boiled eggs.

Source: Captain Hastings Campbell.

Note by H.C.L.: A less sulphurous, indeed a decidedly pleasant variant of the above is the Ethiopian staple dish *wat*. This is a stew of meat, fowl or vegetables, cooked with red peppers and other spices and condiments. It is mopped up with *injira*, the flat, spongy unleavened bread of the country, and is washed down with the national drink *tej*, a fermented mead flavoured with herbs.

143. Fezanjān

>   1 duck
>   ½ lb. shelled dry walnuts
>   rice
>   1 pint pomegranate juice
>
>   butter
>   2 teaspoons ground cinnamon
>   1 pinch powdered nutmeg

Fry the duck whole until golden brown. Then add a cup of water and simmer; as it simmers dry, add more water.

Meantime mince the walnuts in a mincer, fry in a little butter and add to the pomegranate juice, which will draw the oil from the nuts. (If pomegranate juice is not available, lemon or red-currant juice may be substituted provided they are sweetened to taste and are sufficiently diluted to be drinkable while still retaining their tartness.)

Now drain the duck, adding all its juice to the nut-and-pomegranate sauce.

Carve the duck into pieces of a reasonable size, place in the pot, which is nearly full of the sauce, and add 2 cups of water and the spices. Boil slowly with the lid on. When the duck is tender and the sauce thick, turn out and serve with plain boiled rice.

Source: Mrs. Arthur Kellas, British Embassy, Teheran. A well-known Persian delicacy.

144. Salmi de Canard Caribe

>   1 large duck
>   2 slices bacon
>   8 (or more) olives
>   1 large tomato (sliced)
>
>   2 tablespoons Port or Madeira
>   2 tablespoons rum
>   2 tablespoons whisky
>   1 tablespoon vinegar

½ onion	1 tablespoon olive oil
1 clove garlic	1 oz. butter
salt, pepper	2 teaspoons brown sugar

Cut the raw duck into small pieces as for stewing and then remove all large bones. Soak for 1 hour in the mixture composed of the wines, spirits and vinegar, the tomato, chopped onion, garlic, salt, pepper and 1 teaspoon of the brown sugar.

Now remove and brown in the butter and oil with the bacon and the rest of the sugar.

Cover closely in a heavy saucepan with 2 tablespoons of water and cook for 1 hour. Then add the mixture in which the duck was soaked and stew slowly for about another hour, until tender. De-stone the olives and add 5 minutes before serving.

Source: Mrs. Jean Marshall Campbell, Port of Spain, Trinidad. A Trinidad dish.

145. Roast Peacock or Peahen

Clean, stuff as below, truss, rub with salt and ground pepper, and cover breast with slices of fat bacon.

Roast in a moderate oven, allowing 25 minutes to the pound and basting frequently, since peafowl are not fat birds. The peahen should be selected in preference to the cock, who is apt to be dry.

Stuffing:	2 lb. chestnuts	bouquet garni
	1 lb. sausage meat	salt, pepper
	2 oz. butter	1 cup breadcrumbs

Boil the chestnuts, and mash half of them. Fry the sausage meat for 5 minutes, then add the mashed chestnuts and seasoning. When thoroughly mixed, add the whole chestnuts.

Garnish: Whole chestnuts, first parboiled, then sauté in the gravy of the bird, alternating with whole truffles (if available) wrapped individually in greased paper and baked for 1 hour in a hot oven.

Source: First eaten by H.C.L. when staying before the First

World War with Madame Gallet de Koréwo at her Château de la Haute Borde near Chaumont in Touraine. Later was served by him on various occasions in the West Indies to Sir Arthur (author of *A Pattern of Islands*) and Lady Grimble and other friends. The bird is bred for the table in the Dominican Republic.

A juicy peahen as cooked in the French *province* can excel in flavour any other domestic bird, not excluding a goose. But there are those who claim that even the peahen is inferior to a well roast, tender young flamingo.

Remember, when the occasion arises, that in the technical jargon of gastronomy you do not carve a peacock; you disfigure him. Similarly, you

> lift a swan,
> dismember a heron,
> allay a pheasant,
> unbrace a duck,
> thigh a woodcock,
> mince a plover, and
> spall a hen.

What you do to a flamingo is unascertained.

It may be added that in dealing with fish, you

> chine a salmon,
> splat a pike,
> culpon a trout,
> barb a lobster, and
> tame a crab.

146. *The Goose, Domestic and Wild*

The most tasty of the ordinary domesticated fowls, in my opinion, is the goose, a bird vastly superior to duck or turkey. Swedes, who are partial to the bird, are apt to complain that it is too much for one person and not enough for two. A goose should be eaten before it is two years old. A green gosling is one killed before Michaelmas, and the reader may have noticed a reference to a delicious green gosling dish in the Introductory Chapter.

Here is a simple recipe for roast goose:

a goose	*½ pint fresh breadcrumbs*
6 onions	*herbs to taste, preferably without sage,*
2 oz. butter	*and a pinch of lemon thyme*
1 egg	*salt, pepper*

Make a stuffing by chopping the onions and frying them lightly in the butter, then mixing well with the breadcrumbs, herbs, seasoning and whole beaten egg. Fill into the cleaned and trussed bird, rub it well with dripping and wrap in greased paper. Roast in the oven for about 1 hour, according to size. Remove the paper when nearly cooked in order to brown the bird.

Surround with chestnuts that have been cooked with the bird and serve with a good gravy and with cranberry sauce.

That discerning pair of wandering gastronomes, 'Bon Viveur', whose path once intersected mine in Scandinavia, praise (I can well imagine with what justice) a dish of wild goose with wild rice eaten by them in Stockholm. Here, alas, they have the advantage of me so far as the combination is concerned. But I ate wild goose, when staying with Sir Denis and Lady Wright at the British Embassy in Addis Ababa, at a luncheon-party given there on the 13 December 1960 - the day before the outbreak of the abortive revolt against the Emperor Haile Sellassie. It was a Blue Ethiopian goose, dismembered and served as a salmi with a dark brown wine sauce. At first I mistook it for a particularly tasty hare.

Source: H.C.L.

147. *Salted Goose*

a goose	*7 oz. sugar*
2 oz. saltpetre	*3 lb. salt*

Boil up 5 quarts water with the saltpetre, sugar and salt, and pour hot over the goose, which has been cleaned and trussed. Leave the goose lying in this decoction for 3 days, then boil slowly until tender.

The goose should be served cold with a sauce made of lightly whipped cream in which are mixed white vinegar, grated horseradish and a pinch of sugar. The sauce should be frozen in the refrigerator before serving.

A Scanian speciality.

Source: Recipe given to H.C.L. while on a visit to Malmö, capital of the South Swedish Province of Scania, by the British Vice-Consul, Mr. Hans Ekman, M.B.E.

148. *How the Turkey Got His Names*

The turkey is a good bird, although in my opinion he lacks the savour of the goose, quite apart from the goose's superlative sideline, so to speak, in the shape of his liver. Still, since at least the middle of the sixteenth century the turkey has been making his own notable contribution to 'Christmas husbandlie fare', and we are grateful to him for that. As early as 1550 Clarenceux King of Arms had granted the crest of a turkey-cock in splendour to William Strickland of Boynton Hall, Yorks, who as captain of one of Sebastian Cabot's ships had introduced some of these birds from the Spanish Main into England. And to the turkey-hen we should also be grateful for the tastiest of all eggs, their flavour the sublimation of the hen's without the richness of the duck's. Yet, even so, the most interesting thing about the turkey is not his flesh but his name.

The appellations given to this exotic bird from the New World in the languages of the Old are, with one exception, geographically erratic and hopelessly perplexing.

That in English he should be called turkey may be due to sixteenth-century confusion with guinea-fowl and pea-fowl, introduced into England from their respective homes via Turkey at much the same time as the turkey arrived from South America and Spain. Other suggested derivations are, on the one hand, that his gobble sounds like *turk, turk, turk*; on the other, that turkey is a corruption of *furkee*, his name in one of the Amerindian languages.

The French call him *dinde*, and hence *dindon*, because that is how they have contracted *oiseau* or *coq d'Inde*, the Indian bird.

Hence the tongue-twisting French distich:
> *Didon dîna, dit on,*
> *Du dos d'un dodu dindon.*

The official German word is *Truthahn* (fem. *Trute* or *Pute*); but in Germany he is also called *Kalkuttischer Hahn*, actually not the Calcutta but the Calicut cock. The popular Austrian term, again with this apparently irresistible trend towards the Indies, is *Indian*.

Apart, then, from ourselves, the European world generally seems to connect the turkey with Indians, but is extremely hazy about what sort of Indians, whether those of the East Indies or those of the American continent. The French are not only, like the Germans, geographically but also ecclesiastically adrift, because they sometimes call their *dindon* a *jésuite* after one Friar Agapida, the confessor of Cortés, who was one of the first recorded authorities to praise the bird but was not a member of the Society of Jesus. Perhaps the Portuguese are the most ingenious, for they have contrived to hedge and make the best of both worlds, Old and New, since one of their names for the animal is *gallina da India*, but the other, *peru*. The Portuguese were once the most powerful nation in the East Indies, where they still own major portions of the island of Timor; the word *peru* for turkey is one of their legacies to the Malay language.

In point of fact the turkey comes neither from Turkey nor from the Indies. He comes originally from Mexico and Central America, whose aboriginal inhabitants are among the so-called American Indians. This is just one of the many examples of the permanent confusion into which Christopher Columbus plunged the world by thinking that he had reached the East Indies by a new route and so brought it about that his Caribbean discoveries had to remain Indies of sorts, and thus became the West Indies.

The Conquistadores found two kinds of wild turkey in the New World: the ocellated turkey *Agriocharis ocellata* (so called from the eyes on the stag bird's tail), whose home was in Yucatan and what are now Guatemala and British Honduras; and, farther north, the Mexican wild turkey *Meleagris gallopavo*, which the Aztecs had already domesticated for the table. Some of the domesticated variety were shipped to Spain as early as 1498, and from Spain the bird soon spread throughout southern and western Europe. It had been domesticated also by the South American peoples composing the miracle of administrative organization, the Inca Empire, a circumstance which sends the Portuguese to the top of the class with their *peru*.

In the chapel of the castle of Celle is a triptych by Maerten de Vos of 1569, on which a live turkey is depicted. Is this its earliest representation in Western art? As regards the East, the Victoria and Albert Museum possesses a delicately drawn and beautifully coloured miniature of a turkey-cock painted by Ustad Mansur for the Emperor Jahangir in 1612. Perhaps it was in order to emphasize his own Spain's part in propagating this useful bird that Goya painted his brilliant study of a plucked turkey-hen - a picture which formed a part of the loan collection from the Munich Alte Pinakothek to the London National Gallery in 1949. For some strange reason the rather impersonal and remote-control Spanish form of courting - with the swain relegated to the outer side of the *reja* (grille) of the window - is known in Spanish as *pelando la pava* - plucking the turkey-hen.

But has Turkey herself no contribution to make, no solution to offer, regarding this problem of the turkey's name? She has indeed; and her contributions but serve yet farther to darken counsel. For the Turks must needs call this Protean fowl *Hindi* or *Misr tawughu*, the bird from India or from Egypt; so they too have fallen victims to the prevalent geographical confusion, if rather nearer home.

Versatile but long-suffering Egypt. In England she is made the godmother of the gypsy, in Turkey of the turkey; yet in truth she has no more responsibility for the one than for the other. But the Turks are not the worst offenders: the Arabs with their *dik al-Habash*, the Abyssinian fowl, are even wider adrift.

Source: H.C.L.

149. Sliced Turkey en Casserole

Egg and breadcrumb thin slices of cooked breast of turkey and fry lightly. Place half the slices in the bottom of a Pyrex dish, cover with a layer of raw bacon and cover the bacon with a layer of thin slices of Gruyère cheese. Superimpose a layer of each of the three ingredients in the same order and place the dish in the oven until it is thoroughly heated and the cheese has melted.

Source: Mrs. Alan Morton, British Council, Beirut.

150. White Devil

Remove the legs from a turkey, boiling fowl or other gallinaceous white-fleshed bird. Boil the remainder of the bird slowly till very tender, separate the flesh from the carcass and keep warm in the dish in which it is to be served.

Prepare the *sauce* as follows: take 1 pint of cream, add 4 tablespoons of Worcestershire Sauce and 2 teaspoons of English mustard. Mix briskly and bring rapidly to the boil.

When near the boil; place the dish containing the flesh in a convenient place. As soon as the sauce boils, pour it over the flesh and serve immediately.

A boiling fowl will require less sauce than a turkey.

Source: The Recipe book of Lady Coghill, Glen Barrahane, Skibbereen, Co. Cork.

And here, from another source, is a tasty method of dealing with the turkey's legs:

Make a devilled butter as follows: Mix 1 oz. butter with cayenne, black pepper and mustard. Score deeply the legs of the cooked turkey and spread thickly with the mixture. Grill and serve very hot with a Sauce Piquante.

Can also be eaten cold if preferred, in which case the mixture should be left on the meat for an hour before serving.

151. Boned Turkey

(Included for its nostaglic appeal.)

'At the messes of European Regiments in India it is no uncommon thing to bone a turkey and a fowl and to put the one inside the other, filling the interstices with sausage-meat, a small pig being killed for the purpose.'

Source: *A New System of Domestic Cookery*, by Mrs. Rundell, 69th edition, revised by Miss Emma Roberts. John Murray, London, 1846.

152. A Royal Dinner of Roast Cygnets

'Last night (*sc.* on 15 May, 1935) at Vintners' Hall certain Merchant Princes were entertained at dinner by certain other Merchant Princes. Among the guests were a Fishmonger (excellent well, and an honest man, as Hamlet would declare), a Draper, a Mercer and a Clothworker; and, had not illness prevented him, there would also have been a Haberdasher. And it is but in accord with the modern relation between Throne and people that these four guests should be princely by birth and mercantile by election; that the Fishmonger was the Prince of Wales, the Draper the Duke of York, the Mercer the Duke of Gloucester and the Clothworker the Duke of Kent. And the Haberdasher was Prince Arthur of Connaught, and the Vintner, who was the principal host, was the Earl of Athlone, the Queen's brother, and sometime well known by the name of Prince Alexander of Teck.

'The Vintners, mercantile by happy destiny and princely by achievement, are not altogether strange to such company. In one respect they are indeed something like being very nearly Royal themselves. They and the Dyers have an ancient privilege of owning swans on the Thames; and no one else in the world may do that except the King, the Seigneur of Swans. And not swans merely; they own a Game of Swans - a noble phrase, coloured by the lore of the true words of wood and water, a gaggle of geese, a leash of teal and the rest, and by long selection and refinement from the days when Queen Elizabeth kept a game of bears, and a nobleman owned a stately game of red deer in his park. All true Vintners' hearts must have swelled with pride last night when, in the presence of their princely guests, their Swan Warden, with the Swan Mar-

H.C.L. about to share an appetising alfresco luncheon with Queen Salote. Tonga, 1938.

Sacred and Profane. The Proconsul cloaked in the Order of St. John of Jerusalem and the Postgraduate being waggish in Sicily.

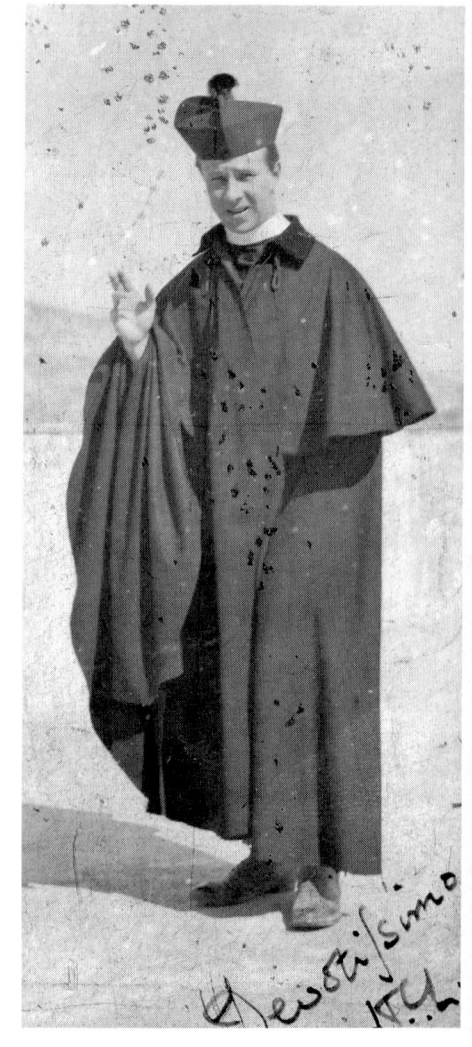

H.C.L. Head of the British Mission with Georgian officers at the Independence Day celebrations. Tiflis (Tblisi), 1920.

H.C.L., the Assistant Governor of Jerusalem, in naval uniform stands beside the Governor, Ronald Storrs, following the 'Liberation Day' Service in the Anglican Cathedral. Palestine, 1924.

kers, Uppers and Banner Bearer, bore in the roast cygnets at the capital moment of the feast.'

Source: Extracted, by kind permission of the Editor, from a leading article in *The Times* of 16 May, 1935.

153. Perdrix aux Choux

Blanch one or two cabbages, and drain them. Melt a little fat in a fireproof dish and braise the cabbage lightly. Hollow out the centre of the dish and therein arrange the partridges which have been tossed in hot butter, a savoury sausage (Frankfurt or Vienna sausages are best) and a piece of fresh unsalted fat bacon. Add a few carrots and small onions, a bouquet garni and peppercorns. Cover the dish closely and braise in the oven for about 1½ hours.

Always take care to remove the game when it is cooked, for the cabbage and bacon will not be spoilt by long cooking. Cut the bacon in pieces and the sausage crossways into thin rounds, and mix in with the cabbage. Arrange this on the serving dish with the partridges cut into joints on top.

A light demi-glace sauce (*q.v.*) may be poured over the dish, for which old birds are best.

Source: Mrs. Neville Lake. A French Recipe, and perhaps the tastiest way of cooking both partridge and cabbage.

154. An Andalusian Method of Preserving Partridges

For each bird (it is economical to preserve several at a time) you require:

1 cup olive oil *1 bayleaf*
1 Sherry glass wine vinegar *salt, pepper*
1 clove garlic

Boil the birds till tender in this marinade, adding more oil if necessary to cover, then place in a porcelain bowl.

Birds thus treated will keep for 10 to 12 months, even in a warm climate.

Source: Mr. Peter Luke.

Of other Spanish partridge dishes, H.C.L. commends one of the bird cooked whole in a blend of olive oil, Spanish white wine and sliced onions. It is the *specialité de la maison* of that agreeable restaurant, 'Venta de Aires', where he enjoyed it on a brilliant late October day in 1953, lunching in the open air on the terrace at the foot of the walls of Toledo with his host Mr. F.A. d'Almeida, O.B.E.

155. The Beccafico (see Recipe 127) and Commandería

The beccafico (literally 'fig-pecker') is a small migratory bird belonging to the genus *Sylvia*, resembling the ortolan in size and flavour.

In the autumn he frequents the shores and islands of the Mediterranean, where he is greatly esteemed after he has fattened on figs and grapes. He is caught by being limed, poor little fellow, in his favourite fig-trees, a more cruel end than that which awaits the ortolan after that delicacy has been artificially fattened for the table. All that is then necessary is to dip the bird's beak in a glass of champagne, whereupon he dies instantaneously from the effect of the effervescent wine on his fattily degenerated heart.

When fresh, the beccafico is eaten roast or, better still, in a pilav or risotto (*cf.* Recipes 26 and 27). In Cyprus, where he is abundant for a short time in the autumn and very popular, the birds not eaten fresh are preserved in a vinegar made of the Cypriote dessert wine which is called Commandería because it is grown on the former Commandery of the Knights of S. John above Kolossi Castle in the District of Limasol. Immersion in this causes the bones to become soft, so that after a while the birds can be eaten whole and in one mouthful.

An article of perfumery popular in Western Europe during the Middle Ages was known as *oiselet de Chypre* because it was fashioned in the shape of the beccafico.

Source: H.C.L.

156. Roast Hare à la Polonaise

Leave the hare in a good marinade (*cf.* Recipe 288) for 2-3 days. Several hours before cooking, add sliced raw vegetables to the marinade and keep in a cool place. Half an hour before cooking discard the vegetables, lard the hare as in the following Recipe, season with pepper and salt, put dabs of butter on top and roast in a hot oven, basting well.

When cooked, beat up ½ pint of sour cream with ½ tablespoon flour and pour it over the hare, replace the pan in the oven to brown, and serve at once.

N.B.: This mixture of ½ pint sour cream beaten with ½ tablespoon flour and heated to boiling point without boiling is added to gravies, soups, etc., in Poland, and is extremely good.

Source: E.G.

157. Larded Saddle of Hare

Draw and truss the hare for roasting, leaving the head. Using a larding needle and prepared strips of fat bacon (*lardons*), lard the back and haunches of the hare in even lines, trimming when finished to give a neat appearance. Cover with buttered paper and roast in a hot oven for about 1½ hours, according to the size of the hare.

Serve on a hot dish garnished with hot, coarsely grated beetroot (which has been cooked, grated and then reheated with a little butter), seasoning and a squeeze of lemon juice.

Add the sour cream sauce as in the preceding Recipe.

Source: The same.

158. A Polish Pâté of Hare or Goose

    1 lb. veal   *bay leaves, nutmeg*
    1 lb. fat pork   *4 eggs*
    1 lb. liver   *fat bacon*

roughly half a hare or the
quarter of a goose, including liver, kidneys, etc.
1 onion

peppercorns
2 small bread rolls

Soak and clean the hare well and place with the other meats in a large pan with the bay leaves, onion and peppercorns, and water to cover. Simmer gently for 3-4 hours, until the meat falls off the bones. Remove bones, gristle, etc., and mince all the meat *three times*, adding two small bread rolls that have been soaked in the stock from the meat. Then sieve the minced meat and add the four raw eggs and half a grated nutmeg. Butter a mould well, sprinkle with breadcrumbs and line with small strips of fat bacon. Fill with the meat mixture, pressed well down until firm and bake in a hot oven for 45 minutes.

Leave to cool in the mould and, when ready to use, heat the mould slightly to turn out.

Source: The same.

159. Pâté of Game

1 pheasant or grouse or 1-2 partridges
½ lb. lean pork
5 oz. streaky bacon
a little Sherry or Madeira
2 onions
herbs, salt, pepper

a few mushrooms
a few chicken livers
2 eggs
4 oz. bacon fat
1 shallot

Bone the birds (old birds will do), cut the meat in fillets and marinade for 6 hours in a little Sherry or Madeira, with slices of onion, bay leaf and parsley, salt and pepper. Meanwhile, make a stock with the carcass, bones and a little water, which you cook slowly until reduced to about ½ pint. Chop or mince the pork, bacon and chicken livers, add the finely chopped mushrooms and shallot, pound well together with the reduced stock and two whole beaten eggs.

Take a deep earthenware dish or terrine, line it with thin slices of pork fat, then arrange first a layer of minced meat, then fillets of game, then mince and so on until the dish is nearly full, finishing with a layer of minced meat and seasoning the whole well. Cover with thin slices of pork fat, put the lid on and cook standing in hot water for 2 hours in a moderate oven. When cooked, remove the lid and let it get cold with a weight on. Cover with a coating of melted lard, and it will keep for several weeks.

160. *Simple Game Pie*

*remains of pheasants, hare,
    rabbits, etc.; livers
½ lb. breadcrumbs
3 eggs
¾ lb. butter
garlic
pepper
fat bacon
mushrooms*

Bone all the meat of the game and make a strong jelly of the bones. Make a forcemeat of the livers rubbed through a sieve, the breadcrumbs, eggs and butter; and season with garlic and pepper.

Line a pie-dish with fat bacon, press in the meat and forcemeat in layers, adding mushrooms. Steam the pie with the lid on. When done, pour in as much stock as it will hold and press with a weight. When cold, make air-tight with hot lard.

Source: Mrs. Philip Martin, Jersey.

161. *A Pork Pâté*

*a piece of good fat pork
2 onions
pepper, cinnamon, garlic
salt
1 gill white wine*

Remove the ligaments from a piece of good fat pork and mince it, but not as finely as for sausages. Mince two onions and mix with the meat. Add salt and pepper with cinnamon and garlic to taste, mixing all well. Place a gill of white wine in the bottom of a fireproof dish, add the prepared meat and cook in a moderate oven until the fat is quite clear, almost like water. Serve cold.

Source: Sister Marie Pierre, a French nun from La Vendée, serving in the Polynesian island of Rotuma, Western Pacific.

162. Fleischkuchen

½ lb. minced or chopped cold meat
1½ oz. butter
2 finely chopped shallots
½ gill stock or gravy
1 dessertspoon flour
salt, pepper, lard

Fry the shallots lightly in the hot butter, sprinkle in the flour, add stock and boil together. Add the meat, with seasoning to taste, and cook for a few minutes.

Make a thin pancake batter, and pour a little into an omelette pan in which ¼ oz. lard has been heated. As soon as this has set, spread over it 2 tablespoons of the meat preparation and cover with another layer of batter and so on. Place the pan in a hot oven and bake until the batter is set and lightly browned. Serve hot, cut into convenient portions, with a green salad.

Source: A German recipe.

163. Stewed Venison or Wild Boar

1 lb. cubed venison or wild boar
½ lb. carrots
½ lb. parsnips (optional)
1 large onion (chopped)
1 large clove garlic (crushed)
2 bay leaves
flour
fresh thyme
10 juniper berries
2-3 tablespoons black olives
½-1 pint stock
½ bottle red wine
salt, pepper

Toss meat in well seasoned flour. Heat olive oil in 4 pint casserole dish and brown meat with onion and garlic. Add vegetables, herbs, stock and wine. Bring to boil skimming any scum off the top. Turn down heat and cook slowly for 1 hour or until tender. Or casserole can be placed in oven. Last 10 minutes add crushed or chopped black olives. Sprinkle with chopped parsley.

Source: Ms. Chloe Luke.

164. Costillas en Adobo

2 lbs. lard
4 lbs. pork spare ribs
sweet paprika pepper
1 head garlic
vinegar

bay leaves
oregano
salt, pepper
cloves

Mix together the lard, plenty of paprika pepper, the chopped garlic, bay leaves, a good handful of oregano (preferably fresh), a couple of cloves, roughly ground black pepper, salt and about a tablespoon of red wine vinegar. Bury the spare ribs well in the marinade and leave overnight. About 2 hours before meal take the whole mixture out of the bowl and fry gently until the lard is clear and the spare ribs are tender. With a slotted spoon lift out the *costillas*. Serve with mashed potatoes and a green salad. The fat left in the pan should be poured into a bowl and set aside to cool. This makes paprika-coloured dripping (*manteca colorada*) with a thick meaty sediment. Delicious with breakfast toast.

Source: Sra. Antonia Cortes, Malaga.

165. To Bake a Gammon of Bacon

(For a joint of about 2 lb.) Soak overnight in cold water. Wrap, without removing the rind, in a double sheet of greaseproof paper or aluminium foil after inserting a bay leaf, and tie up securely with string.

Pour a little boiling water (to start the steaming) into a pyrex casserole with tight-fitting lid, insert the joint and bake in a moderate oven for ½ hour to the lb. and a ½ hour over. Cooking too fast in too high a heat will cause the meat to shrink and spoil.

On removing the joint from the bag, be careful not to spill the accumulated juice, which if not too salty may be made into a light sauce with the addition of Sherry.

Source: Mrs. M.S. Eller.

166. To Cure Ox-tongue or Beef

1 gallon cold water
3 lb. salt
½ lb. pickling sugar
1 oz. powdered saltpetre

Boil all together for ½ hour, skim well and allow to get cold before pouring the mixture on the tongue or beef. Tongues should be well salted overnight and scraped before immersion in the brine, where they should remain from 2 to 3 weeks. If convenient, they should then be smoked for 3 weeks.

167. Boiled Cured Ox-tongue

1 3-lb. cured ox-tongue
2 stalks celery, chopped
a bouquet garni
salt, peppercorns

If fresh from the pickle, soak the tongue in cold water for 2-3 hours; if it has gone hard, for 12 hours.

Then place in fresh water with the above ingredients and simmer from 2 to 3 hours until tender.

Serve hot with Horseradish Sauce (*q.v.*) or a thick, well-sweetened tomato sauce, or both. But subtler than these is the sauce of sieved sorrel thickened with a Béchamel described in Recipe 269.

The tongue should *not* be skinned if it is going to be carved at the table, and particularly if it is going to be used up cold afterwards.

The ideal accompaniments of a hot cured ox-tongue are a purée of spinach or sorrel (unless the sorrel sauce is used), and carrots à la Kazbek (*qq.v.*).

Source: H.C.L.

168. *Spiced Beef*

a large joint of fresh beef of, say, 20 lb.
½ lb. coarse brown sugar

Rub the beef with the sugar, and let it stand for 2 days. Then grind:

2 oz. saltpetre	*¾ lb. common salt*
¼ lb. black pepper	*3 oz. allspice*
4 oz. juniper berries	

Rub these strongly and equally over the beef daily for 3 weeks, turning at the same time. Wash off the spice, and boil. It will keep for a fortnight.

Source: Mrs. Philip Martin (her grandmother's Recipe). Below is a simplified version:

169. *Simple Spiced Beef*

4 lb. fresh silverside   *1½ oz. allspice*
4 large tablespoons dark-   *2 tablespoons vinegar*
  brown sugar   *peppercorns*
4 large tablespoons coarse salt

Cover with water, simmer for 2 hours and allow to stand in the liquor until cold. Press if necessary.

Source: The same.

170. Baked Ham - I

Soak the ham overnight, boil it and skin while hot. When cool, so that the paste will not run, make a thick paste of sticky brown sugar mixed with vinegar. Cover the ham ½ inch thick, and bake in an oven hot enough to brown.
Source: Mrs. Eric Corson, St. Angelo, Malta.
Note by H.C.L.: Adding a pint of white wine or cider and a dessertspoon of Worcestershire sauce to the water in which the ham is boiled is advantageous.

171. Baked Ham - II

Soak skinned ham in cold water for 1 hour, make a thick paste with flour and water, cover the ham thickly with the paste and bake, allowing 15 minutes for each pound of ham, in a medium oven. Allow the ham to cool before removing paste. This method keeps the juices in.
Source: Mrs. Archdeacon Teall, Lolowai, New Hebrides.

172. Baked Ham - III

Remove the outside skin from a cold boiled ham. Criss-cross ham with a sharp knife and insert cloves ½ inch apart.
Cover well with brown sugar, and place in uncovered pan, fat side up, and pour 1 pint ginger ale in bottom on pan. Bake in moderate oven from 1-1½ hours, basting with the liquid every 10-15 minutes.
Source: Mrs. Harold Gatty, Fiji.

173. Baked Ham - IV

Take an 8-lb. ham, skin, and soak overnight in cold water. Make a thick paste of 5 tablespoons brown sugar and 3 tablespoons mus-

tard, mixed very thickly with a few drops of milk, and spread it over the skinned ham. Put in a baking-tin with 1 quart milk and brown in a hot oven for a few minutes, then bake slowly for 3½-4 hours, basting at intervals. Take care that the paste is not too thin.
Source: Lady Wyatt, Tasmania.

174. Hot Ham Soufflé

    3 oz. butter   *10 oz. lean ham*
    4 tablespoons flour   *1 liqueur glass brandy or Port*
    1 pint milk   *4 oz. grated cheese*
    4 eggs

Make a Béchamel with the butter, flour and milk. Season with salt and pepper, add the cheese, stir till smooth and allow to cool. Beat in 4 yolks of eggs, add the stiffly whipped whites, blend together with the finely sieved cooked ham and cook in a well-buttered soufflé dish for 20 minutes in a hot oven. Garnish with small dice of lean ham which have been soaked in a little brandy or Port and cooked in the oven for 20 minutes with a dab of butter on top.
Source: Mrs. Neville Lake.

175. Brawn

Clean a pig's face or sheep's head, place in saucepan with water to cover and simmer with a bouquet garni until the meat leaves the bones. Remove the meat, and continue to boil the liquid until reduced to the amount required, adding additional seasoning as necessary. Strain, add the meat which has been cut into small pieces and pour into a wetted mould. Allow to set. A tongue can be boiled, skinned and put in centre of mould.
Source: Miss Audrey Gainsford. An old Lincolnshire family Recipe.

176. Ox-tail Brawn

Simmer 1 ox-tail in a little water with seasoning for 8 hours, and allow to stand overnight.

Next day, if the jelly is very stiff, pour off some of the liquid (which can be used as stock for jellied soup) and add more water. Take out all bones, chop meat very finely, add chopped parsley, herbs and a good seasoning of salt; for when the brawn is cold it tastes less salty than would be expected. Line a wet mould with sliced hard-boiled eggs, pour in the meat and jelly, and allow to set overnight.

Turn out and garnish with tomato, parsley or cress and serve very cold.

Source: Lady Garvey, Government House, Isle of Man.

177. Ox-tail Cavour

1 ox-tail	onion, garlic
1 calf's foot	a bouquet garni
fried diced ham	red wine
tomato	mushrooms

Parboil the tail, cut in pieces, and add tomato, onion, garlic and a calf's foot. Take out the meat, keeping the liquid in a saucepan with fried diced ham and a bouquet garni. Fry the tail lightly with the calf's foot. Add to the liquor half as much red wine with some mushrooms, reduce and pour over the meat in a casserole.

Source: Sir John Leche.

178. Pepper Pot

1 ox-tail or similar quantity of cow heel	1 bunch thyme
3 lb. fresh pork	2 tablespoons brown sugar
1 lb. salt pork or beef	4 red peppers (in a muslin bag)
	garlic

1 old fowl or duck   1½ gills cassareep
 1 lb. sliced onions

Cut the meat into moderate-sized pieces as for an Irish Stew, place in a large pan, cover with water and put on to boil. When half-cooked, add the condiments, onion and cassareep, and continue to boil until the meat is tender.

The Pepper Pot can be kept going almost indefinitely, certainly for weeks, provided it is cooked and retained in an earthenware pot with a cover, is brought to boiling point every day and is replenished as necessary with the various ingredients. Any left-over cold cooked meat and bird can be added as required, provided it is not seasoned. The addition of seasoned meat will turn the Pepper Pot sour.

Cassareep is the juice of the cassava, the starchy tropical plant of which tapioca is made, and is on the market, ready bottled.

Source: The traditional dish of British Guiana. A Recipe for the Tropics.

179. Barbecued Spareribs of Pork

Let the butcher crack the bones of 3 lb. fresh spareribs of pork in 5-inch pieces to eat with the fingers.

Place the ribs in a shallow pan and sprinkle with salt and pepper. Then roast in hot oven (450° F.) for 30 minutes.

While the ribs are roasting, mix 1 tablespoon butter or margarine, 1 chopped medium-sized onion, 1 8-oz. tin tomato sauce, 1 tablespoon vinegar, 1 tablespoon lemon juice, 2 tablespoons brown sugar, 1 teaspoon salt, 1 teaspoon mustard powder, ½ teaspoon Tabasco sauce, 1 bay leaf, 1 clove of garlic, and bring to the boil in a saucepan in ¼ cup water.

Ladle some of the sauce over the ribs, reducing the temperature to 350° F., and roast for one more hour, basting twice during this period.

Serve with the remaining sauce.

Source: A United States Recipe from Mr. Randall Kirk. While spareribs may not be readily procurable in Great Britain, the recipe is included not only for its intrinsic interest but also because the sauce is equally appropriate to devilled meats generally.

180. Haggis

The word haggis is derived from the French *hachis*, and is one of the Scots Gallicisms of which jigot (*gigot*), ashet *(assiette)* and the Berwickshire meshuntoder (*méchant odeur*) are other examples.

> 1 sheep's paunch and pluck
>   (Liver & lights. Eds.)
> 1 lb. finely chopped beef suet
> 2 finely chopped Spanish
>   onions
> 1½ pints good stock or gravy
>
> 2 tablespoons salt
> 1 teaspoon pepper
> ½ nutmeg, finely grated
> the juice of 1 lemon

Soak the paunch for 6 hours in cold water and salt, then turn it inside out and wash thoroughly in several waters. Wash the pluck, cover the liver with cold water, boil it for 1½ hours and at the end of ¾ hour add to it the heart and lights. Chop half the liver coarsely, the rest with the heart and lights more finely, mix all together and add the oatmeal, suet, onions, salt, pepper, nutmeg, lemon juice and stock. Turn these ingredients into the paunch, sew up the opening, taking care that sufficient space is left for the oatmeal to swell, for if the paunch is overfull there is a possibility of it bursting. Put the haggis into boiling water and boil gently for 3 hours; during the first hour it should be pricked occasionally with a needle to allow the air to escape. As a rule neither sauce nor gravy is served with haggis. But dish up on a foundation of mashed potatoes, as the haggis is very slippery, and this makes for difficulty in serving.

    The above is sufficient for 8-9 persons. If a lesser quantity is required, use a lamb's paunch and pluck, which should suffice for 4-5 people, according to the age of the lamb. The ingredients must not be chopped too finely and, above all, must never be minced, as this tends to make the haggis 'saggy'.

    Source: The recipe of the King's Own Scottish Borderers, which H.C.L. owes to the courtesy of Lt.-Colonel A. Murray and the Officers after dining with the Regiment on S. Andrew's night, 1935.

Sir Ronald Storrs has somewhere a description of the S. Andrew's night banquets at the Savoy Hotel in Cairo, whose Egyptian or Berberine waiters, their long *galabiehs* offering a bizarre contrast to the kilt of the piper, were thrilled to follow the pipes around the dining-room, carrying the haggis above their heads in proper Scots fashion.

181. Cyprus Sausages

Take 8-10 lb. young pork, preferably leg. Separate the lard and pass the lean through the mincing machine. Chop the lard up small, to about the size of peas, and mix together with the minced meat, adding pepper and salt. Add pounded coriander seeds and herbs to taste. Place the whole paste in an earthenware casserole, cover with red wine and soak for 48 hours.

Clean the gut well and soak in vinegar for 2-3 hours, then fill, tying at intervals of 2½-3 inches. Wrap in a muslin bag and hang out to drain for 4-5 days after puncturing the casings with a pin. The sausages may be eaten after 7-10 days, fried or grilled.

If boiled in lard for 10 minutes after draining and then allowed to cool and remain in the lard, the sausages will keep from 3 to 4 months.

Source: A village Recipe from Paphos, of which beautiful and romantic mountain District of Cyprus H.C.L. was once the Commissioner.

182. Liver Sausage

1½ lb. calf's or pig's liver, minced
1½ cups breadcrumbs
1 onion, parboiled and finely chopped
2 eggs
1 teaspoon mixed herbs
1 pinch nutmeg
1 pinch cinnamon
stock

Mix all together, binding with the eggs and sufficient stock. Leave for a few hours, and then roll into a large sausage. Lay this in a greased fireproof dish, top with sliced onion, cover with buttered paper and bake in a moderate oven for 30 minutes. May be served either hot or cold.

Source: An Austrian recipe.

183. Pain de Cervelles

1 calf's brain
1 egg
a little cream

1 Sherry glass Madeira
salt

Put a calf's brain in strong salt water for 1 hour, skin it and cook in cold water, to which a little salt has been added, until tender. Chop finely, add 1 egg, a little cream, a Sherry glass of Madeira and place in a mould.

Serve cold with a Béchamel or, if preferred, a tomato sauce.

Source: Madame Daguet, La Capilla, Colombia. A Recipe from the Auvergne.

184. Rognons au Vin Rouge

Skin and cut the lamb or veal kidneys in pieces, fry lightly with chopped onion, herbs and seasoning, add a little flour and enough red wine and stock in equal quantities to cover them. Put in a few drops of Worcestershire sauce.

This may be eaten either as a separate dish or as filling to an omelette. Chicken livers may be treated in the same way.

Source: Sir John Leche.

185. Tyrolean Liver (or Veal)

  1 lb. calf's liver (or veal) ½ gill sour cream
  1 small onion (chopped) 2 tablespoons flour
  1 dessertspoon capers   2 oz. fat
   (chopped)   salt, pepper
  1 dessertspoon vinegar

Slice the liver or veal and dust lightly with flour. Then fry the slices in the fat and keep them hot in it.

Fry the chopped onion, sprinkle with salt, pepper and a tablespoon of flour, and stir in the chopped capers, vinegar and enough water to make a thick sauce. When this is ready, but without allowing it to boil, add the sour cream. Place the slices of meat in the sauce, heat thoroughly and serve.

Source: Lady Laycock, Sant Anton Palace, Malta.

186. Fondue Bourguignonne

This dish affords an easy means of providing a delicious hot supper for as many people as can sit round a table sufficiently small for everyone to be able to reach to the middle.

The equipment consists of a *metal* chafing dish, which is brought in with the burner lighted and the container filled with boiling fat, either all vegetable or else half butter, half oil; each *convive* is provided with a wooden skewer.

Disposed about the table are sauce-boats filled with Béarnaise, Romano, Tartare and horseradish sauces, tomato ketchup and dishes of finely chopped parsley and onion.

Raw fillet steak - allowing about 1/3 lb. per person - has been cut into ¾-inch cubes.

The diners spear 1 or 2 cubes at a time on their skewers and immerse them in the boiling fat for as long as they like their meat to be cooked; from 1 to 2 minutes should suffice. They then dip the meat into the sauces of their choice (not necessarily confining themselves to one at a time) and eat off their skewers.

A Burgundy will be found as good a wine as any to accompany this Burgundian *Fondue*.

Source: Madame Jeanne Rufer, Berne, Switzerland.

187. Beef Steak à la Victor Hugo

Wipe a porterhouse steak, grill and serve with Sauce Victor Hugo, as follows:

½ teaspoon finely chopped shallot	1 teaspoon lemon juice
1 tablespoon tarragon vinegar	1 teaspoon meat extract
2½-3 oz. butter	½ tablespoon grated horseradish
2 egg yolks	

Cook the shallot in the vinegar for 5 minutes. Divide the butter into three portions. Add one piece of butter to the mixture, with yolks, lemon juice and extract. Cook over hot water, stirring constantly. As soon as the butter is melted, add the second piece and then the third. When the mixture thickens, add the grated horseradish. *Cf.* also Recipe 265.

188. Jugged Steak

Mix together 1 teaspoon each of flour, dry mustard, baking-powder, butter (or margarine) and vinegar, with pepper and salt, until a stiff paste is formed. Cut 1 lb. steak into cubes, and stir into the paste. Pack tightly into a stone jar or small casserole, cover well and cook either by steaming or in a slow oven.

This is an excellent way of dealing with stewing steak that looks tough.

Source: Mrs. J.F. Santer.

189. Hamburg Steak

Chop 1 lb. raw beef steak with a knife (do not put it through the mincing machine), adding 3 oz. raw chopped pork or a raw pork sausage, parsley, black ground pepper, salt, a small piece of soaked bread, and chopped raw onion, shallot or - preferably - chives. Mix together well with a raw egg and shape into cakes about the size of an ordinary tournedos. Roll in breadcrumbs (not too thickly) and cook slowly in a buttered frying-pan for a few minutes on each side. Serve with a lightly fried egg on top.
   Source: H.C.L.

190. Grilled Stuffed Lamb Chops

Cut the lamb chops so that each helping will consist of two ribs to a person. Make a small pocket between the ribs and fill with the following mixture:
   Chop 1 lb. mushrooms and ¼ clove of garlic very fine. Add to 4 tablespoons breadcrumbs, 2 tablespoons melted butter and enough heavy cream to hold the mixture together. Salt and pepper to taste.
   Grill on one side for 10 minutes; turn and grill on the other side for 10 minutes, or longer if desired well done.
   Serve on hot platter with mushrooms grilled whole. Garnish with fresh mint.
   Source: Miss Welden, sometime cook to Mr. and Mrs. Leander McCormick-Goodhart, Bellapaïs, Alexandria, Va., U.S.A.

V

Vegetables

The attempt has been made in this Section to place a certain emphasis on those vegetables which, while tasty, interesting and available, are as a rule strangely neglected in Great Britain.

Among such vegetables are red cabbage, celeriac, chicory (endive), kohlrabi, salsify, seakale, sorrel. Some excellent dishes can be made of each of these.

191. Some Short Definitions in Potato Cookery

Alsacienne: boiled potatoes with fried chopped onions and parsley.

Anna: thin sliced chips baked in a mould or casserole, with butter around them.

Annette: cooked as *Anna*, with chopped onions and cheese.

Ardennaise: egg-shaped potatoes scooped out and filled with a purée of chicken, ham and *fines herbes*, and browned. See Recipe 194.

au beurre: olive-shaped potatoes cooked in a casserole with butter.

au four: baked potatoes with a flavouring of bacon fat and cheese.

Bayonnaise: mashed potatoes mixed with chopped ham, shallots and parsley, browned in oven.

Bonne Femme: sliced and cooked with shredded lettuce, cream and parsley.

Bordelaise: sauté, with fried chopped onions and *fines herbes*.

Boulangère: thick slices baked in layers with sliced tomatoes and a little gravy. Traditionally French women would put their potatoes in the village baker's oven after the bread had been baked. Hence the name.

Bourgeoise: olive-shaped potatoes stewed in brown gravy with sliced onions.

Brabançonne: highly seasoned mashed potatoes with *fines herbes* and cheese, baked in moulds with cheese and breadcrumbs on top, and served browned.

Bretonne: cold sliced potatoes heated with shredded celery and onions, a little cream being added at the end.

Château: large and olive-shaped, blanched, then sauté in butter, and served sprinkled with chopped parsley. Also cut into half-moon shapes.

Chipolata: new potatoes scooped out and stuffed with a mixture of sausage meat, mushrooms and *fines herbes*. Baked in gravy.

Croquettes: Duchesse (q.v.) potatoes made into croquette shapes, egged-and-breadcrumbed and fried.

Dauphinoise: sliced raw potatoes with layers of grated cheese, moistened with milk and baked.

Duchesse: dry mashed potatoes mixed with yolk of egg, a little butter and seasoning, either made into croquette shapes and sauté in butter, or piped into shapes and baked.

Espagnole: blanched olive-shaped potatoes sauté with shredded *pimientos* and *fines herbes.*

Fondant: See Recipe 193.

Hongroise: sliced sauté potatoes mixed with paprika, chopped onions, tomatoes and brown gravy.

Indienne: sauté potatoes mixed with a curry sauce.

Italienne: baked in skins, cut in half, scooped out, filled with rice and Parmesan, and browned.

Lyonnaise: sauté potatoes with sliced fried onions and parsley.

Marquise: Duchesse potatoes *(q.v.)* mixed with tomato juice, piped in meringue shapes and baked.

Menagère: potatoes baked with onions, brown sauce and chopped ham.

Milanaise: baked in skins, scooped out, then blended with yolk of egg and cream. Refill into skins, sprinkle grated cheese and brown.

Mireille: sliced potatoes cooked in butter, served with shredded *fonds d'artichaut* and truffles.

Mousseline: mashed potatoes with whipped cream and butter.

Noisette: olive-shaped potatoes blanched and sauté in butter.

Normande: potatoes cut in squares, and stewed with chopped mint and leeks, milk and butter. Serve browned in a mould.

Parmentier: diced potatoes cooked in a casserole with butter and parsley.

Paysanne: sliced potatoes cooked in butter with dice of lean ham, shredded lettuce, sorrel and parsley.

Pont Neuf: finger-shaped fried potatoes.

Portugaise: potato rissoles served with sauté tomatoes, *fines herbes* and chopped onion.

Provençale: potatoes cooked in oil with chopped onions, garlic and *fines herbes.*

Roberts: Duchesse potatoes with *fines herbes* and chives added.

Russe: sliced potatoes cooked in a mould with layers of soft roes and ham, moistened with a light pancake mixture, cheese on top, and served browned.

S. Florentine: croquettes of mashed potatoes, chopped ham and tongue rolled in vermicelli and fried.

Savoyarde: thinly sliced in a fireproof dish with grated cheese, salt and pepper, and light stock to moisten; grated cheese and cream on top. Baked.

Soufflé: firm potatoes cut 1/8 inch thick and fried. Remove from fat, allow to cool and just before serving plunge in boiling fat for a minute.

Windsor: olive-shaped potatoes blanched, sauté in butter, mixed with shredded mushrooms.

192. Potatoes au Gratin

6 large cooked potatoes
1 oz. butter
1 oz. flour
½ pint milk
4 heaped tablespoons grated cheese
seasoning

Slice the cooked potatoes and sprinkle with pepper and salt. Make a sauce with the butter, flour and milk, add the grated cheese and season to taste. Place layers of potato and sauce alternately in a buttered fireproof dish, finishing with a layer of the sauce and a sprinkling of breadcrumbs. Brown in oven.
Source: **H.C.L.**

193. Pommes Fondantes

Bring some new potatoes to the boil, then drain. Heat some butter in a saucepan and, when very hot, add the potatoes. Stir them round, and add some chicken-bone stock. Season, and put in the oven until the liquid has evaporated.

The oven must not be too hot, or the butter will oil.

194. Pommes Ardennaises

4 oz. fat of an Ardennes ham
1 onion
½ oz. butter
½ leek
½ lb. shredded green cabbage
1 lb. potatoes
salt and pepper
nutmeg

Dice the fat and put in a casserole with the chopped onion and butter. Allow to cook without colouring, add the shredded leek and cabbage, and the potatoes cut in quarters. Cover with hot water, sprinkle with grated nutmeg, cover closely and cook for 1 hour in the oven or on a slow fire. Taste and add seasoning as required. Serve with roast pork or sausages.

Raw bacon fat can if necessary be substituted for that of the ham.

Source: A Belgian dish from the Ardennes.

195. Mashed Potatoes with Horseradish

2 lb. peeled potatoes
½ pint water
¼ pint salad oil
2 raw egg yolks

salt
grated horseradish
a drop of vinegar

Cook and sieve the potatoes, add boiling water and stir until mass is quite smooth. Mix in the oil and drop of vinegar, yolks of egg, salt and grated horseradish to taste. Serve hot.

Source: Dr. Heyrowsky, Mariazell, Austria.

196. Erdäpfelschmarn

Take potatoes that are not too mealy and cook until soft but firm. Cut them in neat slices, melt butter in a casserole and brown lightly over the fire, taking care to stir gently so that they do not burn.

Source: Mrs. J.H. Luke.

197. On Artichokes

The cultivated or 'Globe' artichoke (*Cynara scolymus*) is a glorified thistle, whose name has had a fantastic career and has completed the full circle which has brought it, in a different form, back to the Arabic from which it sprang. Originally *al-kharshuf*, it became in Italian first *alcarcioffo* and later *articiocco*, and then artichoke in English. But that was not the end of its wanderings, for it has now returned to Arabic in a different form as *ardishauki*, which is the literal rendering of the appropriate meaning 'thorn of the earth'. Its Maltese name is *qaqoċċ*.

In this connexion I might mention that a spring delicacy to villagers and other discerning eaters in Cyprus is the small, wild, low-growing thistle - parent of the globe artichoke - known locally as *kavkaroudes*. Visitors to that 'enchanted island' in March and April should make sure of sampling this little known vegetable *bonne bouche*. Cypriotes eat it with scrambled eggs.

When serving hot globe artichokes Mrs. Fraser Wilkins, wife of the first U.S. Ambassador to the Republic of Cyprus, puts some chopped raw sorrel and a touch of dried rosemary into the melted butter.

The artichoke has nothing whatever to do with the tuber known as the Jerusalem artichoke. Among the ironies of language is the fact that, while the globe artichoke grows to greater perfection, perhaps, in Jerusalem than anywhere else in the world, the Jerusalem artichoke is quite unknown in the Holy Land, so that Palestine soup may be eaten almost anywhere except in the country from which it mistakenly takes its name. The origin of Jerusalem in the designation of this vegetable (which in French is *topinambour*) is generally ascribed to a corruption of *girasole*, the Italian for sunflower, to which the Jerusalem artichoke is related.

The vegetable's French name is derived from the Tupinambá tribe of Brazilian Indians, members of which were exhibited in Paris in 1600, just at the time when the plant first reached France.

Source: H.C.L.

198. Fonds d'Artichaut Béarnaise

Place an *oeuf mollet* on a *fond d'artichaut*, cover with 2 tarragon leaves and then with Sauce Béarnaise, and serve cold. Mayonnaise can be used in place of the Béarnaise (*qq.v.*).
    Or the dish can be served warm with a Sauce Hollandaise.
    Excellent as summer luncheon entrées.
    Sources: Madame de Muranyi, Via Rondinelli, Florence.
    Mrs. R.D. Blandy, British Residency, New Hebrides.
    Note by H.C.L.: *Fonds d'artichaut* (one per person) can be good at the bottom of a cheese soufflé, the soufflé mixture being enriched by a purée made of the scrapings of the artichoke leaves.

199. Asparagus à la Viennoise

Boil the fresh asparagus in salted water and sprinkle the ends with well-browned breadcrumbs fried in butter. Serve with additional melted butter.
    Source: The characteristic Austrian way of preparing boiled asparagus.

200. Asperges Vila

Fry lightly boiled green asparagus with a dusting of Parmesan. Serve with semi-hard boiled eggs cut in two.
    Source: Mrs. R.D. Blandy, British Residency, Vila, New Hebrides.

201. Ratatuka

Slice finely 2 *aubergines* (egg-plants or garden-eggs), 4 tomatoes, 3 onions and 4 small marrows. Fry each vegetable separately in oil or butter for a few minutes, then arrange the vegetables in layers in a fireproof dish, seasoning with a hint of garlic, a little pepper and salt. The top layer should be marrow. Add ½ cup stock and cook for 2 hours in a moderate oven. Serve with mutton, pork, game, etc.

Sufficient for 4.

Source: Madame Daguet, La Capilla, Colombia. A Provençal dish.

202. *Broad Beans à la Portugaise*

Fry broad beans whole in any fat, and then fry some onions. The beans must be young and be well browned. Remove part of the fat and add hot stock, 12 peppercorns, sugar, a few fresh peas and some tomatoes. When the vegetables have cooked for about an hour, thicken with flour. The stew should be nearly solid. Serve in a ring of creamed potato, very hot, with a final addition of red wine.

The remains of this stew with added liquid, and sieved, make an excellent thick soup.

Slices of egg-plant (*aubergines*) and French beans can be used in a similar way.

Source: The Misses Warren, Mdina, Malta.

203. *Haricots Verts à la Crème*

Cook the beans in boiling, salted water and drain well. Add a piece of butter to the pan, toss the beans lightly in this, sprinkle with flour and add sufficient milk to make a thin cream sauce.

Carrots are equally good cooked in this way.

Source: Monsieur Henri Sautot, Government House, Nouméa, New Caledonia.

204. Hot Grated Beetroot

Cook 2 lb. beetroots until tender, peel and grate them coarsely. Melt 2 oz. butter in a large pan, add 1 oz. flour and mix in the beetroot. Sprinkle with salt and either lemon juice or vinegar, according to taste, and simmer for 10 minutes. Add about 1/3 pint sour cream before serving.

This dish is delicious with venison, hare or any other kind of game.

Source: E.G. A Polish recipe.

205. Brussels Sprouts with Chestnuts

1 quart Brussels sprouts
½ lb. chestnuts
2 oz. butter or other fat
2 teaspoons sugar
1 tablespoon flour

Peel and blanch the chestnuts and cook in boiling, salted water until the water has evaporated and the chestnuts are tender.

Cook the sprouts uncovered in boiling water for 10-15 minutes until tender and drain, saving 1 cup of the liquor.

Brown 2 tablespoons butter, add sugar and chestnuts and stir constantly, cooking until the chestnuts are well browned. Heat 2 more tablespoons butter, add the flour and brown slightly. Slowly add the sprout liquor, stirring constantly, and cook until smooth. Combine sprouts and chestnuts, season with salt and serve hot.

To *peel* chestnuts, wash them well, cut a slit at the top and cook in cold water until the inner skin is easily removed.

Red cabbage as in Recipe 215 and a purée of spinach are other forms of vegetable that go admirably with chestnuts.

Source: H.C.L.

206. Brussels Sprouts Sautés

Wash the sprouts well in tepid water, then cook in boiling water for 10 minutes with a good deal of salt. Take them out, let them

get quite cold, then put in a pan with cold water and boil for 15 minutes. Remove and drain on a cloth, removing any wilted leaves, put into frying-pan and sauter in butter until well browned.
Source: The same.

207. Calabrese

This delicious vegetable, a member of the broccoli family, is sometimes known as Green Sprouting or Asparagus Broccoli.

Take the long side-shoots and peel them; they peel easily, the leaves coming away at the same time.

Tie together in bunches, and cook conservatively. When tender, serve with melted butter.

Source: Mrs. John Sterndale-Bennett, Oakenwood, Wateringbury, Kent.

208. Cabbage à la Shaw Park

Slice the cabbage finely. Fry with chopped onions in a frying-pan with butter. Make a cream sauce with cornflour and a little milk and cream, mix in the fried cabbage and put in a soufflé dish. Sprinkle with breadcrumbs and bake in an oven for 20 minutes.

Source: Colonel and Mrs. Stewart, Shaw Park Hotel, Ocho Rios, Jamaica.

209. White Cabbage

Shred the cabbage and cook in not more than a bare cup of boiling water with the lid tightly on, for about 5 minutes. The cabbage will keep its colour perfectly and be quite tender.

Sour cream with cabbage, as with carrots and beetroot, is a great improvement.

Source: E.G.

N.B.: H.C.L., at a country picnic near the village of San Pedro in the Guatemalan Highlands, encountered a pleasant dish of fried white cabbage flavoured with dill. He recalls this picnic not only with culinary but with aesthetic satisfaction, as it happened to take place on the *fiesta* of the village. The women of San Pedro, all Maya Indians, came past in a gaily coloured procession, dressed in their most brilliant *huipils* (blouses) and carrying images of Our Lord, the Blessed Virgin and the village's patron saints, which were decked in beautifully embroidered Maya costumes - one of the most decorative forms of dress in the world.

210. Cabbage with Wine

1 white cabbage
1 onion
3 oz. butter or lard
2 tablespoons castor sugar
½ pint meat stock
1 tablespoon flour
3 tablespoons red wine or wine vinegar
caraway seed
salt

Slice the onion finely and fry to a golden brown, adding half the sugar.

Then add the cabbage which has been cut into thin strips and seasoned with salt and caraway seed, place cover on pan and stew in the stock for 1 hour.

When the cabbage is soft, stir into it the flour which has been lightly fried, the wine or vinegar and the remainder of the sugar.

Serves 4.

Source: Frau Frischmuth, Hotel am See, Alt-Aussee, Styria, Austria.

211. Paprika Cabbage (Paprikakraut)

1 white cabbage
1 onion
3 oz. butter or lard
1 large green pepper
vinegar
caraway seed
salt, black pepper, paprika

Cut the cabbage into strips and leave it for 12 hours in a marinade of vinegar, caraway seed, salt and black pepper.

Then slice and fry the onion, add the marinated cabbage, sprinkle with paprika and stew for 1 hour or until soft. When ready, mix into it the raw green pepper, thinly sliced.

Serves 4.

Source: The same.

212. *Polish Stuffed Cabbage*

  a large Savoy cabbage   1 oz. butter
  1 lb. stewing beef   1 oz. flour
  1 egg   1 pint liquor from cabbage
  2 onions   3 tablespoons sour cream
  salt and pepper

Put the cabbage in cold water and bring it gently to the boil. Remove the cabbage, allow it to cool and separate each leaf from the rest.

Mince the meat, fry the finely chopped onion with a little fat, season well and bind with a raw egg. Fill this mixture into each cabbage leaf, making a little roll or envelope with the ends folded in. Place in a fireproof dish with a little water at the bottom, add a dab of butter, and simmer for about 1½ hours until the leaves are tender and the meat cooked.

Make a sauce with the flour, butter and liquid in which the cabbage was cooked; add the cream and a little tomato paste if liked; pour over the cabbage rolls to serve.

Enough for 4.

Source: E.G.

213. *Faar-i-Kaal*

  1 cabbage   peppercorns
  2 lb. neck of mutton chops

Put a layer of cabbage leaves in a large saucepan, sprinkle with salt and a little flour, then arrange a layer of meat sprinkled with salt and flour, and fill up the saucepan in this way. Put about 1 oz. peppercorns in a small bag in the middle of the pan, add ½ cup water, cover and simmer for at least 8 hours. When ready, the dish should be of a light-brown colour. If the liquid has not evaporated, simmer for a time with the lid off the saucepan.

Source: Lady (Ragnar) Hyne, sometime of the British Solomon Islands. A Norwegian recipe.

214. Fylt Kaalhade

1 small cabbage
1 lb. minced beef
salt and pepper

Cut the top off the cabbage, scoop out the centre, stuff with the minced meat, replace the lid, and tie up securely. Simmer in a little clear stock or water for at least 4 hours. Serve with a rich cream sauce.

Source: The same.

215. Red Cabbage à la Bruxelloise

Here is an excellent Belgian recipe for that delicious vegetable, red cabbage, which in Great Britain is so rarely seen on the table otherwise than as a pickle. Hot red cabbage is an admirable accompaniment to roast duck, goose and most forms of game.

1 good-sized red cabbage
2 lb. apples
½ lb. lard
3 fair-sized onions
thyme
bay leaf
sugar, pepper, salt

Cut up the onions and brown in the lard. Add the shredded red cabbage, also a little water, the herbs, pepper and salt; cook slowly for 2 hours.

Peel and cut up the apples, add them raw, together with 3 tablespoons sugar, and cook for 1 more hour.

Source: Mlle. Yvonne L'Été, cook to Mr. and Mrs. Randall Kirk, 172 Avenue Louise, Brussels.

216. *To Stew Red Cabbage*

Wash, pick and shred what will fill a pint-size basin. Melt some butter in a saucepan, and put in the red cabbage with only the water that hangs about it and an onion sliced. Season with black pepper, cayenne, salt and sugar.

Stew, keeping the saucepan closely covered; and, when almost ready, add a glass of vinegar, which may just be brought to the boil.

Source: Mrs. John Sterndale-Bennett, Oakenwood, Wateringbury, Kent. An English recipe of c. 1820.

217. *Carrots à la Kazbek*

First cut up some onions or shallots (in quantity at least half of that of the carrots) and fry a deep brown in butter. Then cut the carrots crosswise into thin rounds, put in the same pan with salt and sugar, and bake for 30-45 minutes, shaking the dish at intervals.

The carrots should be well browned on both sides without being allowed to become crisp.

Source: H.C.L.'s Georgian cook, British Mission, Tiflis.

218. *Celeriac (also Kohlrabi) au Gratin*

1 lb. celeriac (or kohlrabi)	1 cup stock or water
¼ lb. grated Parmesan	breadcrumbs
4 tablespoons butter	salt, pepper

Butter a fireproof dish well. Put a layer of sliced celeriac (French *céleri-rave*) on the bottom and sprinkle with grated Parmesan, salt and pepper. Repeat the process until the dish is filled. Press down and pour on the stock or water. Sprinkle breadcrumbs and more grated cheese on the top and add the melted butter.

Cook in a moderate oven for ½ hour.

This is also the best way of preparing that serviceable vegetable kohlrabi.

Celeriac is excellent as a salad, either raw ('matchsticks' dressed with Mayonnaise) or else cooked like potatoes in a potato salad.

Source: H.C.L. A Recipe of his grandfather's house. The celeriac makes a delicious vegetable entrée.

219. *Celeriac au Jus*

Take 3 or 4 celeriac roots, clean them well, wash them in fresh water, cut them in more or less equal pieces, place for 4-5 minutes in boiling water and dry. Then place in a frying-pan with a good piece of butter over a slow fire. When they have begun to brown, season and allow them to cook with some good stock and some meat gravy. At the moment of serving sprinkle with chopped parsley.

220. *Sliced Kohlrabi*

Pare some young kohlrabi and cut in thin slices. Place in covered saucepan with water, butter and salt, and steam slowly until the liquid has begun to thicken. Stir in a dusting of flour, adding bouillon or more water.

Take the smaller of the sprouting green leaves (the largest ones are too coarse), chop them finely and boil separately in water with salt and a little soda.

Pour this water away and add the leaves to the kohlrabi. Then heat up once more before serving.

Source: Frau Frischmuth, Hotel am See, Alt-Aussee, Styria, Austria.

221. Chicory

There is much confusion around the name chicory, which sometimes refers to the vegetable discussed here, namely that also known as witloof and in Italy as *insalata Belga,* sometimes to the ground-root so lamentably mixed with, and even substituted for, coffee.

The confusion becomes particularly acute as between the former kind of chicory and endive, because what we call chicory the French call *endive*, while the French for the curly-leafed salad we call endive is *chicorée frisée.*

222. Chicory Ardennaise

Wash 12 small firm heads of chicory, chop up ¼ lb. smoked raw ham. Butter a fireproof dish, put in half the quantity of the chopped ham, cover with chicory and season with a little grated nutmeg.

Add the remainder of the ham and cover with a plate, on top of which replace the lid of the dish. Leave to cook for at least ½ hour.

Serve in a vegetable dish, sprinkling with a little of the water in which the chicory has been cooked.

Source: A Belgian dish from the Ardennes, where is produced an excellent smoked ham, normally intended, like Westphalian ham, to be eaten raw.

223. Chicory au Gratin

Wash the heads, remove discoloured leaves, cook for 5 minutes in boiling salted water, drain and then cook in fresh boiling water until tender. Arrange the heads in a gratin dish, cover with a good cheese sauce, sprinkle with grated cheese and brown in the oven or under the grill.

224. Braised Chicory

Wash 4 or 5 heads of chicory, remove any discoloured leaves, put them in boiling salted water, cook for 5 minutes and strain. Put in a casserole with 2 oz. melted margarine, salt and pepper, and cook in a moderate oven until tender and nicely browned, basting and turning from time to time.

Serve either as a vegetable dish or with roast veal or other meat.

225. Chicory in Cheese Sauce (Endives à la Mornay)

2 lb. chicory
1 pint Béchamel sauce
½ lb. Gruyère cheese
3 oz. butter

Wash the chicory and lay it in a well-buttered casserole. Sprinkle with salt (and lemon juice if liked), add the butter, cover tightly with a well-fitting lid and cook in a moderate oven for 30-35 minutes. Lay the cooked heads in a shallow fireproof dish, cover with the Béchamel, to which most of the grated cheese has been added, sprinkle with grated cheese and dabs of butter and brown under the grill.

Source: Mrs. Neville Lake.

226. Chicory in Cream Sauce (Endives à la Crème)

4 large heads of chicory
1 oz. butter
1 teaspoon chopped onion
½ pint cream (or Béchamel) sauce
1 egg yolk

Remove any green leaves, wash the chicory and cut into small shreds. Melt the butter in a casserole, add the onions, cook together till the onion is opaque, then add the chicory by degrees, keeping it at simmering point. Then cover with a lid and cook till tender.

Replace over a quick fire to allow any liquor to evaporate, add the cream (or a Béchamel) and bring to the boil.

Before serving, blend in the yolk of egg and seasoning.

Source: A Belgian recipe.

227. *Chicory Asolano*

>8 large heads of chicory
>3 oz. butter
>1 teaspoon meat extract
>1 pint Béchamel sauce
>salt, pepper

Remove any green leaves, wash the chicory and strain well. Lay the heads in a casserole sufficiently large to accommodate them in one layer, add pepper, salt and the butter which has been melted. Pour over them a glass of water in which has been dissolved a teaspoon of meat extract.

Cover the casserole and let it cook in a moderate oven for about 1 hour, adding a little water if necessary. Ten minutes before removing the casserole from the oven make a light Béchamel sauce. Place the chicory on a hot dish, cover with the Béchamel and then with the liquor from the casserole. Serve very hot.

Source: This is a North Italian variant of the above as prepared by Signorina Giulietta Olivieri in the house of the Maestro Francesco and Signora Malipiero, Asolo, Province of Treviso, where it was enjoyed by Freya Stark and H.C.L.

228. *Leek Tart (Flamiche aux Poireaux)*

>1 lb. leeks
>½ pint Béchamel sauce
>4 oz. grated cheese
>3 egg yolks

Remove the leaves and base of the leeks, slit lengthways without dividing entirely and wash well. Cook in boiling salted water, remove, rinse in boiling water and drain thoroughly. Line a flan case with short pastry, lay the cooked leeks inside, cover with the sauce to which the cheese and two yolks have been added, cover with a pastry lid, brush with beaten egg and bake in oven till golden brown - about 45 minutes.

Source: Mrs. Neville Lake, Furneux Pelham, Herts. A speciality of Picardy.

229. *Young Leeks au Gratin*

Boil the required number of young, small leeks till tender in veal or other meat stock. Trim and arrange in baking-dish with a little of the stock. Season with salt, pepper and a pinch of nutmeg. Sprinkle well with grated cheese (preferably Parmesan), and place under the grill until the cheese runs and is slightly browned.

Source: Madame Gallet de Koréwo, Château de la Haute Borde, Touraine.

230. *Mushrooms à la Caucasienne*

Cook the mushrooms whole in butter, then cover with sour cream, thickening with a little flour, and simmer. Serve very hot.

Source: H.C.L.'s Georgian cook, British Mission, Tiflis.

231. *Peas with Lettuce*

> 1 lb. young (unshelled) peas
> the hearts of 2 lettuces
> 1 large sliced onion
> parsley, mint
>
> 2 oz. butter
> 1 dessertspoon flour
> 1 tablespoon cream
> a pinch of sugar

Put the peas with the shredded lettuce hearts, onion, parsley and mint to taste, in a pan, cover closely and cook until tender, shaking the pan occasionally to prevent sticking. Mix the butter smoothly with the flour, cream and a pinch of sugar, and add to the cooked peas.

Source: H.C.L.

232. Aubergine Pureé

4 aubergines, cubed, salted and drained
2 cups white wine
1 red ball pepper, chopped
1 large onion, chopped
4 tomatoes, chopped
4 courgettes, sliced
4 cloves garlic
1 tub Greek strained yoghurt
thyme
rosemary
lemon juice
pepper

Toss aubergines, onion and garlic in hot olive oil. Add pepper, courgettes, tomatoes and herbs and 2 cups of white wine. Cook gently till soft and season with pepper. When cool, purée with blender. Add the yoghurt. Squeeze lemon juice over to prevent discolouring.
Source: Ms. Chlöe Luke.

233. Purée of Lettuce (Kochsalat)

3 heads Cos lettuce
2 oz. butter
1 gill milk
½ cup arrowroot (or flour)
salt, pepper
a pinch of sugar

Boil the lettuce thoroughly, strain well and put through a sieve or mixer.
Make a sauce with the butter, arrowroot and milk; and, while hot, add the sieved lettuce and stir well. Add the seasoning, and serve hot in a heated vegetable dish.
Flour can, if necessary, be substituted for the arrowroot.
Source: Prince Charles Victor de Rohan.

234. Duveć (Pimientos with Meat and Rice)

Sweet peppers are frequently miscalled *pimentos*, whereas their Spanish name is *pimiento*. *Pimento* is the bay-tree, which flourishes, for example, in Jamaica and produces allspice from its berries.

½ lb. sweet peppers (pimientos)	4 oz. rice
1 lb. tomatoes	cooked meat
1 onion	salt, pepper
¾ pint water	

Cut up the sweet peppers and tomatoes. Fry the sliced onions golden brown in a little fat. Take a fireproof dish and put in first a layer of onion, then of peppers, then tomatoes, rice and pieces of meat such as beef, pork, mutton or chicken, repeating until all the ingredients are used. Add salt, pepper and water. Cover and bake for an hour. Before it is quite cooked, remove lid so that a crust may form.

For 4 persons.

Source: Mr. R.T. Smallbones's Croatian cook Felix, Island of Koludarz, Dalmatia.

235. *Pimientos Asa'o*

1 large red pepper	olive oil
1 large green pepper	lemon juice
1 large yellow pepper	salt/pepper
1 whole head garlic	

Sear the peppers and the garlic on a charcoal grill or hot plate *(plancha)*, turning them on all sides till charred and tender. When done wrap in kitchen paper towels. Leave for a few minutes, then wipe off the worst of the char. Do not entirely de-skin or de-pip them. Peel the garlic and separate the teeth. Now with your fingers tear the *pimientos* into not too small pieces, taking care not to lose the juice. Put them and the garlic into a bowl and whilst still hot pour over olive oil, lemon juice, salt and plenty of black pepper.

Source: Miss June Tobin, Jimena de la Frontera (Cádiz), Spain.

236. Piperade and Satraš

Cut up the requisite quantity of sweet peppers (*pimientos*) which can be red, green or both. Remove the seeds and add a shallot or small onion and (if liked) a clove of garlic, all finely chopped. Then cook slowly, without frying, in olive oil or pork fat.

When almost cooked, add an equal quantity of tomato flesh with salt, pepper and a pinch of sugar. Cook for another 20 minutes and stir from time to time to make the mixture into a purée.

Lastly, break in, singly and without beating, one egg per person, and stir again over the fire till the eggs are cooked.

The dish should have the consistency of a Welsh Rarebit.

Source: A Basque dish.

Similar to Piperade is the Serbian dish Satraš (pronounced Satrash), the difference being that Satraš also contains a well-chopped bunch of parsley and a good pinch or two of ground paprika, but no eggs.

Source: Frau Dr. Arthur Satter, Heiligenkreuz-am-Waasen, Southern Styria, Austria.

237. Salsify, Fried and Otherwise

Salsify (with its related Scorzonera) is sometimes called the oyster-plant - rather fancifully, for its flavour bears little resemblance to that of the oyster (but see below). On the other hand, it resembles quite closely that of the *fond* of a globe artichoke.

Scrape the salsify, throwing each piece as soon as it is scraped into a basin of water, to which some vinegar has been added to keep the colour. Then place in boiling water, adding a little salt and 1 dessertspoon flour. When cooked, dry and place in a tureen with pepper and vinegar for a few minutes before serving, then dip in batter, fry until brown and serve.

Salsify is also good *au jus*, as in the celeriac *au jus* (Recipe 219); or blanched in water to which vinegar has been added, and served with a Béchamel and a squeeze of lemon. It can, however, convey a suggestion of oyster when served as an entrée with anchovy sauce, a family recipe of Major-General J.M. Renton, C.B., D.S.O.

Salsify is a gnarled, lumpy root, outwardly white to yellow; scorzonera is long, straight and outwardly black. If the salsify is small and too ill-shapen, sieve, mould it into flat cakes, roll in flour, fry and serve as fritters.

Source: H.C.L.

238. *Seakale*

This winter and spring vegetable, a relative of the asparagus, has a very delicate flavour, which must not be overpowered by highly flavoured accessories.

Tie up the seakale in small bunches and boil in salted water for about 25 minutes till tender. Season, and serve with a Béchamel or, if preferred, with melted butter slightly browned.

239. *Spinach and some Substitutes*

Spinach (French *épinards*) is a valuable, nutritious and palatable article of food, easily digested, cooling to the blood and with iron content.

It is equally good either whole (*en branches*) or sieved; alone or in combination, *e.g.* with eggs, chestnuts, or blended with sorrel, lettuce or water-cress.

It should be washed several times and lifted out of the rinsing waters so that the grit may not remain in the leaves.

If eaten sieved, it is well to mix with it some cream or milk, meat or chicken stock and finely chopped onion.

A good substitute for spinach (and for sorrel) is the wild mallow (*Malva sylvestris*). In the first century B.C. a Chinese poet wrote:

'I'll pluck the mallows and make soup',
From A. Waley, *170 Chinese Poems*. London, 1923.

and that is what villagers in Cyprus do to this day. And very good is the result, almost as good as the soups of Recipes 87-89.

As a vegetable, Cypriotes make its young leaves into something in no wise inferior to *epinards en branches*. In the same way, also, do they treat the young leaves of the bladder campion (*Silene inflata*), which they call *strouthoudia* ('sparrow-grass').

Source: H.C.L.

240. *Cream of Spinach au Parmesan*

Place the spinach in a pan with the water which adheres to the leaves, sprinkle with salt, cover the pan, and cook for 20-30 minutes over low heat, frequently stirring with a wooden spoon.

Then drain well, expressing all the moisture, and sieve.

Return to the pan, add 2 tablespoons cream, 1 oz. butter, some finely chopped onion, salt, pepper ground from the mill and, if liked, a pinch of nutmeg.

Reheat and serve in a fireproof dish with a good sprinkling of grated cheese, Parmesan for choice.

241. *Epinards au Gratin*

2-3 lb. spinach	2 tablespoons breadcrumbs
1 pint Béchamel sauce	salt, pepper
½ lb. grated cheese	

Shred and wash the spinach. Cook in boiling salted water for 15 minutes, drain, rinse in cold water and dry in a clean cloth. Make 1 pint good Béchamel sauce, adding 6 oz. of the cheese, and arrange alternating layers of spinach and cheese sauce in a fireproof dish. Finish with a layer of sauce topped with breadcrumbs, grated cheese and dabs of butter. Brown in the oven.

Source: Mrs. Neville Lake.

242. Sorrel

Sorrel (French *oseille*) is a cooling and refreshing vegetable with a tart and highly individual flavour. Properly appreciated in France, it is not as well known in Great Britain as it deserves to be.

It makes excellent soups *(q.v.)*, and as a vegetable should be used when young and fresh. It may be cooked in all ways suitable for spinach, with which it can also be blended, as with lettuce leaves and/or water-cress. Sorrel Sauce *(q.v.)* is, as has been noted, the perfect accompaniment of a hot boiled tongue.
Source: H.C.L.

243. Purée of Sorrel

Wash the sorrel in several waters and, after drying, put in a casserole with 2 oz. butter. Cook until tender, thicken with a little flour; add salt and butter and ½ teaspoon Bovril or meat extract, melted in a little hot water. Add gradually some beaten eggs. Serve with hard-boiled eggs, quartered.

244. Sorrel (or Spinach) Pancakes

Pancakes: 2 tablespoons flour for each person
 1 egg for every 2-3 persons
 a little salt
 enough equal parts of milk and water to make a thin batter
Filling: 1 lb. sorrel or spinach
 2-3 teaspoons cream
 6 tablespoons grated cheese
 1 lb. small mushrooms (failing which, liver, kidneys or chicken)
 salt and pepper to taste

Make a purée of the sorrel or spinach, chopped and sieved. Add cream to make a thin paste, then the cheese, salt, pepper and the mushrooms (or their alternative), which have been cooked in butter and chopped fine. When all is thoroughly mixed to a paste, 1 tablespoon is allowed to each pancake.

The pancake batter must be thin, and very lightly cooked. Stuff with the filling as soon as it leaves the pan, and place in a buttered fireproof dish. Sprinkle with dabs of butter and grated cheese, and bake for just long enough to melt the cheese. If mushrooms are not available, use liver, kidneys or chicken.

245. Sweet Corn à la Irene

1½ cups cooked sweet corn kernels
1/3 cup sour cream

½ teaspoon curry powder
pinch of salt

Boil the requisite number of corn cobs for 20 minutes. Then cut the kernels off the cobs, mix with the other ingredients and heat.
Source: Mrs. R.A. Wellington, Fazenda Os Marmeleiros, Atibaia, State of São Paulo, Brazil.

246. Tanya Fritters

1 lb. tanyas
1 egg

grated onion, salt, pepper
oil

Grate the raw tanya and add to it the beaten egg and seasonings. Whip until light and of a creamy consistency. Drop by spoonfuls into hot oil, cook until golden brown, drain on glazed paper.

A Recipe included in case this book should find its way to the Tropics. Tanyas and eddoes are small varieties, much grown in the West Indies (where the larger one is called *dasheen*), of the starchy root *Colocasia esculenta*, which under the names *taro* and *dalo* is one of the staple foods of South Seas Islanders, grows also in Cyprus, and in South Africa is known as the 'elephant plant'.
Source: Family of Mr. Justice Perez, Trinidad.

247. Tomato Jelly and Ice

    1 lb. tomatoes   1 bay leaf
    ½ oz. gelatine   salt, pepper, sugar

Cut the tomatoes in quarters and cook with a little water until soft. Sieve, and add enough of the water in which the tomatoes were cooked to make up 1 pint purée. Dissolve the gelatine in a little boiling water and add to the mixture with seasoning and a little sugar. Pour into a wetted mould and allow to set.

Source: Lady (Stanley) Fisher, Cyprus.

Major-General J.M. Renton serves, at summer luncheons, tomato water ices covered with a good sprinkling of grated Parmesan.

248. Truffles

Truffles may be black or white; and the better known to the world at large is doubtless the *black* truffle of Périgord, familiar as the essential concomitant of all *foies gras* worthy of the name. Can the popularity of this elusive subterranean fungus, which has to be nosed out of the ground by pigs and poodles, have originated in its alleged aphrodisiac qualities, on which Brillat-Savarin has an interesting dissertation?

In 1933 *The Times* printed a delightful anonymous article on the Truffle Fair of Alba in Piedmont. The Fair is held annually in November, and lasts for three days; it is attended by truffle-fanciers not only from all parts of Italy but also from across the Alps. The truffle that is the object of this gathering is not the black but the pungently scented *white* variety of Piedmont; and between the Wars, according to the writer of the article, it would fetch over 30s. a lb. from the assembled connoisseurs. But in 1953 it fetched the then record price of £4 7s. 6d. a lb.

For over two centuries Alba has supported a school for truffle dogs, mostly poodles and similar breeds; and these dogs 'are as fond' - I quote from the article -

> 'of the truffles as their owners are, and it would be useless to try to train a dog unless it had this taste. The writer has seen an English pedigree wire-haired fox terrier walk round the kitchen on his hind legs begging for a small piece of white truffle and devour it in an ecstasy; but the father of this terrier, when offered a piece, wrinkled up his nose in disgust, and walked stiffly out of the kitchen.'

Truffles are prepared by being wrapped individually in greased paper and baked for 1 hour in a hot oven.

A coarse variety of the white truffle is found in many parts of the Middle East, from the Qatar Peninsula on the Persian Gulf northward along the Green Crescent, and by the western edge of the Syrian Desert. Here the Bedu women are practised at detecting with their bare feet the slight bulges that betray their presence.

These truffles, looking externally like small potatoes and known in Arabic as *kima*, can be bought in the spring in the *suqs* of Syrian cities such as Homs, Hama and Aleppo, where they fetch the equivalent of about 2s. a lb. Although nothing like as delicate in flavour as the European varieties, they are highly esteemed locally when eaten, for example in a pilav.

Source: H.C.L.

249. Vegetable Marrow à l'Hongroise

The vegetable marrow is all too often little more than a watery, tasteless vehicle for an equally tasteless white sauce. In the following simple recipe it will be found to undergo a remarkable metamorphosis:

1 large vegetable marrow
1 oz. butter
1 tablespoon flour
1 tablespoon vinegar

1 egg
2 teaspoons sugar
½ gill milk
salt

Take a large but tender vegetable marrow, peel, remove seedy part and slice the fleshy part into thin, spaghetti-like strips.

Place in a bowl, add salt and leave for ½ hour; then squeeze out the moisture.

Pour on the melted butter and the vinegar, stir gently and then dust with the flour. Stew for 20 minutes, adding a little water if not sufficiently moist.

Prepare (but do not cook) a mixture of the egg, milk and sugar. Place the marrow in a bowl and turn the mixture into it. Stir gently and keep hot until ready to be served.

Source: Mrs. Stanton, Sam Lord's Castle, Barbados.

250. Small Marrows à la Brésilienne

12 small marrows (courgettes)
2 medium-sized onions
salt, pepper
6 tablespoons lard
several bay leaves

Wash but do not peel the marrows, cut off and remove both ends, and slice into rounds. Chop the onions fairly fine.

Heat the lard in a deep frying-pan and fry the onions a golden brown. Add the sliced marrows and cook for about ½ hour over a very low flame, constantly shaking the pan to avoid burning.

Five minutes before removing from the fire, add the bay leaves, salt and pepper.

Avocado Marrows can be treated in the same way.

Source: Mrs. R.A. Wellington, Fazenda Os Marmeleiros, Atibaia, State of São Paulo, Brazil.

Signora Emma Menegon, Mrs. Freya Stark's cook at the Casa Freia, Asolo, Province of Treviso, Italy, makes a good dish, *au gratin*, of *courgettes* and of tomatoes (cut in half lengthways, peeled and seeded), laid in a pie-dish in alternate layers, with a Béchamel mixture between the layers.

251. Hot Cucumber with Dill

Chop finely ½ small onion, fry in butter but do not brown. Add a peeled cucumber cut in cubes, not salted and not previously squeezed, a little stock and salt, and cook until tender.

Meanwhile stir 1 tablespoon flour in a little stock or water, bring to the boil and reduce until most of the liquid has evaporated, then mix with the cucumber. Add 1 tablespoon finely chopped dill, cook again for a few minutes, finally adding a little - preferably sour - cream.

Source: Miss Genia Hordliczka, São Paulo, Brazil.

VI

Sauces, Salad Dressings, Salads and Herbs

'It takes four persons to make a salad dressing: a spendthrift to squander the oil, a miser to dole out the vinegar, a wise man to dispense the salt, a madman to stir.'

Spanish saying.

252. Sauce Béchamel

This basic sauce, which can be varied by the addition of grated cheese, cooked mushrooms, etc., is made by melting 1½ oz. butter in a pan, adding an equal weight of flour and cooking together for a few minutes without colouring. Then work in ½ pint milk flavoured with salt, pepper and a slice of onion or shallot. Bring to boiling point, stirring constantly, strain and use.

253. Sauce Hollandaise

½ cup butter (4 oz.)
2 egg yolks
1 tablespoon lemon juice
¼ teaspoon salt

1/3 cup (2½ oz.) boiling water
1 oz. wine vinegar
cayenne pepper

Divide the butter into three pieces; put one piece in the pan with the eggs and juice, stand pan in boiling water and whisk until the butter is melted; add the second piece of butter and, when melted, the third, whisking all the time. Add water and vinegar, cook 1 minute and season with salt and cayenne. The sauce should have a velvety consistency and be served warm. If the mixture curdles, add 2 tablespoons boiling water.

To make the sauce additionally tasty, add a touch of grated horseradish.

For boiled fish, cauliflower, globe artichokes, etc.

Source: H.C.L.

254. Sauce Mousseline

To the Sauce Hollandaise, as above, add some whipped cream just before serving.

Source: The same.

255. Sauce Maltaise

Work into a Sauce Hollandaise as above the juice of one or two blood-oranges (which grow particularly well in Malta) as may be required, together with pieces of the rind cut exceedingly fine.

Source: The same. The last time H.C.L. encountered this sauce in a restaurant was in 1957 when lunching with Mr. and Mrs. Robert Taylor at the elegant Hotel Aviz in Lisbon. It was the perfect accompaniment to the boiled turbot, a dish preceded by thin slices of cold smoked duck as an unusual and agreeable *hors d'oeuvre*.

256. Concerning Mayonnaise

The name 'Mayonnaise' is a corruption of the Spanish 'Mahonesa' and was introduced into France, together with the sauce to which it is applied, by Marshal the 3rd Duke of Richelieu (1696-1788) after his capture of Port Mahon in Minorca in 1756.

This Duke as a boy was a Page of Honour to Louis XIV towards the end of the life of *le roi Soleil*; and it was his widow - whom he married as his third wife when he was an octogenarian and she quite young - who was heard to remark to the Empress Eugénie at tea in the Tuileries in 1867: '*Oui, Madame, comme mon mari disait à Louis Quatorze* - as my husband *used to say* to Louis XIV.'

It was, as his mother recounted in her *Letters from Samoa*, while helping his wife to mix a Mayonnaise for dinner in the large downstairs hall of his house Vailima, which later became the Government House of Western Samoa, that Robert Louis Stevenson suffered his fatal cerebral haemorrhage on 3 December 1894.

N.B.: The easiest way of working oil into a Mayonnaise and similar sauces is to cut a small slit from the side of the cork so that it drips evenly from the bottle. Two yolks need about a ½ pint oil, though more can be worked in.

Source: The same.

257. A Victorian Mayonnaise

>2 egg yolks
>½ pint olive oil
>1 teaspoon plain or tarragon vinegar
>veal jelly
>pinch of salt
>pinch of cayenne pepper
>1 clove garlic
>capers

Put into a large basin the yolks only of two large fresh eggs with a little salt and cayenne pepper. Stir these well together, then add a teaspoon of the best salad oil and work the mixture round with a wooden spoon until it appears like a cream.

Pour in by slow degrees nearly ½ pint of oil, continuing to work the sauce as at first until it has the smoothness of a custard and not any of the oil remains visible. Then add a tablespoon of plain or tarragon vinegar and 1 tablespoon of cold water to whiten the sauce. A lump of clear veal jelly the size of an egg much improves it, and a morsel of garlic not larger than a pea. A few French capers may be added.

Source: Major-General J.M. Renton, Rowfold Grange, Billingshurst, Sussex, from the MS. Recipe Book of his grandmother Mrs. Charles Taylor.

258. Kent House Mayonnaise

>2 egg yolks
>½ teaspoon mustard
>½ teaspoon sugar
>½ teaspoon salt
>¼ cup oil
>3 tablespoons vinegar
>½ tablespoon lime juice
>a little milk

Rub mustard, sugar and salt into the yolks, then add the oil drop by drop, then the vinegar, followed by a little milk, finally adding the lime juice.

Source: Lloyd, butler at Kent House, Port of Spain, Trinidad.

259. Mayonnaise - a Chilean Variant

The luxurious Union Club of Santiago, the capital of Chile, serves with its cold *langoustes* (which are brought to the mainland from Robinson Crusoe's island of Juan Fernandez, 360 miles out in the Pacific) an anonymous sauce of a Mayonnaise consistency but browny-pink in colour and of a subtle, intriguing flavour.

Persistent inquiry through Robert Taylor and other friends who have entertained H.C.L. there finally elicited that it is compounded of ordinary Mayonnaise with a little Pan Yan pickle worked into it. It is as simple as that - and very good.

260. Sweet Mayonnaise

  1 cup sugar   1 teaspoon salt
  ½ cup flour   1 teaspoon mustard, dry
  ¾ cup vinegar   1¼ cups water
  2 eggs   1/3-½ cup oil

Sift sugar, flour, salt and mustard together, add water and vinegar. Bring to boiling point in a bain-marie, stirring occasionally. Beat the eggs and add the oil to them, pour into the pan with the rest of the Mayonnaise, and cook until thick.

This sauce will keep indefinitely in the refrigerator.
Source: Marine Hotel, Hastings, Barbados.

261. Green Sauce

Make a Mayonnaise with 4 tablespoons oil, 2 tablespoons vinegar, 4 yolks of egg, water, salt and mustard. Stand this mixture in a pan containing hot but not boiling water, stir until the mixture starts to solidify, remove from the bain-marie and add more vinegar and/or oil as required. Stir until it cools. Add the following herbs, extremely finely chopped and well mixed: cress, parsley, borage, dill, chervil, tarragon.

Exceedingly good with cold fish such as trout and salmon-trout.

Source: Mr. R.T. Smallbones, C.M.G., British Consulate-General, Frankfurt-am-Main.

262. Sauce Rémoulade

2 egg yolks
olive oil
1 teaspoon castor sugar
1 heaped teaspoon finely
  chopped parsley
½ teaspoon chopped capers

a sprinkling of finely chopped
  chives
½ teaspoon finely chopped onion
1 saltspoon salt
1 teaspoon chili vinegar
2 tablespoons tarragon vinegar
1 tablespoon malt vinegar

Put the yolks in a pudding-basin with a small bottom to it, stir for a few moments with a wooden spoon, then add, drop by drop, sufficient oil to make a mixture as stiff as butter, stirring all the while. When the spoon will stand upright in it work in the remaining ingredients and stand in a cool place.

For 6-7 people.

263. Sauce Tartare without Capers

1 egg yolk
1 heaped teaspoon sugar
½ teaspoon salt
½ teaspoon dry mustard

1 tablespoon vinegar
2 gills salad oil
2 tablespoons finely chopped
  chives
1 tablespoon finely chopped
  parsley

Put the yolk, sugar, salt and mustard in a basin, and stir in the oil drop by drop, adding at intervals a few drops of vinegar. Beat until the mixture is of the consistency of very thick cream and, when finished, add the chopped chives and parsley. Chopped-up plain pickles instead of chives and parsley make an equally good sauce.

An excellent form of Sauce Tartare when capers are unavailable - indeed, as tasty as any with capers.
Particularly good with prawns at cocktail parties.
Source: Lady Blackall, Kyrenia, Cyprus.

264. Accident Sauce

2 egg yolks
1 tablespoon white sugar
pinch of salt
3-4 tablespoons olive oil

1 tablespoon vinegar
½ cup cream
1-2 tablespoons tomato sauce

Beat together yolks, sugar and salt, add the oil slowly, and then the vinegar, followed by the cream and finally the tomato sauce. Strain through a muslin before serving, chilled, with fish.
Source: Sir Gordon Lethem, K.C.M.G., Government House, British Guiana. So called because originally made by accident.

265. Romano Sauce

4 oz. butter
2 eggs
1 saltspoon salt

1 tablespoon tarragon vinegar
a little finely chopped onion, or onion juice

Melt the butter in a saucepan, add salt and the eggs well beaten and strained. Stir over the fire until thick, but do not allow to boil.
Add the vinegar and onion, and serve with steak. *Cf.* also Recipe 186.

266. Sauce Béarnaise - I

3 egg yolks
1 gill cream
¼ lb. butter

a little finely chopped onion and tarragon
salt, pepper, a few drops lemon juice

Beat the eggs and cream with onion, tarragon and seasoning. Stir over a gentle flame until frothy, then add the butter in small pieces. When the butter has dissolved, return to the fire and stir briskly until thick and creamy. If kept waiting, keep warm in a bain-marie, and if it curdles add a drop of water and stir quickly.

For 3-4 people.

For beef steaks, fish, *oeufs mollets*, artichokes, etc.

Source: Madame de Muranyi, Via Rondinelli, Florence.

267. Sauce Béarnaise - II

½ pint white wine
½ pint vinegar
4 teaspoons chopped onion
1 oz. bruised tarragon

6 egg yolks
1 lb. butter
cayenne, parsley, tarragon

Reduce by two-thirds ½ pint white wine and the same amount of vinegar with 4 teaspoons of chopped onion and about 1 oz. bruised tarragon; add salt and pepper. Let it get cold, add the egg yolks and the 1 lb. butter little by little, stirring all the time. Add a pinch of cayenne pepper and complete with a little chopped parsley and tarragon.

Source: Sir John Leche.

268. Tomato Sauce (for Bottling)

½ sieve of tomatoes
4 Spanish onions
2 oz. shallots
¾ oz. garlic
¼ oz. mace

¾ oz. bruised ginger
3 drachms cayenne pepper
1 quart good vinegar
1 quart strong old ale

Wipe the tomatoes with a soft cloth. Slice them; peel and slice the onions, shallots and garlic. Put them into a tight iron pot with the spice and vinegar.

Simmer for 2 hours, skimming and stirring frequently. Add the ale, then boil moderately fast for ½ hour or till the sauce thickens.

Rub the whole through a coarse hair sieve. When cold, put into dry wide-mouthed bottles. Cork tightly and seal on top. The bottles should be small so as to hold sufficient for once or twice only, as, once the bottles are opened, the sauce becomes mouldy.

Source: Mrs. T.E. Hussey, Bishop's Waltham. The Recipe is dated 1869.

269. *Sorrel Sauce (for Hot Boiled Tongue)*

Either:

Chop the leaves and stew for a few minutes in butter and stock; they get tender very quickly. Then dissolve 1 or 2 tablespoons (according to the quantity of sorrel used) flour in cold stock, pour into the pan and simmer for a few minutes, adding a little cream, pepper and salt.

Or:

Make a rich white sauce with butter, flour and stock, bring to the boil and then add the sorrel leaves, letting them cook until tender. Before serving add the cream, pepper and salt.

In either case the sauce may be sieved before serving. Diluted with more stock it makes a good soup.

Source: Miss Genia Hordliczka, São Paulo, Brazil.

270. *Sauce Espagnole*

a little lean bacon or ham, diced	1 tablespoon flour
a little onion	butter
1 carrot	tomato purée or whole tomatoes
1 bay leaf, sprig of thyme parsley	stock
	1 glass white wine

Cut in dice a little lean bacon or ham, a little onion and a carrot. Add a bay leaf, sprig of thyme and parsley, and the flour. Cook for a few minutes in butter, stirring well to prevent burning, then add tomato purée or whole tomatoes, some stock and the white wine.

Let it cook until all the vegetables are soft, then pass through a fine sieve.

This is the base of all brown sauces.

Source: Sir John Leche.

271. Sauce Demi-glace

The same as for Sauce Espagnole, reducing quantity and adding equivalent proportion of meat juice or meat extract.

Source: The same.

272. Tarragon Sauce - I

Season some thick cream with pepper and a little salt, whip slightly and mix in a small quantity of finely chopped tarragon and chervil. Serve cold, but not iced.

For hot roast birds.

273. Tarragon Sauce - II

2/3 oz. tarragon leaves	veal stock or Sauce Espagnole
½ pint white wine	(q.v.)
	a little chopped tarragon

Put the tarragon leaves in boiling white wine and allow to boil for 10 minutes. Add very strong veal stock of Sauce Espagnole, complete with a little chopped tarragon.

Source: Sir John Leche.

274. Brown Chaudfroid Sauce

>1½ pints Demi-glace or Sauce Espagnole
>essence of truffle (if available)
>1½ pints jellied stock (or ordinary stock and a little gelatine)
>1 glass Port or Sherry

Combine 1½ pints Demi-glace or Sauce Espagnole, the essence of truffle and the stock. Reduce by one-third and add the wine.
Source: The same.

275. White Chaudfroid Sauce

>1½ pints Béchamel Sauce a little gelatine
>1½ pints chicken or veal jelly ½ pint cream
> or stock

Reduce by one-third 1½ pints Béchamel sauce, 1½ pints chicken or veal jelly or stock, and add gelatine and ½ pint cream.
To cover cold boiled chicken.
Source The same.

276. Maître d'Hôtel Butter

Melted butter combined with chopped parsley or tarragon, mustard and lemon juice. Refrigerate to harden.
Source: The same.

277. Black Butter Sauce

Melt and brown the butter without burning, and mix with a small quantity of wine vinegar. Serve very hot.
Excellent with boiled fish, sweetbread, brain, etc.
Source: Mrs. J.H. Luke.

278. Sauce Bruxelloise

1 egg, hard-boiled	salt, pepper
butter	lemon juice

Melt the butter until slightly browned. Add the condiments and lemon juice to taste. Chop the egg finely, add to the browned butter and serve hot.

For fried fish, *fonds d'artichaut*, hot asparagus.

279. Sauce Prince Lieven

5 pieces Gervais cheese	raspberry jelly
¾ liqueur glass French mustard	some juniper berries
½ tinned peach	paprika or cayenne pepper
2 onions	sugar, salt

Pass all these through a fine sieve and beat to a froth.
Serve with game.
Source: Count Haupt Pappenheim, São Paulo, Brazil.

280. Sauce Madère

2 glasses Madeira	½ pint chicken stock
1 tablespoon chopped shallots	2 tomatoes
1 sprig of thyme	cayenne pepper
1 gill thick cream	lemon juice

Reduce the wine and shallots with the thyme, by half; add the stock, cut-up tomatoes, pepper, salt and a squeeze of lemon juice. Bring to the boil, cook for 10 minutes, strain and add 1 gill fresh thick cream. Serve with ham, tongue, etc.

Source: Vice-Admiral Dubois, French Navy. (*Cf.* Recipe 110).

281. Cumberland Sauce - I

>   red-currant jelly   2 tablespoons Port
>   1 orange   a little ground ginger
>   1 lemon

Cut the rinds of the orange and lemon in strips, cook until soft in a little water. Strain off the water and mix the rind with jelly, ginger, Port and fruit juices, stirring well so that the jelly is not lumpy.

Delicious with cold game, guinea-fowl, salt and pressed beef.

Source: Mrs. Philip Martin, Jersey.

N.B. General Sir John du Cane's Polish chef at Sant Anton Palace, Malta, added some English mustard.

282. Cumberland Sauce - II (in Jelly Form)

>   peel of 1 orange   1 gill stock
>   a small piece of lemon peel   1 teaspoon Worcestershire sauce
>   2 tablespoons red-currant jelly

Peel the orange very thinly and bring all the ingredients slowly to the boil; strain through muslin into a small glass bowl, and allow to set. Serve with cold meats or ham.

283. Wine Sauce

>   2 lb. raspberry jam   cayenne pepper
>   1 quart Port or Sherry

Warm the jam, then pass through a sieve. Add the wine and cayenne pepper, and bottle ready for use.

For hot and cold ham.

Source: Mr. F.H. Jarvis, R.N., Chief Steward to Admiral of the Fleet Sir John de Robeck, H.M.S. *Iron Duke*.

284. Horseradish Sauce - I

Wash and scrape or grate the horseradish finely. Whip 1½ gills cream lightly, add 1 tablespoon wine vinegar (or chili, if preferred rather hot), salt, 1 teaspoon French or English made mustard and a trace of sugar. Stir in the grated horseradish to taste.

Alternatively, the sauce can be built on a base of Béchamel Sauce, *q.v.*

285. Horseradish Sauce - II

> ½ teaspoon mustard
> 1 teaspoon sugar
> 1 teaspoon tarragon vinegar
> 2 tablespoons grated horseradish
> 1 gill cream whipped to a thick consistency

Mix the ingredients in the order given, stirring in the cream very lightly. Stand on ice, and serve cold.

286. Horseradish Sauce - III (Iced)

> ½ pint fresh or sour cream
> 1 tablespoon grated horseradish
> 1 teaspoon sugar

Mix, freeze stiff, and serve sliced.

N.B.: Some other good horseradish recipes are given in that excellent little book *Culinary and Salad Herbs*, by Eleanour Sinclair Rohde.

287. Curry Sauce and Powder, and Rijstafel

> 1 dessertspoon good curry powder such as Vencatachellum's, or of Daw Sen's
> ½ oz. butter
> ½ gill milk

curry paste
2-3 dessertspoons tomato sauce

Melt the butter, add the remaining ingredients and boil together for a few minutes. Serve with hard-boiled eggs or as a sauce for boiled fish.

Source: H.C.L.'s West African cook, Sierra Leone.

In Brunei, in 1956, H.C.L. accompanied Mrs. John Gilbert, wife of the British Resident, who prefers to mix her own curry powders, on a marketing expedition for this purpose. She bought, separately and in varying quantities, the following ingredients to add to black pepper: aniseed, cardamom, chillies, cinnamon, cloves, coriander, cumin, mace, nutmeg, poppyseed, saffron, tamarind, turmeric.

Every traveller in the Far East has sampled the famous Rijstafel, the traditional Sunday midday meal gradually evolved by the early Dutch settlers in Java and Sumatra around the basic curried chicken or beef (which is often buffalo) and rice.

The accompanying *sambals* (relishes) comprise various forms (including pastes) of prawns and shrimps, spiced whitebait and other small fish, salted ducks' eggs, spiced mutton, fried cabbage, beans and okras, grated coconut, fried plantains, buttered toasted peanuts and the like, all seasoned to the limit of human endurance, and of course chutneys.

288. Marinade

Slice finely 3 oz. carrots, 5 oz. onions, 1 oz. celery, and brown them with 2 crushed cloves of garlic, a bouquet garni, pepper, salt, cloves, juniper berries, basil and rosemary.

Add 3 pints red or white wine (red for dark, white for white meat) and ½ pint vinegar.

Cook for ½ hour and allow to cool.

This marinade may be used many times, but must be boiled up and, if necessary, added to, every 2 days.

Source: Sir John Leche.

289. Vinaigrette Sauce

3 tablespoons olive oil
1 tablespoon lemon juice
1 tablespoon tarragon vinegar
1 dessertspoon chopped capers
¼ teaspoon salt
¼ teaspoon sugar
½ teaspoon made mustard
a dust of black pepper, freshly ground
chopped herbs: parsley, chives, tarragon, chervil

Mix the herbs and seasonings, adding the oil and beating well, then the vinegar and finally the lemon juice. If chives are not obtainable, add finely grated onion, or onion juice.

290. Sauce Banu

1 large onion
2 hard-boiled eggs
as much parsley as onion
2 oz. vinegar (¼ breakfast cup)
2 oz. oil
1 teaspoon mustard

Chop onions, eggs and parsley finely, add the mustard, vinegar, oil, salt and pepper.
 Serves 6 people.
 A piquant Vinaigrette for cold meat, iced asparagus, globe artichokes, etc.
 Source: Monsieur Banuelos, landlord of the inn at La Foà, interior of New Caledonia.

291. Chives

Chives (*Allium schoenoprasium*), finely chopped, are an appetizing adjunct to a lettuce salad, to scrambled eggs and an omelette, and to cream cheese. A hot consommé gains much by being poured over chopped chives before serving.
 Chives should, in fact, be used much more in Great Britain than they are, especially as they are said to originate in England.
 Source: H.C.L.

292. Chive Sauce - I

>   3 eggs
>   ¼ lb. butter
>   a good handful of chopped chives
>   2 tablespoons wine vinegar
>   salt
>   pepper

Beat in a bain-marie over boiling water the yolks of the eggs with the vinegar and a tablespoon of water, adding salt and pepper to taste.

When the mixture begins to cream add the butter in small pieces, bit by bit, beating all the time until it is thick and creamy. When it has almost cooled, fold in the white of the eggs, stiffly beaten, and the chopped chives. Do not let the sauce become too cold.

To be served with cold meats.

Source: Mrs. Reginald Davies, Stratton Audley Manor, Bicester.

293. Chive Sauce - II (Schnittlauch-Sauce)

>   2 hard-boiled eggs
>   the crumb or inside of a roll
>   chives
>   wine vinegar
>   oil
>   salt
>   sugar

Sieve one whole egg and the yolk of the other, also the bread; stir well with the oil, vinegar, salt, a pinch of sugar and a fair quantity of chopped chives. Serve cold. The sauce should have the consistency of a vinaigrette.

Served in Austria with the forms of hot boiled beef described in the Introductory Chapter.

Source: Mrs. J.H. Luke.

294. Anchovy Sauce

Make as for Chive Sauce II, adding two sieved anchovies.
 Source: The same.

295. Salsetta Verde per Bollito

<table>
<tr><td>1 lb. capers</td><td>parsley</td></tr>
<tr><td>3 anchovies</td><td>oil</td></tr>
<tr><td>the crumb of a roll soaked in vinegar</td><td>juice of half a small lemon
pepper</td></tr>
</table>

Chop the capers, anchovies, bread and parsley finely together and mix with the oil, pepper and, if liked, the lemon juice. For boiled beef, hot or cold.
 Source: Signora Emma Menegon, cook to Mrs. Freya Stark, Casa Freia, Asolo, Italy.

296. Aspic Jelly

<table>
<tr><td>2½ oz. gelatine</td><td>1 sliced onion</td></tr>
<tr><td>1 quart hot water</td><td>2 tablespoons tarragon vinegar</td></tr>
<tr><td>1 tablespoon salt</td><td>2-3 bay leaves</td></tr>
<tr><td>sprig of thyme</td><td>2 whites of eggs, slightly whipped</td></tr>
</table>

Put all the ingredients into a large pan and whisk together until boiling. Remove whisk, simmer for a few minutes so that the eggs may cake and clear the jelly, strain through a jelly bag.
 This makes a strong jelly that can be used for lining moulds, slicing or chopping, mixing with cream and vinegar to form aspic cream, etc.
 Source: E.G.

297. Fish Aspic

Sieve the requisite quantity of fish stock, clarify with white of egg, add gelatine and a little red wine.
    Source: Lady Laycock, Sant Anton Palace, Malta.

298. Jellied Salad

Soak

>1 tablespoon gelatine

in ¼ cup cold water, then add   While this is cooling add

>1 cup boiling water   cooked diced vegetables and
>¼ cup tarragon vinegar   cooked peas
>¼ cup sugar   quarters of skinned raw tomatoes
>1 teaspoon salt   hard-boiled eggs (sliced)
>2 tablespoons lemon juice

A thick Remoulade sauce (Recipe 262) can make a satisfactory addition.
    Source: Mrs. J.F. Santer.

299. Tomato Aspic Salad (A Variant of the Above)

>2 cups tomato juice   1 teaspoon salt
>1 small onion, chopped   A dash of celery salt and of
>2 tablespoons gelatine   cayenne pepper
>1 tablespoon lemon juice   a few celery leaves and a bay leaf
>1 teaspoon castor sugar

Soften the gelatine in half a cup of cold water. Simmer the remaining ingredients (except for the lemon juice) in a saucepan for 15 minutes. Then strain, add the gelatine and lemon juice and stir until well dissolved. Allow to cool, then pour into either 6-8 individual moulds or into one 6-inch ring mould. Chill until firm, then remove on to lettuce leaves and serve with a Mayonnaise.

Source: Mrs. Dade, cook to Mr. and Mrs. McCormick-Goodhard, Bellapaïs, Alexandria, Va., U.S.A.

300. My Favourite Lettuce Salad Dressing

¼ teaspoon mustard
¼ teaspoon salt
1 teaspoon castor sugar
3 teaspoons tarragon vinegar

3 teaspoons olive oil
mint sauce
meat or chicken gravy

Mix together with chopped celery, shallots, chives, tarragon leaves and a little parsley. Over the lettuce salad thus dressed pour some fairly well-sweetened mint sauce, and finally some meat or chicken gravy. Mix well.

Source: H.C.L.

301. A French Salad Dressing

3 tablespoons olive oil
3 tablespoons cream or top of milk
1 tablespoon malt vinegar

2 teaspoons castor sugar
½ teaspoon mixed mustard
salt, pepper

Mix and stir well, adding the cream last.

Source: Gwenllian Lady Palmer, the Dower House, Farley Hill, Berks.

302. Another with Herbs

1 heaped teaspoon sugar
a pinch each of mustard, pepper and salt
1 teaspoon French wine vinegar

  2-3 teaspoons best olive oil or cream
  chopped chives, parsley, thyme, mint, marjoram and (if liked) sage

Mix some hours before serving.
  Source: Madge, Lady Bonham-Carter.

303. Irish Salad Dressing

  the yolks of 2 hard-boiled eggs   *4 tablespoons salad oil*
  1 teaspoon salt   *2 tablespoons tarragon vinegar*
  1 teaspoon castor sugar   *1 tablespoon malt vinegar*
  1 teaspoon mustard   *4 tablespoons cream*

Mix the sieved yolks, salt, sugar and mustard well together, add the oil, beating thoroughly, then the vinegars and the cream. Bottle and cork. It will keep for some weeks.
  Source: Count Haupt Pappenheim, São Paulo, from an Irish Military Mess in the 1870's.

304. A Salad Dressing without Oil

  1 lb. brown sugar   *½ teaspoon Worcestershire sauce*
  1½ gills brown vinegar   *½ teaspoon salt*
  2 additional tablespoons vinegar   *3 dashes white pepper*
  2 teaspoons Colman's mustard

Put the mustard and salt in a mixing-bowl, and stir into it the 2 tablespoons vinegar until the mustard is well mixed. Add the brown sugar, Worcestershire sauce and pepper. Stir into this the 1½ gills vinegar until the sugar is melted to a thick syrup.
  Let it settle for a few minutes, after which it is ready to serve. Should be kept in the refrigerator.
  Source: Bridgetown Club, Barbados.

305. Trinity Salad

Cos lettuce, washed and
  drained very dry
spring onions, shredded and
  washed in water
Cheddar cheese, grated
olive oil

Orleans vinegar
garlic vinegar
tarragon vinegar
salt, pepper

Blend the grated cheese with the oil, vinegars and condiments as if for a Mayonnaise; then mix with the lettuce and onions when ready to serve.

Source: A speciality of Trinity College, Oxford.

Attributed to R.W. Raper (1842-1915), Fellow, Bursar and Vice-President of the College, who is said to have found its inspiration in Homer, in lines 628 *sqq.* of the XIth Book of the *Iliad*, where a drink is flavoured with cheese and onions.

306. Chicory Salad

An excellent winter salad is made by washing the chicory well, removing any green leaves, shredding finely and mixing with a dressing made from 2 tablespoons oil, 1 tablespoon lemon juice, 1 saltspoon each of salt and sugar, and a sprinkling of freshly ground black pepper.

Source: E.G.

307. Jerusalem Artichoke Salad

Boil small, young Jerusalem artichokes and place on ice. Lay each artichoke on a crisp lettuce leaf and serve very cold with a covering of Mayonnaise or Sauce Béarnaise.

308. A Beetroot Salad

A good and unusual salad is made by dicing the beetroot and mixing it with chopped celery and shallot, a touch of finely grated horseradish and a clove or two. Then add French dressing or a Mayonnaise, as preferred.

Source: The Dowager Viscountess Galway, formerly of Government House, Wellington, New Zealand.

309. South Styrian Cucumber Salad

The cucumber, peeled and thinly sliced, is dressed with wine vinegar and sour cream, and is liberally sprinkled with caraway seed and grated paprika.

Source: Frau Dr. Arthur Satter, Heiligenkreuz-am-Waasen, Southern Styria, Austria.

When salad-oil is required in this part of the world, both north and south of the Austro-Yugoslav frontier, that extracted from pumpkin seed is generally preferred to olive oil. It is much darker in colour, but has quite a pleasant flavour.

310. Tabuli

¾ of a ½-pint cup burghul (a porridge of barley)	3 bunches parsley
	1 bunch mint
2-3 tomatoes	1 gill olive oil
3 spring onions	juice of 2 lemons
2 inches of chopped cucumber	

Chop all the ingredients finely together, then mix with the *burghul*, adding the oil and lemon juice. Serve with lettuce. If an old onion has to be used, rub salt in after chopping so that it will dissolve.

This is a favourite Lebanese salad, included here for its unusual composition.

Source: Eaten by H.C.L. at Homs in Syria in 1955 at the house of Livingstone of Bachuil and Mrs. Livingstone.

311. Salt Cucumbers (Salzgurken)

Take some middle-sized green cucumbers, cut off the ends, make a small incision with a knife in the middle of each, and place in cold water. Take a small wooden barrel or a large stone jug and cover the bottom with vine leaves, cherry leaves, tarragon leaves, bay leaves, the leaves of cucumber or of dill, salt, cloves and peppercorns, together with a few grains or seeds of mustard. Place two layers of cucumbers on this, then more spices and leaves, and so on until the barrel is full. Add cold water (with 4 teaspoons salt to every quart used) to cover, and put on a lid with a heavy weight so as to keep the cucumbers well pressed down and covered with salt water.

Stand in a warm place from 8 to 10 days, removing the scum as it forms and adding more freshly salted water when necessary to prevent the cucumbers from protruding.

Source: Mrs. J.H. Luke. An Austrian recipe.

312. Dill Pickles (To Serve with Cocktails)

6 dill pickles
2¾ cups sugar
1 teaspoon salt
1 teaspoon mustard
1 teaspoon celery seed
5 cloves
1½ cups vinegar

Cut the pickles in thick slices, place in bowl with sugar and seasonings. Stir every few hours until the sugar is dissolved, then add the vinegar and stir well. Allow to stand 2-3 days, by which time the pickles are ready for use.

Source: Marine Hotel, Hastings, Barbados.

313. Pickled Watermelon

Remove from the watermelon rind all the dark green skin and most of the pink flesh, then cut into oblong pieces about ½ by 1½ inches.

Soak for 24 hours in a brine made of ¼ cup salt to 8 cups water. Rinse thoroughly in clear water, then boil gently until tender in fresh water with a scant teaspoon alum to preserve crispness.

Drain, then simmer again until translucent in a syrup made of 2 cups each of water, white vinegar and sugar together with 2 tablespoons cinnamon bark or 1 tablespoon cloves and whole allspice. The spices should be tied in a piece of cheese-cloth.

Bottle in sterile jars and seal.

Source: Mrs. F.J. d'Almeida, São Paulo, Brazil.

314. Banana Chutney

2½ ripe bananas
1 medium unripe pawpaw or apple
2 fairly large red chillies
1 breakfast cup malt vinegar
2 medium onions
3 cloves garlic (crushed)
2 knobs small green ginger
1 teaspoon ground ginger
1 handful raisins
1 breakfast cup brown sugar
1 tablespoon salt

Chop all the ingredients together and boil for 2 hours.

Source: Mrs. A.H. Russell, Samatau Plantation, Island of Upolu, Western Samoa.

Note by H.C.L.: In this connexion H.C.L. would like to make mention of a pleasantly piquant Peach Chutney he ate when lunching in 1962 with Brigadier and Mrs. Daniel Sandford at their farm of Mulu some 42 miles from the Ethiopian capital, Addis Ababa. To the hosts' fresh, sliced home-grown peaches was added a decoction of onions, green tomatoes and not too vitriolic red peppers.

315. On the Use of Herbs and Spices

A *sine qua non* in the intelligent preparation of food is the judicious use of herbs and spices. Among the former the following in particular will improve even well-cooked dishes, and can change dull and cloying ones out of all recognition: bay leaf, chervil, chives, marjoram, parsley, summer and winter savory and thyme. So can the vinegars flavoured, for example, with tarragon, basil and chervil become valuable adjuncts to salads. My friend Major-General J.M. Renton (see Recipe 237) serves saucers of freshly chopped tarragon, chervil, sorrel, fennel, alecost and 'English Mace' (not the mace of the nutmeg-tree but the herb *Achillea decolorans*) with his curries, to their advantage. The menu of Amyas Leigh's supper party at the Ship Inn described in Chapter VIII of Charles Kingsley's *Westward Ho!* included a remarkably comprehensive selection of the plants and herbs that went into Tudor salads.

Horseradish can be an important purveyor of zest and tang not only to a sirloin of beef but also to a wide range of other foods, including mashed potatoes and even apple sauce (see Recipes 195 and 317). Mint and dill communicate their distinctive flavours with advantage to the appropriate surroundings. On the other hand, sage, with its powerful savour, should be used with discretion and be confined to richly flavoured dishes such as roast duck.

Garlic is best allowed to exert its pungent and stimulating influence in an indirect manner, *e.g.* through the burial of a clove in the knuckle of a leg of lamb or mutton during the process of roasting, or by being rubbed round the inside of the salad-bowl, or in the form of garlic vinegar and garlic salt. Not a bad method is to enlist the aid of a garlic-squeezer, a gadget made inexpensively in France under the name *pressail*.

To turn to spices, mace - that aesthetically beautiful by-product of the nutmeg-tree, a network husk of deep and brilliant lacquer-red while it is still fresh on the nut - enriches thick soups and the stock-pot generally with its singularly piquant aroma. Nutmeg itself, grated, is also a help in soups (as had been noted elsewhere) no less than in bread sauce and a rum punch. Saffron is as indispensable to a good Milanese risotto as it is to a bouillabaisse and a *paella*. A touch of cardamom or coriander seed transforms a humdrum stew with the aroma of a Middle Eastern *suq*. And what a rich evocative aroma they have, those ancient vaulted bazaars of

Aleppo and Damascus and the Old City of Jerusalem, of Qazvin and Meshhed and Isfahan, as you approach the streets of the vendors of spices. Here you inhale an amalgam of all the aboriginal savours and smells of the Orient: the pepper and cloves; the cinnamon and turmeric and coriander; the sweetness of myrrh correcting the pungency of the urine of camels.

For caraway seeds, rightly cherished by those with the wit to appreciate its Protean capabilities (from bread to beetroot, cake to Kümmel, cabbage to a pork chop), refer to the following item. For chives see Recipes 291-293.

How pleasant if Kipling had thought of adding a verse on culinary herbs to 'Our Fathers of Old'. In tarragon, marjoram, thyme and bay he could have found an antiphon not unworthy of

'Basil, Rocket, Valerian, Rue,

. . . .

Vervain, Dittany, Call-me-to-you.'

Source: H.C.L.

316. Caraway Seed

If you dislike caraway seed, very well, you dislike it. Or do you? I have often found that persons who say they do only *think* they do do, because they confuse caraway with aniseed, a very different proposition.

When I ask these people if they dislike Kümmel as well as disliking Anisette, and how they react to seed-cake, the answer to the first question is more often than not a negative one, and that to the second favourable.

So for their benefit let me urge the enormous improvement effected in a pork chop by grilling or frying it with a good sprinkling of caraway seed.

Braised vegetables such as white and red cabbage are all the better for it, also beetroot hot and as a cold salad. Sauerkraut is unthinkable without it; while it is a delicious ingredient of certain forms of Continental bread, both white and black. This is especially true of Austria with its long white *Salzstangel*, its light brown, pointed *Bier-Wecken* formerly known as *Bosniaken*, and the flat dark brown Tirolese *Finschger-brot*.

It will be recalled that caraway figures between apples and cheese in the Elizabethan grace before meat quoted in the Introductory Chapter.

Source: The same.

VII

Sweets

317. Cooked Bananas

I am not one of those who appreciate the practice, so popular in Creole (*i.e.* Caribbean and New Orleans) cooking and elsewhere, of stewing bananas or plantains with chicken or ragouts of meat. To my mind the mixing of fruit with savoury meats and with salads is to spoil two good things. I dislike, for example, apple sauce with meat and bird; indeed, in any company except when mixed with horseradish as *Apfel-Kren*, a popular accompaniment of Austrian boiled beef, and as a similar Swedish sauce. I certainly like cranberry sauce with hare, venison, goose and turkey; chutney with a curry; red-currant jelly with indifferent mutton that wants helping along. But otherwise I approve of the mixing of fruit with meat only when both are uncooked, as in the excellent Venetian combination of raw smoked ham with cantaloupe melon, and the equally interesting South American combination of the same ham with fresh figs (*cf.* Recipe 1).

If you *must* eat your bananas cooked and hot, then lay them, *in their skins*, in an open dish, and place in the oven for 20-30 minutes, according to the heat of the oven. Serve with sugar and cream.

Or peel the requisite number of bananas and sauter them in butter. Then place them in a well-heated dish, sprinkle well with sugar and flamber with brandy or rum.

Much can, of course, be done with raw bananas. There is, to go no farther afield than Eton, that establishment's delicious Banana Mess (a sliced banana with vanilla ice-cream dressed with sugar and fresh cream. *Eds.*); while more exotic, and certainly less teetotal, is the seductive Hawaiian composition known as Banana Cow, of which I will say no more than that it is offered as an anodyne to a hangover in *Trader Vic's Book of Food and Drink*.

Source: H.C.L.

318. The Apricot

The word apricot (French *abricot*) has had a life-history as pleasant as it is interesting. From the Latin for early-ripening, *praecoquus* (from which is also derived the word precocious), it passed through Byzantine Greek into Arabic as *al-barquq*. From the Arabic-speaking world it passed on to Portugal and Spain as *albaricoque*, thence to France and finally assumed its English form by false analogy with the unconnected Latin word *apricus*, meaning sunny.
Source: The same.

319. Apricots or Peaches Flambés

Empty a tin of apricots or peaches into a colander placed over a bowl, and drain thoroughly. The fruit must be lifted out on to a dish, ready to serve, as dry as possible.
Pour hot rum over the fruit and a little into the hollow of each half and light. If the fruit is not very well drained the rum will not flame up; and, once it goes out, it cannot be rekindled.
The juice can be kept for adding to fruit salads, jellies, etc.
Source: Mrs. Stanton, Sam Lord's Castle, Barbados.

320. Plum or Apricot Dumplings (Zwetschken or Marillen-Knödel)

2 lb. potatoes
½ lb. flour
5 oz. breadcrumbs
2½ oz. fat
1 egg
salt

Boil, peel and sieve the potatoes. When cool, mix with the flour, the egg and a pinch or two of salt, and roll out thin on a pastry board. Cut into squares of the requisite size to enclose a fresh plum or apricot, and shape into dumplings.
Place the dumplings in boiling salted water and boil for 10 minutes, stirring frequently. Remove and drain. Fry the bread-

crumbs in the fat and cover the dumplings with them.
Source: A popular Viennese recipe.

321. Crêpes aux Abricots

Make some thin pancakes, spread them with hot apricot jam, roll up and serve on a hot dish, pouring more apricot jam over each pancake before serving.

322. Crêpes Suzette

Recipes for Crêpes Suzette, celebrated among pancakes and become the traditional French dish for Shrove Tuesday, are to be found in most good Cookery Books. So, apart from the following note on their origin, all that need be said of them here is that their exclusive characteristics are, first, their flavouring of orange juice, secondly, the Cognac or Armagnac with which they are finally set alight.

The Mademoiselle Suzette immortalized in these crêpes was an actress of the Comédie Française at the turn of the last century, who in the eighteen-nineties was taking the part of a maidservant required at one moment in the play to serve pancakes. These were supplied every night from the adjoining Restaurant Marivaux, whose proprietor, the Monsieur Joseph who was afterwards manager of the Savoy Restaurant in London, conceived the idea of igniting them with a glass of brandy so that the audience could assure themselves that the pancakes were genuine.

Although Crêpes Suzette are an essentially Parisian dish, I have never eaten better ones than at Hélène Cordet's 'Maison de France' at 6 Hamilton Place in London.
Source: H.C.L.

323. Omelette Rossini

In contrast with Verdi, who wrote his finest operas, *Othello* and *Falstaff*, in extreme old age, the composer G.A. Rossini (1792-1868) produced *The Barber of Seville* and *Cenerentola* before he was twenty-five and never wrote another opera after he was thirty-seven. Become rich and idle and concentrating thenceforth on good living, he settled in France, the gastronomer's paradise, and devoted the last forty years of his life to culinary rather than musical composition. On accidentally dropping a wing of truffled chicken into Lake Como at a water-picnic he is recorded to have burst into tears.

Some of Rossini's recipes became as famous as his *Barbiere*, among them 'Côtelettes Rossini' (lamb cutlets served with slices of truffle and *foie gras*) and the 'Omelette Rossini' which follows:

Source The same.

6 eggs
1 tablespoon potato flour
4 oz. castor sugar

3 oz. butter
peel of half a lemon

Beat the yolks of the 6 eggs with the scraped lemon peel for ¼ hour until the mixture becomes frothy. Then add the whites, which have been well whisked, together with the potato flour.

Now pour the mixture into a fairly deep pan which has been warmed and lined with butter. Bake for a ¼ hour in a very moderate oven, then turn out into the dish with the browned side uppermost. Sprinkle liberally with sugar and glaze this with a red-hot toasting-fork.

Source: G.A. Rossini.

324. Rum Omelette

2 eggs
2 tablespoons guava jelly

1 tablespoon lard
1 liqueur glass rum

Break the eggs into a bowl, add 1 teaspoon cold water and beat slightly. Drop the lard in an omelette pan and, as soon as it is hot, toss in the eggs, spread out as for a pancake.

When set and golden brown, turn out on to plate and allow to cool slightly. Then add the guava jelly, fold the omelette over it, place in a hot dish, pour the rum over, light and serve burning.

For 1 person.

Source: Bridgetown Club, Barbados.

325. *Guava Fool*

    2 tins Golden Glory guavas
    1 pint yoghurt
    2 tablespoons thick cream

Sieve the guavas. Add the yoghurt and cream gradually, then stir thoroughly. Pour into champagne glasses and keep in a cool place until required to be served. Sufficient for 5 people.

Source: Mrs. James Welch.

326. *Zabaglione - I*

4 eggs	*2 tablespoons Marsala or sweet*
2 tablespoons sugar	*Sherry*
	4 tablespoons hot milk

Beat the eggs with the sugar, add the milk and wine, stand the bowl in a bain-marie and whisk until it becomes thick and foamy. Serve at once. It is important that it should not be allowed to boil.

A Graves or Sauterne may be used if a drier wine is preferred.

Serves 4.

Zabaglione is the Italian counterpart of the old-fashioned English sillabub.

327. Zabaglione - II

Egg yolks (one per person)
Shortridge Old Malmsey (or similar) Madeira
Hock
Castor sugar
*(*for amounts of sugar and wines see below*)*

Zabaglione, when allowed to get cool, can be used as a filling for cakes, éclairs, etc., but if served as a sweet should be eaten warm. So the serving bowls or glasses should be warmed before you start.

It is important that, once the beating of the egg-yolk mixture over heat has begun, there should be little or no pause; it is also important that the heat be kept constant. So have the water at simmering point in the bain-marie and do not turn the heat up or down once the beating has started.

When the water is simmering, the bowls or glasses have been put to warm and everything is ready, separate the yolks from the whites of large eggs (placing the yolks in the top of the bain-marie) and putting the whites aside for other purposes.

To each yolk add one good dessertspoon of castor sugar and, using one evenly broken half-eggshell as a measure, add one measure of hock and one of Madeira for each yolk. The wines should not be measured in a metal spoon, and it is possible by using the half-eggshell as a measure to get the wines exactly right in proportion to the size of the eggs.

Stir the yolks, sugar and wine once or twice with a wooden spoon - just enough to break the yolks and blend them with the other ingredients. Place the container with this mixture over the simmering water in the bain-marie and start beating at once with an egg-whisk or electric hand-beater. The yolk mixture should be whisked until almost white and very fluffy, that is for about a quarter of an hour. When ready, pour into the warmed serving bowls or glasses and send to the table at once, serving sponge fingers separately.

Source: Mrs. James Holladay, Trinity College, Oxford.

328. Marrons à la Crème

    2 lb. chestnuts   1 pint cream
    ½ lb. bitter chocolate   sugar to taste

Cook the chestnuts whole for 2 hours, then skin and sieve. Just before serving, mix in the grated chocolate, sugar and the whipped cream.

With this may be handed a compote of orange flavoured with Maraschino (*cf.* Recipe 337).

Source: Lady Leche, British Embassy, Santiago, Chile.

At a luncheon-party given at the Iranian Embassy in Ankara by General and Madame Arfa in 1961 and attended by H.C.L., the hostess served a *purée* of chestnuts of this type, but shaped into tall and narrow cones surmounted by the cream. The dish figured appropriately on the menu as 'Damavand', the name of Persia's highest peak, whose striking outline and snow-capped summit the sweet ingeniously suggested.

329. Chestnuts Flambés

Slit the requisite quantity of chestnuts, roast in the oven ½-¾ hour and then shell.

Meanwhile make a syrup of rum, 1 tablespoon pure alcohol and an adequate quantity of sugar. Cook this slowly for 15-20 minutes.

When the syrup is sufficiently thick, boil it up. When it has boiled for 2 minutes pour it over the chestnuts and set the dish alight when about to serve.

Source: Contessa de Lord, Il Galero, Asolo, Province of Treviso, Italy.

330. Chestnut Soufflé - I

2 lb. chestnuts
3 oz. castor sugar
a vanilla pod
3 eggs

1 pint milk
1 oz. butter
½ pint water

Slit the chestnuts and place on baking-sheet in a moderate oven until the skin can be removed, or boil and skin. Put shelled nuts in pan with ½ pint milk, ½ pint water, add vanilla pod and cook until tender. Remove pod, and sieve chestnuts. Melt the butter in a stew-pan, add the sieved nuts, then work in the remaining ½ pint of milk, the sugar and the yolks of the eggs, mixing well. Beat the whites stiff and fold in lightly.

Put mixture in a buttered mould, cover with buttered paper and steam for 1 hour. Serve with hot jam sauce.

Serves 4.

Source: H.C.L.

331. Chestnut Soufflé - II

4 lb. chestnuts
4 eggs
6 oz. castor sugar

½ cup cream
2 oz. butter

Shell and skin the chestnuts, then boil for about 15 minutes in salted water until just tender. Drain and sieve. Add the sugar, cream, butter and the yolks of the eggs, and mix well. Beat the whites stiff and fold in lightly.

Put the mixture lightly in a buttered mould and bake for about 20 minutes in a moderate oven.

Serves 6-8.

Source: A United States recipe.

332. Chestnuts and Grapefruit

A surprisingly good combination for a cold sweet is skinned 'pigs' of fresh grapefruit sprinkled with grated chestnut.

Source: The Dowager Viscountess Mersey, late of Bignor Park, Pulborough, Sussex.

333. On Medlars and Persimmons

In my early days the medlar (French *nèfle*) must have been much more popular as a fresh fruit than it is today. Its appearance in the London fruit-shops of my childhood in its little round punnets used to be a regular and consoling herald of autumn; and I for one would look forward eagerly year after year to enjoying the tang of its tart yet mellow taste after the fruits of summer had gone their way. Between the wars an anonymous correspondent of *The Times* wrote pleasantly of how

> 'this curious little brown fruit has the quintessence of autumn in it - colour, smell and taste - and its subtle sub-acid flavour blends perfectly with most red wines, a secret Professor Saintsbury revealed to many in his *Notes on a Cellar Book*'.

Critics of the medlar decry it because, they say contemptuously, you cannot eat it until it is rotten. In support of their thesis they quote the old doggerel

> *'The medlar, be it not forgotten,*
> *Is never ripe until it's rotten',*

but this, like many other old rhymes, is fallacious. You eat the medlar when - to use the technical term - it has 'bletted', that is to say when it has begun to 'go to sleep' like the pear to which it is related and has been subjected to frost; at the moment when the skin is still unbroken and the flavour at its best; at the moment before decay has really set in.

The medlar's botanical name is *Mespilus* or *Nespilus German-ica* and, despite its apple-like structure, it belongs to the Pyrus family. It is not related to the yellow, smooth-skinned, plum-shaped loquat or 'Japanese medlar'.

Nowadays more people eat the medlar in jelly form (for which a Recipe follows) than fresh; and here I might add that when jellies such as medlar and guava are intended to be used with meats and game they are vastly improved by the inclusion of a little Worcestershire sauce and fresh lemon juice in their composition.

The one other fruit I know that can be eaten only when it has gone soft and has 'bletted' is the persimmon, that beautiful 'golden apple' which should clearly have hailed from the gardens of the Hesperides. In point of fact it hails from Japan *(Diospyros Kaki)* and the Southern States of the United States *(Diospyros Virginiana)*. Is it not strange that flesh which in both cases, until that stage is reached, is so harsh and wryly astringent as to be utterly uneatable should thereafter be transmuted into substances so agreeable to the taste?

The persimmon tree is of large and noble growth - with the mulberry it is among the tallest fruit-trees in the world - and in the European summer the 'plums' (for that is what they look like), still of a pale apricot hue, gleam coldly luminous among the leaves. The trees are certainly handsome enough at this season of the year in their natural beauty; but in late November and in December, when the fruit has ripened into edibility, they assume the tinge of another kind of beauty: the boughs, now entirely stripped of leaves, are weighed down under their burden of fruit, by this time no longer just a pale reflection of lunar austerity but richly, warmly glowing - great balls of orange-brown amber - against the sharp clear blue of the Italian winter sky. They look like toy trees - if anything so large may be likened to a toy - to whose naked branches the children of a race of giants have tied the golden globes for a Christmas party in Brobdingnag.

Source: H.C.L.

334. Medlar Jelly

1½ lb. medlars
1½ pints water

1½ lemons
sugar to equal weight of juice

Wash the medlars and cut them in quarters. Place in a pan with the water, thinly sliced lemon rind and the pith from the lemons cut in rough pieces. Cook together for about 2 hours, stirring and pressing the fruit occasionally.

Strain through a jelly bag, measure the liquid and put aside an equal weight of sugar. Boil the juice for 7 minutes, add the sugar and reboil, stirring till the sugar has dissolved. Test on a cold plate for jellying in the usual way, bottle in clean, heated jars and cover at once.

Source: The Dowager Viscountess Mersey, late of Bignor Park, Pulborough.

335. Strawberry-grape Jelly

Pick the grapes when nearly ripe. Boil until soft and strain through a jelly bag. Take 1 lb. sugar to each pint of juice, boil together quickly for ½ hour or until it sets on a cold plate.

The jelly can, of course, be made from any variety of grape, the only difference being that a lesser quantity of sugar will be needed for very sweet grapes such as Muscats. The real reason I have headed this recipe 'Strawberry-grape Jelly' is to invite attention to what is in my opinion the most piquant of all grapes - the grape with the true wood-strawberry flavour.

This round, purply-blue little grape, which pops so neatly and completely out of the skin when gently squeezed, grows abundantly in Central and South-east Europe (under the name *Isabella*), in New England (as *Catawba*), in a corner of North Island, New Zealand, under the Maori name *Te Kauwhata*, in South Africa and in other parts of the world. I have also encountered a pink strawberry-grape, exceptionally large, juicy and sweet and known locally as Marengo in addition to the usual purple varieties in the south of

Brazil, where both are extensively cultivated in the States of São Paulo and Rio Grande do Sul. I have grown it with success in my garden in Malta; and it has been known to do well in the south of England.

The strawberry-grape is a grape to be recommended; and I for one have done my best to chase it around the globe.

Source: H.C.L.

336. The Mulberry

The mulberry, when it is fully ripe and spurting with purply red juice, is to me the most delicious of all berries. So it should be, seeing that its drupelets are filled with the mingled blood of those fabled lovers Pyramus and Thisbe. I speak, of course, of *morus nigra*, the black mulberry, with which James I planted the area now occupied by Buckingham Palace and its gardens, hoping thereby to encourage the spinning of silk. The King meant well, and did indeed benefit the citizens of London, although not as he had intended. For with all his learning, the monarch failed to realize that what the silkworm delights in is not the black mulberry but the leaf of the white one, *morus alba*, whose dehydrated, dirty-white little berries are tasteless and of no use to man.

Don't cook mulberries unless you have more than you can cope with fresh. For one reason, their flavour is far too delicate for them to be eaten otherwise than fresh. For another, more general, reason all fruit when cooked is apt to become acid-, instead of alkali-forming. I have found that the best use for a surplus of mulberries is to turn it into water-ices (sorbets), which are of exquisite taste and an ideal form of refreshment for a summer party.

Source: The same.

337. Orange Compote

Remove the rind and outer pith from your oranges, then with a knife cut each segment lengthwise, removing all the skin. Put in a dish with layers of sugar, stand for 2 hours, then add a good syrup of sugar and water flavoured with Maraschino. Stand the dish in the refrigerator for ½ hour, basting occasionally, and serve.

The fruit should be no more than chilled; if iced, it loses flavour.

Here may be mentioned parenthetically the marmalade of piquant tangerine flavour made at Saint Augustine (Florida) of the calamondin (*Citrus mitis*). This tiny and acid fruit has the colour and shape, in miniature, of a tangerine and is, with the kumquat, the smallest of the citrus family.

Source: The same.

338. *Plum and Orange Roll*

½ lb. sugar
½ lb. plums
1½ oz. shredded orange peel (*arancini*)
3 oz. dried hazel-nuts

Wash the plums and cook till tender and easily broken up. Dissolve the sugar in a little water, add the plums and cook together till a thick paste results. Add the nuts, which have been chopped, and the orange peel finely shredded, and form into a sausage-shaped roll. Stand in a cool place to dry off, sprinkle with sugar and serve cut in thin slices for tea, or whole as a sweetmeat.

Source: Mrs. J.H. Luke.

339. *Ginger and Fig Pudding*

8 oz. crystallized ginger
8 oz. dried figs
8 oz. sugar
¼ oz. gelatine

Simmer the figs and ginger in 1½ pints of water for as long as possible, in fact all day if convenient.

Add the sugar and a pinch of *powdered* ginger. Melt the gelatine in hot water and add to the rest. Stir well and leave to set in a ring mould.

Serve cold with whipped cream.

Source: Mrs. John Brewis; a Shropshire Recipe.

340. Pineapple Cake

¼ lb. butter
1 cup sugar
2 cups flour
1 teaspoon vanilla essence
2 eggs

4 slices of pineapple
1 cup pineapple juice
1 cup brown sugar
2 oz. butter

Put the pineapple in a baking-pan with the juice, brown sugar and 2 oz. butter, cook for a little and leave until cold. (If fresh pineapple is used it must be boiled for the juice, so it is better to use tinned pineapple.)

Make a cake mixture with the creamed butter, sugar, flour, eggs and vanilla, pour over the pineapple and bake. Turn over on a plate to serve.

Source: Mrs. A.A.L. Tuson, British Legation, Port-au-Prince, Haiti.

341. 'Indians' (Cookies)

2 oz. chocolate ⎫
½ cup butter   ⎬ melt together over hot water
                ⎭
2 eggs
1 cup sugar
½ cup flour
1 cup chopped nuts
1 teaspoon vanilla

Remove chocolate-butter mixture from heat. Add sugar, eggs, flour, vanilla and nuts in the order given. Bake for 20 minutes at

400°F. Cut in squares while hot. They will look raw inside, but they are done.

Source: Miss Welden, cook to Mr. and Mrs. Leander McCormick-Goodhart, Bellapaïs, Alexandria, Va., U.S.A.

342. *A Delicious Coffee Cream Cake*

In the first place take

>   6 oz. hazel-nuts
>   6 oz. castor sugar
>   3 egg whites

brown the nuts in the oven and remove the skins, then grind in a 'Mouli'.

Make a meringue mixture with the stiffly beaten egg whites and sugar, fold in most of the ground hazel-nuts, leaving enough to coat the top when finished.

Divide the mixture between two well-buttered and floured, loose-bottomed sandwich tins, bearing in mind that the meringue is fragile and difficult to remove. Then bake in a medium (350°) oven for about 25 minutes until pale brown, remove from the tins at once on to paper and dry on a wire tray.

Next, prepare a cream with

>   3 egg yolks (whisked)
>   4 tablespoons strong coffee
>   4 oz. well sieved icing sugar

mixed over boiling water until thick and creamy. Let it cool, stirring occasionally.

Now cream

>   4 oz. butter

in a bowl and add the coffee-egg mixture gradually, stirring gently.

This completed, place the cream between the nut-meringue cakes, with the addition of a little on top, and dust with the balance of the ground hazel-nuts.

Source: Mrs. Reginald Davies, Stratton Audley Manor, Bicester. This is one of the best sweets H.C.L. has ever tasted.

343. Meringue Cake - I

```
4 eggs                          1 tablespoon finely ground coffee
4 oz. butter                    4 oz. almonds
13 oz. castor sugar             cream
4 teaspoons baking powder
```

Beat the whites of the eggs very stiffly. Add, gradually, 9 oz. sugar sieved with the baking-powder, and go on beating. Drop this mixture, a teaspoon at a time, on a buttered baking-sheet, place in a cold oven and bake - to start with - under slow heat for from 30 to 40 minutes.

Meanwhile make the following cream: beat together the 4 yolks, 4 oz. sugar, the 4 oz. butter and the coffee in the electric mixer until smooth and creamy; then add a little whipped cream. Line the bottom of a 7-inch round baking-tin with the small meringues, spread over them half of the cream, cover with another layer of meringues flat side up, spread the rest of the cream over these, cover again with meringues and place in the refrigerator for an hour or two.

Then take the cake out of the tin, cover with sugared whipped cream and skinned, chopped and slightly browned almonds.

Source: Miss Genia Hordliczka, São Paulo, Brazil.

344. Meringue Cake - II

```
½ cup butter                    ¾ cup sifted cake flour
½ cup sugar                     1 teaspoon baking-powder
4 egg yolks                     ½ teaspoon vanilla
¼ cup milk
```

Cream butter, sugar and vanilla well. Add egg yolks, then flour, milk and baking-powder. Divide in two, and put into greased floured pans.

```
4 egg whites                    ¼ cup blanched and shredded
1 cup sugar                         almonds
½ teaspoon almond extract       a pinch of salt
```

Beat egg whites until stiff but not dry. Slowly beat in sugar, a tablespoon at a time. Fold in extract and almonds. Pile on each pan on top of cake batter. Bake for 45-50 minutes at 350º F. Turn out meringue side down. When cold spread one layer with whipped cream and crushed pineapple or apricot jam. Put other layer in place with meringue side up.

Source: Miss Welden, Bellapaïs, Alexandria, Va., U.S.A.

345. *Tea Cake*

2 cups sifted flour	1/3 cup shortening
4 teaspoons baking-powder	1 egg
2 tablespoons sugar	milk
½ teaspoon salt	

Mix and sift dry the ingredients. Cut in shortening until well mixed. Break egg into cup, and fill with milk until cup is ¾ full. Toss *lightly* in bowl until all is mixed well. Place in greased and floured pan. Spread well with pineapple or apricot jam. Bake in hot oven (450ºF.) for 15 minutes. Reduce heat and bake for 10 minutes or until nicely browned.

Remove from pan and place on serving plate. Cut in wedges and serve hot with whipped cream.

Source: The same.

346. *Fruit Cake*

1 lb. butter	1 lb. chopped dates
1 lb. sugar	1 pint grape juice
1 lb. flour	2 lb. mixed chopped nuts (walnuts, pecans and almonds)
1 dozen eggs	
4 lb. seeded raisins	1 tablespoon cinnamon
2 lb. crystallized pineapple	1 teaspoon nutmeg
1 lb. crystallized cherries	1 teaspoon allspice
1 lb. shredded citron	½ teaspoon cloves
1 glass grape jelly	1 tablespoon almond extract
1 pint preserved pears	1 tablespoon brandy extract

Soak fruit, pear preserves, grape juice and jelly overnight.

Cream butter, sugar and egg yolks. Add stiffly beaten egg whites. Sift spices with half the flour and add to above mixture. Mix remainder of flour into fruit. Add fruit to batter a little at a time so as to mix well. Add nuts last. Bake for 4-6 hours, depending on the size of each cake, in greased and papered pans at 200°F. or less. Start cakes in cool oven. It is better to underbake them than to overbake them, but they should be baked enough in order not to mould. Will keep a year if stored in a cool place.

(A good substitute for pear preserves: 1 lb. dates stoned and cut, 1 cup sugar and 1 cup water. Cook until thick.)

Source: The same.

347. *Frangipane Tartlets*

2 ½ oz. butter	4 oz. sugar
2½ oz. margarine	4 oz. ground almonds
5 oz. flour	2 eggs
4 oz. butter	vanilla essence

Make a short crust pastry with the flour, butter and margarine; cream the 4 oz. butter, add sugar and eggs, the ground almonds and essence, beating to a smooth batter. Line small patty tins with thin pastry, put a small teaspoon of apricot jam in each, and then a spoonful of batter. Cook at 370° F. for about 20 minutes.

This quantity makes 50 tartlets.

Source: E.G.

348. *Smaa Aebleskiver (Small Doughnuts)*

¾ lb. wheaten flour	½ lb. butter
5 eggs	1 pint milk

Stir the flour into the tepid milk, add the yolks and the butter and, finally, the lightly beaten whites of the eggs.

Fry the resultant batter in a special pan containing seven hemispherical depressions, producing as many spherical *'skiver'* at a time. These are eaten warm, with sugar, jam and, if desired, whipped cream.

Source: An eighteenth-century book of Recipes which is an exhibit in the Gamle By ('Old Town'), a collection of original houses of the sixteenth to eighteenth centuries assembled as an open-air museum at Aarhus, Jutland, Denmark.

349. Crème Brulée

10 egg yolks
1 pint fresh cream
3 oz. castor sugar

Beat the yolks and the sugar together, bring the cream to the boil and mix. Return to saucepan and cook slightly, not allowing the mixture to boil. Pour into dish and set in slow oven.

When cold, cover top with castor sugar and place under salamander. A gas grill or a clean, hot coal shovel will make the salamander.

Decorate with whipped vanilla cream and serve.
Serves 6.
Source: The Manciple, Corpus Christi College, Cambridge.

350. Spanish Cream

1 carton natural yoghurt
¼ pint double cream
dark mollasses sugar

Whip the cream and spoon it into a shallow dish. Fold the yoghurt into it and top the mixture with ½ inch of dark mollasses sugar. Leave in refrigerator for the minimum of 8 hours.

Source: Mrs. Nelson Paine, Jimena de la Frontera, Spain.

351. Cream Puffs

¼ pint water   2½ oz. flour
2 oz. butter   2 eggs

Boil the butter and water together, add the flour, beat in thoroughly until smooth and allow to cool slightly. Add the unbeaten eggs one at a time, beating well, and then put spoonfuls of the mixture on a greased baking-sheet, about 1½ inches apart, shaping with the spoon. (Or use a forcing bag, for éclairs.) Bake for 20 minutes in a hot oven.

It is wise to have nothing else in the oven at the same time, as cream puffs fall at once if they are not cooked; and it is unwise to open the oven door too frequently. Take one out, to test, and if cooked remove the rest and place on a cake-tray.

Cut a slit in the side of each, fill with whipped cream and ice, or for a dinner sweet serve with hot chocolate sauce.

This quantity makes 12 puffs or 15 éclairs.

352. Pureé de Fruits au Fromage Rose

2 lb. fresh strawberries   2 egg yolks
1 lb. fresh raspberries   kirsch   ⎱ to taste
2 small cream cheeses   castor sugar ⎰

Put on one side the biggest of the strawberries (destined to be placed on top of the sweet) and leave them to absorb a liberal sprinkling of kirsch and sugar.

Rub the remainder through a tammy (*cf.* Glossary) together with the raspberries, then work the mixture with a fork into the cheese until this has completely absorbed the fruit.

Add the egg yolks, sugar and kirsch to the *purée*, arrange it in rounded form in a glass dish, cover with the whole strawberries and surround with small finger biscuits.

Source: Mrs. J.C. Adamson's adaptation of a Belgian Recipe.

353. Chocolate Mousse

>6 oz. sweet chocolate
>6 eggs
>½ liqueur glass brandy

Melt the chocolate in a bain-marie. Beat the egg yolks and stir into the chocolate, adding the brandy.
Whisk the whites very stiffly and fold into the chocolate. Put in a cool place to set, but do not leave more than 6 hours before eating. Serves 6.
Source: Mrs. Wilfred Bolton, Kyrenia, Cyprus.

354. A Similar Chocolate Sweet

>1 lb. bitter chocolate   fried almonds
>9 eggs

Whip whites and beat yolks of eggs separately. Melt chocolate in a little water, pour on to yolks, mix well together. Fold in the whipped whites lightly, and serve with chopped brown almonds on top.
Source: Mrs. Edward Lefroy, Coleherne Court, London, S.W.

355. Hungarian Chocolate

>2 egg whites   4 oz. bitter chocolate
>2 tablespoons castor sugar 2 tablespoons strong coffee

Whip the white very stiff, add the sugar carefully. Melt the chocolate in the coffee, and mix together lightly. Serve when cold in separate glasses, topped with whipped cream.
Source: E.G.

356. Hot Chocolate Sauce

1 square bitter chocolate
1 tablespoon melted butter
1/3 cup boiling water
1 cup sugar

Melt the chocolate in a bain-marie, add the butter; when blended, add water by degrees and the sugar. Bring to the boil and boil 15 minutes, cool slightly and flavour lightly with vanilla.

357. Chocolate or Coffee Mousse

3 oz. chocolate or 4 tablespoons strong (liquid) coffee
1½ gills cream
whites of 4 eggs
¼ oz. gelatine
2 oz. sugar
1 teaspoon rum or kirsch

Melt the gelatine in 2 tablespoons water and keep warm. Whip the cream slightly and put aside. Whip the whites of egg to a very soft froth, add the warm gelatine and whip well again.

Then add the sugar, cream, rum (or kirsch) and the chocolate or coffee mixed with a little milk.

Mix very lightly together, turn into a small basin rinsed out with cold water and allow to set.

Source: Mrs. S. Barrowclough, Penn Oast, Hollingbourne, Kent.

358. White Coffee Ice

½ pint milk
½ pint cream
4 oz. freshly roasted whole coffee berries
3 oz. castor sugar
1 teaspoon vanilla essence

Put all these ingredients into a bain-marie and bring slowly to boiling point. Then keep hot at the back of the stove for ½ hour, strain and when quite cold freeze in the usual way.

This ice has an unusual, smoky flavour.

Source: E.G.

359. *Black Currant and Red Currant Water Ice*

  2 punnets black currants 1½ cups sugar
  2 punnets red currants   1 lemon

Simmer the currants, sugar and the juice of the lemon until the fruit is soft. Then pour the contents of the saucepan into a 'Mouli' and sieve into a bowl. Put the juice into trays in the refrigerator and leave to freeze.

  Source: The Hon. Mrs. Michael Luke.

360. *Rolled Oats Biscuits*

  1 cup brown sugar   4 oz. butter
  2 cups rolled oats   1 teaspoon soda dissolved in
  2 tablespoons flour   2 tablespoons milk

Mix sugar, oats and flour, add the soda dissolved in milk and mix well. Lastly, pour in the melted butter. Put small teaspoons of the mixture on a greased baking-tin, flatten slightly and bake in a fairly hot oven for 10 minutes. Remove from tray while hot.

  Source: E.G.

361. *Rolled Oats Fingers*

  8 oz. rolled oats   2 oz. sugar
  4 oz. butter   a pinch of salt

Mix all together well and spread on a greased baking-sheet - the mixture will be stiff and require flattening to the tin. Bake in a moderate oven until slightly golden, cut into fingers and leave on the tin until cold.

Source: The same.

362. Gubbeen Cheese

And for the many who, for diverse reasons, do not eat puddings or sweetmeats, what better than the best farmhouse semi-soft cheese ever to come out of Ireland. Gubbeen cheese is made from the unpasteurized milk of the pedigree Gubbeen herd and is the product of Mr. and Mrs. Tom Ferguson, Gubbeen House, Schull, Co. Cork, Ireland. The latter, Giana Ferguson, is the eldest granddaughter of the author. Gubbeen cheese has won many national and international prizes, including 3rd. Prize at the International Cheese Convention, Switzerland, 1991. At the time of going to press, Giana Ferguson is on a sponsored lecture tour of the U.S.A. on behalf of Irish farmhouse cheeses.

Source: Mr. and Mrs. Tom Ferguson, as above.

VIII

Drinks

363. Apricot Brandy

    2 lb. apricots   1 cup sugar
    1 bottle brandy

Cut the apricots, which should be on the unripe side, into quarters and soak them in brandy for 4-5 weeks with some of the apricot kernels. At the end of this time make a thick syrup of sugar and water, strain off the apricots without squeezing them, and add syrup to the brandy according to taste.
Source: H.C.L.

364. Orange Brandy

    peel of 18 Seville oranges   4 lb. white sugar
    4 bottles brandy

Cut the orange peel very thin and mix with the sugar and brandy in a stone jar. Cork well, and leave for a week, shaking several times a day. Then remove peel.

    Can be drunk in six months, but it is best kept two or more years, and it is an advantage to stand it near a fire before serving, as this draws out the flavour.

    The pulp can be used to make marmalade if the rinds of 3 ordinary oranges are added.

365. Mickey's Finn

This is a summer cup.

    Plymouth Gin   fresh mint
    strong dry fizzy cider   lemon or lime peel
    Angostura bitters

Mix in a big jug the above ingredients in proportions according to thirst and sense of well-being.
    Source: Mr. Michael Luke, Eaton Square, London.

366. Clover Cup Cocktail

> 1 part lemon juice
> 1 part Grenadine
> 2 parts dry gin
> white of one egg

Frapper well with ice, add stiffly whipped white of egg and float mint leaves on top, or chop mint leaves and shake with cocktail in shaker. Do not use too much ice.

367. Corson's Cocktail

> ½ lemon
> 1/3 gin
> 1/3 Sherry
> ice
> a dash of the following: Italian vermouth
> French vermouth
> Curaçao
> cherry brandy
> Crème de Cacao

Shake well and serve cold.
    Source: Rear-Admiral Eric Corson, S. Angelo, Malta.

368. Gin Cocktail (for Small Shaker)

> juice of ½ lemon
> juice of ½ orange
> 1 teaspoon sugar
> 2 claret glasses gin
> liqueur glass brandy

Ice the mixture, shake it well and garnish with lemon peel.
    Source: Mr. Peter Luke.

369. Grapefruit Cocktail

Mix together 2 parts grapefruit juice, 1 part vodka and a squeeze of lime.
    The name of this cocktail, like that of the next one, is a little misleading.
    Source: Sir Edward Cunard, Bart., Barbados.

370. Pineapple Cocktail

Mix together the juice of 1 pineapple, ¼ bottle each of Curaçao and Bacardi rum, and a bottle of fizzy lemonade. Serve iced in deep claret glasses.
Source: The same.

371. Iquique Cocktail

To 4 claret glasses gin add 1 claret glass lemon juice, 3 heaped soupspoons *icing* sugar, 2 full teaspoons Angostura bitters, plenty of ice; then shake well.
Source: Sir James Dodds, K.C.M.G., British Embassy, Lima.

372. Alexander Cocktail (Variant)

>   equal parts of: *vodka*
> *Crême de Cacao*
> *cream*

373. Mosul Mist

Fill a claret glass, in equal quantities, with

>   *brandy*
> *crême de menthe*

Source: A speciality of the R.A.F. Mess in Mosul, Northern Iraq, in the time of the British Mandate. It was there administered to H.C.L. on a grilling day in 1924 on top of a late Sunday luncheon consisting, not altogether seasonably, of mulligatawny, curry and beer.

Mosul Mist must be just wonderful in an Arctic blizzard, but it is not the liquid with which to wash down a heavy repast in the middle of a broiling Mesopotamian afternoon.

374. Georgetown Rum Swizzle

    4 measures rum
    2 shakes Angostura bitters
    ¾ measure water
    crushed ice

Pour above into a jug and swizzle well, then strain into another jug to get rid of the ice. Swizzle again before serving. (Some brands of rum do not swizzle well, and if the water is hard it will not swizzle.)

    This is supposed to be swallowed at one gulp. The same applies to whisky and gin swizzles.

    Source: Captain P. Jeffs, Government House, British Guiana.

375. 'Christopher's Mother'

    2 measures gin
    1 measure rum
    ½ measure orange juice
    juice of ¼ lemon
    3 shakes of whisky (to bind)

Shake well, and serve cold.

    Source: Mrs. H. Pirie-Gordon, Polesacre, Lowfield Heath, Crawley, Sussex.

376. Pisco Sour

Those whose way takes them to South America will be well advised to sample the Peruvian grape spirit called Pisco from the town near which it is made. Pisco is as well known in those parts as is whisky elsewhere, and is an admirable base for all sorts of cocktails, cups and sours.

    Here is one of the sours:

    Pisco
    fresh lime (or lemon) juice
    white of egg, beaten up
    a dash of Angostura or orange bitters
    sugar to taste

    Source: H.C.L.

377. A Fresh Tomato Cocktail and a 'Bloody Mary'

<blockquote>
2 lb. fresh tomatoes
1 shallot or small onion
1 small lemon or, better still, 1 lime
2 dessertspoons castor sugar
Worcestershire sauce to taste
celery salt
</blockquote>

Squeeze the juice of the tomatoes, chop the shallot or onion up finely, add the other ingredients, including the juice of the lemon or lime, shake vigorously in the cocktail shaker until the shallot is dissolved and serve cold.

So much for the Fresh Tomato Cocktail, in which the discerning palate will accept tinned tomato juice only as a *pis aller* for the fresh.

For those who prefer their Tomato Cocktails to be alcoholic the New World has devised various combinations of tomato juice with vodka and other, minor, ingredients in the proportion of 1 to 1½ measures vodka to 1 pony-glass tomato. One of these mixtures bears the undeservedly forbidding name of 'Bloody Mary', for it is in truth a highly effective apéritif. In H.C.L.'s opinion it becomes even more attractive with the addition of Worcestershire sauce.

Source: The same.

378. 'Cold Duck' (Kalte Ente)

<blockquote>
1 bottle champagne
2 bottles Moselle
½ bottle soda water
peel of 1 lemon
</blockquote>

Ice the wines and soda water, then mix and immerse for 5 minutes the lemon peel sliced very thin.

This very refreshing hot-weather luncheon or dinner drink should only be prepared immediately before use.

Source: Mr. R.T. Smallbones, C.M.G., British Consulate-General, Frankfurt-am-Main, Germany.

379. Cruchon (Georgian Wine Cup)

The favourite summer drink among Georgians and other Trans-Caucasians is the wine cup they call Cruchon, for which they use some of their full-bodied amber-coloured wines and for which their superlatively fine fruits are admirably adapted.

Cruchons are mixed with the usual accessories, such as liqueurs, herbs, lemon and cucumber peel, and the like; but they differ from our Cups in that the large glass jugs in which they are made and served are more than half-filled with the fruit, and the fruit is ultimately eaten off plates. The wine-impregnated fruit is, in fact, as important as the liquor.

The most delicious Cruchon, in my opinion, is that made with wild wood-strawberries; the most redoubtable (for what reason I do not know), that made with the famous Georgian peaches.

Source: H.C.L.

380. A Wine Cocktail

3 parts Burgundy   1 part brandy
Maraschino to taste   slice of lemon

381. Sangaree

1 Sherry glass Madeira   1 lime
½ pint water   a pinch of nutmeg
sugar to taste   ice

Squeeze the juice of the lime into the Madeira and water, mix in the sugar and nutmeg, add the ice and serve in a long glass.

For 1 person.

Source: A traditional eighteenth-century Barbadian middle-of-the-morning or luncheon drink, as now served at the Bridgetown Club.

An eighteenth-century Sangaree glass originally made for the owner of the Windsor Plantation, Barbados, and inscribed 'Success to Windsor', was the wedding-present of the women and girls of Barbados to H.M. Queen Elizabeth II.

382. *A Prize-Winning 'Old-Fashioned'*

Into an 'Old-Fashioned' tumbler or other broad-based glass pour:

>½ *teaspoon castor sugar*
>3 *drops Angostura bitters*

and just sufficient soda-water to mix the sugar and bitters into a liquid paste.
    Cut slices of

>*apple*
>*orange*
>*pineapple*

and pack together artistically in the glass. On top of this pack small cubes of ice completely covering the fruit. Then pour the

>*Bourbon whisky*

up to the ice level and add a maraschino cherry (not *glaçée*) on a toothpick.
    Source: Group-Captain Dudley Honor, D.F.C., who won the prize with this recipe (against competing Americans) at a competition held at the Hotel Granada, Bogotá, Colombia.

383. *Barrosa Cup*

1 *bottle liqueur brandy*	1 *glass Kümmel*
1 *bottle peach brandy*	*the rind of two lemons*
½ *bottle cherry whisky*	*the peel of one cucumber*

½ bottle brown Curacao
½ bottle Maraschine
1 glass Sherry
1 teaspoon bitter almond essence
4 tablespoons sifted sugar
1 pint champagne

Mix all together except the champagne, remove the rind and peel after a few minutes, stir well and add more sugar if necessary. Before serving strain, and add the champagne just before serving.

Source: The traditional loving-cup of the Royal Irish Fusiliers, which is passed round the Officers' Mess on 'Barrosa Night', while the Officers recite a doleful poem commemorating the victory and the junior subaltern makes a speech on the same topic under a fusillade of rolls and apples. (A British force under Sir Thomas Graham defeated the French at La Barrosa, near Cádiz, on 5 March 1811. *Eds.*)

H.C.L. owes the Recipe to the courtesy of the Commanding Officer and Officers when he dined with the Regiment on 'Barrosa Night' on 5 March 1938.

Contrary to what might be supposed, the comforting effect of this remarkable and very smooth composition does not degenerate later into a hangover.

384. On Punches and Grog

There are cold Punches and hot Punches, the former consumed in the tropics, where the drink originates, the latter round about Christmas in damp, foggy Britain and snow-bound Scandinavia.

The name is probably derived from the Hindustani *panj*, meaning 'five' (*cf.* Panjab), and the drink introduced from India, where the five original ingredients were arrack, tea, lemon juice, sugar and water. As punch established itself in the West, rum became its normal principal alcoholic ingredient in the place of arrack.

In this connexion may be mentioned the derivation of grog (rum and water), namely from the cloak of grograin (a coarse fabric of silk, wool and mohair) habitually worn by Admiral Vernon ('Old Grog'), who ordered the mixture to be issued to his men in place of the neat spirit.

Source: H.C.L.

385. Cold West India Punch (Gwernvale Recipe)

12 lumps sugar
limes (failing which, lemons)
1 tablespoon guava jelly
tea

1 bottle (or according to the quantity required) of: rum, gin, claret, brandy, Port, Burgundy, whisky, Sherry

Rub the zest from the skins of limes (or lemons) with twelve lumps of cane sugar, until they turn greenish and hold the oils. Melt the sugar and 1 tablespoon guava jelly in boiling water, using as little water as possible. Put the resulting syrup in a large bowl, and add the spirits and wines in the order given. Stir in 2 tablespoons very strong cold tea. Serve cold.

Source: Mr. H. Pirie-Gordon, Polesacre, Lowfield Heath, Crawley, Sussex (formerly of Gwernvale, Crickhowell, South Wales).

N.B.: A bottle of each brew should be carefully corked and set aside to be poured into the next brew, which will be improved thereby.

386. Roman Punch

juice of 12 lemons
2½ Sherry glasses rum
2 liqueur glasses Curaçao
2 liqueur glasses Maraschino di Zara

1 quart champagne
2 pints cream
¾ lb. sugar
the whites of three eggs, beaten stiff

Place all the ingredients in an ice machine and freeze for 1 hour before dinner. Turn out, and serve immediately in deep claret glasses.

Makes 14 glasses.

Source: General Sir David and Lady Campbell, Sant Anton, Malta.

387. Hot Punch

    1 quart whisky
    1 quart rum
    1 quart Benedictine
    1 quart cherry brandy
    China tea
    bananas
    grapes
    apples
    oranges
    lemons
    cloves, nutmeg, cinnamon
    brown sugar

Cut up the fruit and place on fire in a pint of China tea freshly made with boiling water. Simmer for 2 hours with the spices and sugar. Then add the spirits and liqueurs.

    Source: Mr. F.H. Jarvis, R.N., Chief Steward to Admiral of the Fleet Sir John de Robeck, H.M.S. *Iron Duke*.

388. Bishop

'You take a bottle of that noble liquor (*sc.* Port) and put it in a saucepan, adding as much or as little water as you can reconcile to your taste and conscience, an orange cut in half (I believe some people squeeze it slightly), and plenty of cloves (you may stick them in the orange if you have a mind). Sugar or no sugar at discretion, and with regard to the character of the wine. Put it on the fire and, as soon as it is warm and begins to steam, light it. The flames will be of an imposingly infernal colour, quite different from the light blue flicker of spirits or of claret mulled. Before it has burned too long pour it into a bowl, and drink it as hot as you like.'

    Source: Professor George Saintsbury's *Notes on a Cellar-Book*.

389. Another Hot Brew for a Cold Christmas

    4 gallons red vin ordinaire
        (Bordeaux)
    2 bottles Port
    1 bottle brandy
    several shakes of Angostura bitters
    1 clove-studded lemon (whole)
    grated peel of 1 tangerine
    ground ginger, mace, nutmeg,
        cinnamon

Mix and heat, but do not at any stage allow to boil. Serve in tumblers. The above quantities should suffice for a Boxing Day morning party of from thirty to forty.

This composition, while generating a feeling of *bien-être* and even allaying an appetite for solid food, claims to be hangover-proof.

Source: Mr. Michael Luke.

390. Athol Brose

>1 bottle Scotch whisky
>¾ of a 1-lb. jar of liquid honey (not matured or opaque)
>12 oz. cream
>12 oz. oatmeal water

Pour all into whisky bottles, cork and shake gently before serving.
Source: Lady Burrows, British Embassy, Ankara.

391. A.1 Pick-me-up

>6 eggs   ½ pint good old rum
>6 lemons   ½ lb. rock sugar

Break the eggs, shells and all, into a jug, squeeze on to them the juice of the lemons. Cover with a cloth and allow to stand for 3 days, when the acid will have dissolved the shell.

Strain through muslin into a larger jug. Boil the rock sugar in the rum and a quart of water. Mix all together, and bottle.

Source: Mrs. Ernest Fisher (aged ninety-four), for whose grandmother Sir William Gull prescribed this stimulant.

392. 'Igloo Cocktail' (Hot Buttered Rum)

rum
2 teaspoons maple syrup
1 teaspoon butter
1 squeeze orange juice
1 pinch nutmeg

Warm a wineglass and fill with very hot rum and boiling water in the proportion of 2 to 1. Float the butter on the top, and add the maple syrup, orange juice and nutmeg.

To be taken in the winter after a day on the ice or snow.

Source: Miss Penny Chipman (Mrs. Maxwell-Fisher), Oka, Province of Quebec, Canada.

393. Some Seventeenth-century Dutch Liqueurs

Those whose interest in drinks embraces their historical aspect will be well advised to visit the venerable city of Amsterdam, justly called 'the Venice of the North'. When they have savoured the unusual, ship-like architecture and the superb cooking of the 'Five Flies' Restaurant, where Jan Janszoon Vijffvliegen was already plying his trade of innkeeper in 1627; when they have paused to sample a glass of mellow Schiedam at the even older (1614) bar of 'De Silveren Spiegel'; then let them end their day, if still full of enterprise, at the 'Rembrandt Tavern', which dates from 1642.

Here they may be offered the choice of the following liqueurs, whose intriguing names and composition date from the same century as the tavern that stocks them:

>Bride's Tears
>Consolation in Bitter Suffering
>Forget-me-not
>Half and Half
>Quarter to Five
>Eau de ma Tante
>Goldwater
>Silverwater

Damsel in Green
Midwife's Aniseed
Jack in the Cellar
Pull up your Shirt
The Longer the Better
Three Times Three
Rose without Thorns
Venus Oil
Perfect Happiness.

Source: H.C.L.

394. Spiced Ale

Heat without boiling 1 quart beer and 1 wineglass brandy, 1 tablespoon sugar, a pinch of ground clove, nutmeg and ginger.
Source: Sir John Leche.

395. A Good Soft Drink

1 tin pineapple juice	1 tablespoon sugar
the juice of 3 oranges	2 tablespoons passion fruit juice,
the juice of 3 lemons	if available

Add iced water at the last minute. Makes 1½-2 jugs.

396. A Good Coffee Blend

1 part Mocha	3 parts East Indian
2 parts Puerto Rico	

Source: Hon. E.R. Mifsud, C.M.G., Malta.

397. Turkish Coffee

Coffee, according to a Syrian legend of the early days of Islam, was first used as a beverage when the Sheikh of some Moslem confraternity, observing his goats becoming livelier after nibbling the berries of a certain tree in the neighbourhood, made a brew of the berries to keep the members of his brotherhood awake at their evening devotions. The word is derived from the Arabic *qahweh*, which in its turn comes, according to the Ethiopians, from the name of their Province of Kaffa, where the *Coffea arabica* grows abundantly.

The Arabs, especially the Beduin of the Arabian peninsula and the Syrian desert, like their coffee thin, bitter and powerfully flavoured with cardamom; the Turks prefer theirs unadulterated, thick and sweet. Turkish coffee, said some Frenchman - it could have been Talleyrand - should be

> 'Chaud comme l'enfer,
> Noir comme le diable,
> Pur comme un ange,
> Doux comme l'amour.'

The process of attaining these objectives is as follows: Turkish coffee is made in and served from a long-handled brass pot, tapering towards the top so that the coffee may boil up quickly and form the requisite heavy froth.

Put into the pot 2 teaspoons powdered coffee and 1 Turkish coffee-cupful cold water for each person to be served. Bring to the boil, then remove from the fire to allow the froth to subside. Do this twice; and serve when brought to the boil for the third time.

Only a little coffee should be poured into each cup at a time, to ensure the froth and the sediment being evenly distributed.

In the Near East the guest is asked before his coffee is made which of three grades of sweetness he prefers, as the sugar has to be added to the coffee *before* boiling.

So much for the *mécanique*. The *flavour* will depend upon how you have blended your coffee and on how freshly you have roasted and how finely you have powdered your beans. For while for French coffee the beans are ground, for Turkish coffee they must be pounded to a fine powder.

Source: H.C.L.

398. On Café au Lait and the Croissant

The Turks make their coffee in the manner that has been described; the Austrian Court in the seventeenth century breakfasted on hot milk. In 1683 Vienna, the Imperial city, was besieged by the Grand Vizier Kara Mustafa, defended by Prince Starhemberg and relieved by John Sobieski with the support of the Duke of Lorraine. The vast camp of the invader, bursting with supplies, fell into the hands of the defenders and the citizens of Vienna, and the booty included countless sacks of coffee.

Soon the city's inns had learned how to roast and brew the fragrant bean and the Archdukes how to add a little of the strange infusion to their hot breakfast milk. So originated the 'Princes' Coffee' which was the precursor of café au lait.

And coffee may be mixed not only with milk. It is worth while to note that the addition of a teaspoon or so of cocoa powder to the coffee-pot produces the same piquantly fragrant effect as does the converse, namely the addition of a suggestion of coffee to 'bitter' chocolate.

Reference may appropriately be made here to the involuntary Turkish inspiration of the crescent-shaped *Kipfel* (the French *croissant*), first made by a Viennese baker during the Siege. This man was granted a monopoly for his *Kipfel* as a reward for having warned the defending garrison that the Turks were driving a mine under the fortifications. He had heard the tapping of their sappers while working late one night in his bakery by the city wall, and thereafter shaped his light and dainty breakfast rolls from the Turkish national emblem of the crescent moon.

Source: The same.

399. On How Coffee Came to England

Into England, however, coffee was introduced not via Vienna but direct from the Levant. In the reign of George I the English Consul in Smyrna was a certain Edwards, married to a Greek lady of the well-known Mavrocordato family of Chios. On his retirement to

England Mr. Edwards brought with him his servant 'Pasqua Rossi' (?Paschales Roussos), a Smyrniote Greek, whose coffee as he made it for his employers was so popular among their friends that the demand for it became somewhat of a burden on the Edwards household. Mr. Edwards thereupon allowed 'Rossi' to set up a public coffee-house in S. Michael's Alley, Cornhill, bearing a sign with his portrait and the inscription: 'The first who made and publicly sold coffee drink in England.'

Source: H.C.L. owes these details to his former colleague Mr. Hugh Paget, O.B.E., British Council Representative in Mexico, a direct descendant of Richard Kemble, English Consul in Salonika in 1718, who married a sister of Mrs. Edwards. They are printed in *The Kemble Papers* (2 vols., New York Historical Society, 1883-84), which deal mainly with the military career of Richard's grandson Colonel Stephen Kemble, Adjutant-General of the British Forces in North America.

400. Café Brulôt

Soak the peel of a fresh orange in rum (or brandy) with cinnamon, cloves, allspice and sugar to taste. After the peel, spices and sugar have been well steeped in the spirit warm this and set it alight.

Then add the *hot* black coffee, let it simmer a little and serve.

Source: Mrs. Rex Cheverton, Guatemala.

N.B.: In South America and the Caribbean you may sometimes encounter that tasty and stimulating blend, a cup of hot chocolate laced with cinnamon.

CONCLUDING CHAPTER: DON'TS

What I have to say as regards DON'TS is really a commentary on the menus of the type of dinner where, in the words of Disraeli, 'everything is cold except the ice'. Or of that dinner which one of the guests, when asked how he had fared, described as follows: 'If the soup had been as hot as the claret, the claret as old as the bird, and the bird had had the breast of the parlour-maid, it would have been a damned good dinner.'

Clear Soup

This is generally tepid (whether intended to be hot or iced), the colour of pale Sherry, the consistency and flavour of light-brown water. Clear soup can be delicious, but it requires much labour and many ingredients to achieve this result, as witness the State Bouillon of the Habsburgs. Except on occasions when you can provide the necessary labour and ingredients, stick to thick soups, in which some sort of flavour can more easily be achieved. And serve them *hot*.

Steamed Fillet of Fish - White Sauce

Don't fillet dinner fish, as filleting dissipates flavour. Smaller fish should, unless the size of the party makes this inconvenient, be served on the bone. Larger fish should be cooked whole. *Never* produce White Sauce, at least of the seaside boarding-house type. Retain, in the appropriate cases, the skin on the fish and serve boiled fish with Hollandaise or a good Béchamel sauce or melted black butter.

Breast, or Wing, of Chicken

In the 'Disraeli' type dinner above, often only the white meat is served. A bad habit of which some hostesses are unreasonably proud is 'wings only', the most tasteless part of the fowl. One can only hope the justification for this to be that the hosts want to eat the thighs and drumsticks devilled for breakfast the next morning.

At this sort of dinner the birds may even be skinned before being cooked, which not only has no conceivable advantage but lets out all the flavours. And even if they are suffered to retain their skins in the pot or oven, it is sometimes considered more genteel to peel them before serving. In effect, this practice, far from being more genteel, makes the birds look naked and ashamed. It is legitimate - in fact correct - to skin for a Chaudfroid, but not otherwise.

In birds, as in many kinds of fish, much of the flavour resides in the skin. You would require, no doubt, to skin an ostrich or an 800-lb. tunny; but it is scarcely necessary to legislate for cases such as these.

At these dinners I have often known tinned peas (dyed an arsenical green and as hard to assimilate as bullets) to be served when fresh marrowfats were on the market; and it goes without saying that the French beans are chopped up before being boiled (thereby losing most of their flavour) instead of being cooked and served entire, browned in butter in the frying-pan after boiling.

Don't chop up, or skin, French beans unless they are really old, but confine yourself to stringing.

Don't chop up good, hearted cabbage, but quarter, or prepare with the leaves separated.

Don't, consequently, serve cabbage in compressed squares or lozenges.

Don't cut lettuce leaves into narrow strips.

Don't dice carrots. These should, size permitting, be cooked whole, or if sliced (but never diced), be fried in butter.

Don't throw away the pods of your green peas or the shells and remnants of lobster and crayfish. Sieve or pound them and use for Pea Soup and Bisque respectively. Or serve peas and their pods together, since the pods of young peas are delicious and tender.

Don't imagine, because you may read American thrillers in which the detectives say 'Uh-huh' and talk incessantly about Vichyssoise, that this is the only French soup. It is more popular in New York restaurants than it is in France.

Don't go through life under the delusion that the flavour of a chicken or similar bird resides in the wing. On the contrary, this is, as has been said, the least flavoured joint. The most highly flavoured, as the French so rightly recognize, is what they call the *cuisse*, the thigh.

Don't put meat for Hamburg steaks into a mincing machine, but chop it with a knife.

Don't put potatoes through the rice-machine.

Don't forget that potatoes must be peeled - not cut; and be boiled before, not after, peeling. This seems obvious, but obviously it needs saying.

Don't perpetrate false quantities in the word paprika by mispronouning it paprika with the accent wrongly placed on the second syllable.

Don't in hotels, if you can avoid it, tolerate prefabricated breakfast, cooked hours before they are destined to be consumed.

Don't waste good food and wine on those so ignorant of the art of living that they smoke between, and even during, courses.

Don't, therefore, encourage such barbarians by allowing cigarettes and ash-trays on the dinner-table.

But

Do add sugar when cooking peas, tomatoes, carrots and when preparing the soups and salads made of these. Also add a pinch of sugar to green salads and more than a pinch to mint sauce.

Do baste roast meats and birds.

Do be herb- and spice-minded.

Do prefer peppercorns freshly ground in a pepper-mill to pre-ground pepper, and rock-salt to prepared 'table-salts'.

The same principle applies, *mutatis mutandis*, to coffee.

And *do* remember that the Lord intended wine to be drunk *with* our food. How uncivilized is the practice of filling up with hard liquor for an hour or two before dinner, only to sit down to table facing, as regards liquids, a forbidding tumbler of water ready filled to the brim.

APPENDIX

A NOTE ON SAINT ZITA
Patron of Cooks and other Domestic Workers

The future Saint Zita was born in 1218 in the Tuscan village of Monte Segrati, eight miles from the city of Lucca (source of the best olive oil), whither at the age of twelve she was sent to work in the house of a prosperous weaver, one Pagano di Fatinelli. Coming of a pious family - her uncle was a hermit with a reputation of holiness, her sister became a nun - and herself deeply devout from childhood, she now heard Mass daily in San Frediano, even then old among the churches of Lucca and today second only to the Duomo in beauty and interest. She also formed the habit of giving to the poor the good food provided by her employer, keeping but the barest necessities for herself.

One year there was famine in the land, and Zita, having nothing more of her own to give away, made inroads for this purpose on her master's store of beans. Then came the day when Messer Pagano, who was a hot-tempered man, made inspection of his supply, for he was minded to sell his beans at a good profit. Zita, terrified that her depredations (for all that they had been made in the cause of charity) would come to light, prayed earnestly for help, and her prayer was answered: no loss was found, for the stock had been divinely replenished.

On another occasion, having forgotten that it was baking day, she unduly protracted her devotions at San Frediano, then hurried home expecting to find the loaves burnt to cinders. What she found was a new row of loaves all ready laid out for the oven. Indeed, it is the tradition in Lucca to this day that angels took charge of the baking of her bread and cakes and the cooking of her meat whenever she was absent in church.

She died in 1278, having served the same family for forty-eight years, and is buried in her beloved San Frediano. Her feast is kept on the 27th April.

INDEX

A   Recipes and Ingredients
B   Places of Origins

A

RECIPES AND INGREDIENTS

Ajo Blanco, 85
Albondigas, 54
Ale, spiced, 238
Alligator, dried and salted, 2
Allspice (*cf. pimento*), 160
Apfel-Kren, 200
Apricot, 201-202
Apricot Brandy, 226
Aspic, 100, 104, 188, 189
Athol Brose, 236
Aubergine, 160
Avocado Pear, 38, 39

Bacalao, 100
Bananas, cooked and otherwise, 200
Baqlawa, 14, 19
Barrosa Cup, 232
Bears' hams, 15
    paws, 2
    steak, 31
Beccaficos, 101, 122
Beef, boiled, 30
    cured, 128
    spiced, 129
    steak, 3, 10, 137-139
Bee's Toast, 43
Bobotie, 50
Brain, calves', 136, 181
    squirrel's, 12
Brawn, 25, 131, 132
Breakfast dishes, 20-21

Calamondin, marmalade, 211-212
Camel's hump, 32
Cantaloupe, melon, 11, 38
Caraway seed, 25, 40, 95, 197
Cardamon, 72, 184, 195

Carving of birds and fish, technical terms in, 114
Cassava, Cassareep, 132, 133
Cheese, forms of eating, 61-64, 223
    Quiches, 56
    soufflé, 47
    wafers, 60
    Welsh Rarebit, 61
    with eggs and tomatoes, 45
    and see under Soups
Chestnuts and Chestnut Sweets, 113
Chicken dishes, 108-111
    livers, *see under* Livers
Chinese and Manchu *cuisine*, 2, 68
Chives, 30, 187
Chocolate and chocolate dishes, 30, 220-221, 240, 241
Chutneys, 184-185, 195
Cinnamon, 72, 241
Cocktails:
    Alexander, 228
    'Bloody Mary', 230
    'Christopher's Mother', 229
    Clover Cup, 227
    Corson's, 227
    Gin, 227
    Grapefruit, 227
    'Igloo' (Hot Buttered Rum), 237
    Iquique, 228
    Mosul Mist, 228
    Pineapple, 228
    Tomato, 230
    Wine, 231
Coffee, Brûlot, Turkish, etc. 238-241
    Sweets, 214-215, 221
Commandería Wine, 122
Coriander, 51, 135, 184, 196

249

Costillas, 127
Cream Puffs, 219
    Spanish, 218
Crème Brulée, 218
Croissants (Kipfel), 240
Currant, Black and Red, Water Ice, 222
Curry, 38-39, 43, 59, 96, 184
Cyclamen Leaves, 51

Dill, 72, 150, 170, 194, 195-196
Dolma, 51
Doughnuts, Danish, 217
    Turkish, 28
Duck, 2, 75, 112
Dumplings, apricot and plum, 201

Eggs, 40-42, 43-45, 59
    and see under Omelettes, Soufflés

Fennel, 75, 77, 81, 195-196
Figs, 11, 38
Fish, Shell-fish, etc.:
    Bacalhao (dried cod) pudding, 105
    Bêche-de-mer, 12, 68
    Caviare, 15-17, 98
    Char, 103-104
    Crab, 96
    Crayfish, 88, 93, 95
    Dentice (gilt-head), 100
    Dolphin, 23
    Dublin Bay prawns, 23, 94
    Lobster, Langouste, *Langostina*, 4, 88-93, 94, 95
    Lote (burbot, eel-pout), 99
    Mbalolo, 12
    Mussels, 99
    Prawns, 38, 95-96
        and see under Soups
    Fish Pudin, 58
    Raw Fish, 105-106
    Salmon, Salmon-trout, 15, 98, 101
    Sardines, fresh and tinned, 43, 59, 101
    Scallops, 97
    Scampi, 23, 94
    Sea-bream, 100
    Smelts and *Pejerreyes*, 23, 101
    Smoked fish *au Gratin*, 105
    Sole, 102
    Trout, 103-104
    Turbot, 102

Fleischkuchen, 126
Foie gras, 23, 57, 167
Fondue Bourguignonne, 137
Francolin, 32
Frangipane tartlets, 217
Fruit cake, 216

Gammon, 72, 127
Gardenia petals, 51
Garlic, 196
Gazpachuelo, 73
Gazpacho Andaluz, 84
Goose, domestic and wild, 5, 114-115, 123
    liver, *see under* Liver
Gosling, green, 23, 115
Grapefruit and chestnuts, 208
Grouse, 23, 124
Guavas, 203-204, 208, 234
Guinea-pig, 111
Gubbeen Cheese, 223
Guinea-pig, 111

Haggis, 134
Ham, baked, curing of, raw, souffle, etc., 38, 45, 56, 72, 130-131, 144, 156
Hare, 71, 74, 123, 125, 149
Herbs and Spices, 190, 195, 197
Horseradish, 103, 105, 115, 128, 138, 145, 193, 195, 200
    and see under Sauces

Iguana, 1
'Indians', 213

Jelly, *see under* Aspic, Guava, Medlar, Salad, Stawberry-Grape

Kebabs, 28
Kidneys, 70, 71, 136
Kipfel (Croissant), 240
Kumquat, 211-212

Lamb Chops, Stuffed, 139
Liqueurs, 17th-century Dutch, 237
Liver, calf, 70, 137
    chicken, 41, 43, 48, 57, 59, 60, 71, 136
    goose, 23, 57, 116
    sausage, 135

Macaroni and Spaghetti, 55, 73
Mace, 72, 178, 195, 235
Madeira, 23, 231
Marrow-bones and fat, 48, 59
Mart, 3
Medlars, 208-209
Meringue Cake, 215
Mint, 85, 195
Moussaká, 46
Mulberries, 211
Muskrat, 31

Nockerln, 56
Nutmeg, 71, 156, 195

Oats, rolled, 222
'Old-Fashioned', 232
Omelettes, savoury, 40
    sweet, 203
Orange and plum roll, 212
    blood, 173
    brandy, 226
    compôte, 206, 211
    peel, 241
Ortolan, 3, 122
Ox-tail, 132-133

Paella, 49
Palm, heart of, 93
Pancakes, savoury, 165
    sweet, 202
Partridge, 5, 15, 121, 124
Peaches Flambés, 201
Peacock and peahen, roast, 113
Pepper Pot, 132
Persimmons, 209
Pheasant, 5, 15, 124, 125
Pilav, 49, 96
Pimiento, 160, 161
Pineapple cake, 213
    drinks, 228, 238
Pisco sour, 229
Pomegranate juice, 112
Pork pâté, 125
    spareribs of, 133
Pudding, Ginger and Fig, 212
Pumpernickel, 63
Pumpkin-seed, 193
Purée de Fruits au Fromage Rose, 219
Punch, cold and hot, 233-234

Quenelles, 69
Quiches Lorraine, 56

Rattle-snakes, 2
Rice (including Bobotie, Dolma, *Duveć*, Fezanjan, Paella, Pilav, Risotto), 3, 48-51, 94, 109, 112, 160
    wild, 31-32, 115
Rijstafel, 184
Risotto, 48, 90
Rosemary, dried, 72, 103, 146
Rum drinks, cold and hot, 229, 237, 241
    and see under Punches

Sachertorte, 30
Saffron, 48, 49, 66, 184, 195
Salad dressings, 190-191
Salads:
    Beetroot, 193
    Chicken and Rice, 109
    Chicory, 192
    Cucumber (including pickles), 193, 194
    Jellied, 189
    Jerusalem Artichoke, 192
    Tabuli, 193
    Trinity (College, Oxford), 192
Saltsticks, 40, 197-198
Sangaree, 231
Sauces:
    Accident, 177
    Anchovy, 188
    Béarnaise, 10, 45, 147, 177-178, 192
    Béchamel, 172
    Black Butter, 181
    Bruxelloise, 101, 182
    Chaudfroid, 181
    Chive, 30, 187-188
    Cumberland, 183
    Curry, 184
    Demi-glace, 180
    Espagnole, 179
    Green, 100
    Hollandaise, 172
    Horseradish, 184
    Madère, 182
    Maître d'Hôtel Butter, 181
    Maltaise, 173
    Marinade, 185
    Mayonnaise, 61, 100, 173-175
    Mousseline, 172
    Périgourdine, 11

Prince Lieven, 182
Remoulade, 100, 176
Romano, 177
Salsetta Verde, 188
Sorrel, 179
Sour Cream, 123
Tarragon (*and see under* Béarnaise), 180
Tartare (without capers), 176
Tomato (for bottling), 178
Vinaigrette, 186
Wine, 183
Worcestershire, 24, 119, 130, 209, 230
Sausages, 135
Schinkenfleckerln, 56
Sesame oil, 17, 111
Sheep's head, 131
'Small chop', West African, 39
Soufflés, 131, 147, 207
Soups:
    Ajo Blanco, 85
    Artichoke, 72
    Beef and Liver Bouillon, 70
    Birds' Nest, 68
    Bisque, 24, 67, 90
    Bonne Femme, 78
    Bortsh, Barscz, 75-76, 77
    Cabbage, 76-77
    Cheese Cream, 73
    Chicken Liver, 71
    Consommé, 69
    Creole (Okra), 83
    Dieting, 75
    Dorich, 72
    Dormers, 80
    Gazpacho, 84
    Germiny, 82
    Groundnut, 83
    Hare, 71
    Iced, 70, 84-85
    Jugo Doble, 71
    Kangaroo, 12
    Kidney, 71
    Madrilène, 70
    Onion, 78-79
    Pea-pod, 82
    Petite Marmite, 10, 74
    Pot-au-Feu, 74
    Prawns, Bisque of, 67
        Cream of, 66

Sharks' Fin, 2
Sorrel, 78, 81-82
Spinach, 82
Springfield, 80
Stock, 69
Toheroa, 12
Tomato and Egg, 83
Turtle, 69
Squirrel's brains, 12
Strawberry-grapes, 210
Sucking-pigs' tails, 94
Suzette, Crêpes, 202
Swans and Cygnets, 113-114, 120

Tarragon, 40, 78, 147, 177-178, 195
Tea-cake, 216
Tongue, duck's, 2
    ox-, 15, 21, 128, 131
    reindeer, 21
Turkey, 19, 20, 116
Turtle, *see under* Soups

Veal, 137
Vegetables:
    Artichokes, globe, 19-20, 41, 93-94, 146-147
        Jerusalem, 72, 146, 192
        wild, 146
    Asparagus, 28, 147, 182
    Avocado Pears, 38
    Beans, baked, 94
        broad, 148
        French, 24, 148
    Beetroot, 149, 197
        and see under Bortsh, *etc., and* Salads
    Brussels Sprouts, 149
    Cabbage, green, red, white, 150-154
        and see under Soups
    Calabrese, 150
    Carrots, 128-129, 148, 154
    Celeriac, 154-155
    Chicory (Endive), 156-158
    Cucumber, hot with Dill, 170
        in soup, 78
    Egg-plants (*Aubergines*), 28, 46, 51, 147-148
    Endive, *see under* Chicory
    Kohlrabi, 154, 155
    Leeks, 158-159
    Lettuce, 159-160

Mallow, wild, 163
Marrows, Vegetable, 19, 147, 168, 169
Mushrooms, 4, 11, 15, 159
Peas with Lettuce, 159, 160
Peppers, hot red, 10-11, 111
    sweet *(pimientos)*, 108, 160-162
Potatoes, 42, 142-145
Ratatuka, see under Egg-plants
Salsify, 162
Satras, see under Peppers, Sweet
Scorzonera, 162
Seakale, 163
Sorrel, 163, 165
    and see under Soups, Sauces
Spinach, 163-164, 165
    and see under Soups
Sweet Corn, 44, 96, 166
    and see under Soups

Tanya Fritters, 166
Tomato, jelly and ice, 167
    with eggs and cheese, 45
    and see under Soups, Sauces, Drinks
Truffles, 17, 93, 167
Venison, 149, 126
Vine leaves, 51, 194
Vodka, 15, 98, 227, 228, 230

Watermelon, pickled, 194
Welsh Rarebit a la Green Jacket, 61
Wild Boar, 126

Yalanji Dolma, 51
Yoghurt, 204

Zabaglione, 204, 205
Zakuski, 15

B
PLACES OF ORIGIN

Aleppo, 19-20, 168, 197
Amsterdam, 237
Andalusia, 44, 73, 84, 85, 109-110, 121, 127, 161
Ardennes, 144, 156
Armenia, 15, 98
Athos, Mount, 16-17
Austria (*and see under* Vienna), 4-5, 29-30, 40, 45, 56, 69, 135, 137, 145, 147, 151, 155, 160, 187, 188, 193, 197, 200, 201, 212, 240
Auvergne, 136
Aztec Empire, 38, 117

Baku, 3, 98
Baltic States, 182
Basque Provinces, 162
Bavaria, 6-8
Bazaars (*suqs*), oriental, 197
Belgium (*and see under* Ardennes)
Bohemia, 95
Bolivia, 70, 111
Borneo, 68
British Guiana, 132, 177, 229
British Honduras, 94
Brittany, 89
Buenos Aires, 3, 11
Burgundy, 137

Cambridge, 22, 218
Canada, 237
Caspian Sea, 98
Chile, 71, 175
China, 2, 68, 163
Circassia, 108
Colombia, 57
Congo, 27
Cyprus, 32, 46, 51, 122, 135, 146, 163, 176, 220
Dalmatia, 26-27, 88, 94, 160
Denmark, 66, 217
Dominican Republic, 114

Ecuador, 2, 10-11
England, 20-25, 29, 43, 58-59, 61, 80, 104, 110, 114, 119, 124, 125, 126-129, 131, 132, 138, 154, 162, 163, 174, 178, 183-184, 186, 187, 189, 192, 208, 210, 212, 214, 217, 218, 220, 221-222, 229, 232, 235, 236, 238
Ethiopia, 111-112, 115, 118, 195
Eton, 55, 200

Fiji, 2, 11, 12, 69, 105
France (*and see under* Auvergne, Brittany, Burgundy, La Vendée, Marseilles, Paris, Picardy, Provence), 6-7, 9-10, 29, 40, 74, 78, 81, 82, 92, 93, 95, 99, 102, 113-114, 121, 137-138, 148, 157, 158-159, 164, 167, 173, 182, 190, 202

Georgia (Transcaucasia), 15-16, 154, 159, 231
Germany (*and see under* Bavaria), 29-30, 126, 139, 175, 230
Granada, 44
Guatemala, 2, 150-151, 241

Haiti, 213
Hawaii, 25
Hungary, 168, 220

Inca Empire, 118
India, 119
Indonesia, 184
Iran, 98, 112
Iraq (*and see under* Mosul, Yezidis), 108, 228
Ireland, 119, 191, 223
Italy, 29, 38, 48, 158, 167, 169, 188, 204, 205, 206, 247

Jamaica, 27, 150
Juan Fernandez, 88, 175

Konya, 18-19

255

Lapland, 21
Lofoten Islands, 21
Lorraine, 56

Madrid, 58
Malta, 14, 32, 55, 90, 100, 173
Man, Isle of, 97
Marseilles, 66
Mexico (*and see under* Aztec Empire), 38
Monaco, 75
Mosul, 17, 228

New Caledonia, 12, 186
New Zealand, 12, 104, 193
Norway, 21, 59, 152-153

Oxford, Trinity College, 21-22, 192

Pacific, the *(and see under* Fiji, New Caledonia, Samoa), 12, 32
Paris, 6-7, 10
Patagonia, 3
Persian Gulf (*and see under* Qatar), 102
Peru, 116, 228, 229
Picardy, 158
Poland, 76, 77, 81, 123, 149, 152
Portugal, 27, 105, 117, 148
Provence, 147

Qatar Peninsula, 168
Quito, 10-11

Russia, 16-17, 75-76, 77, 98

St. Kitts, 80
St. Lucia, 93
Samoa, 106, 173

Scotland, 20, 236
Sicily, 102
South Africa, 50
South America (*and see under* Bolivia, Brazil, British Guiana, Buenos Aires, Chile, Colombia, Ecuador, Inca Empire, Patagonia, Peru), 38, 101, 241
Spain (*and see under* Andalusia), 27, 38, 49, 95, 116, 121, 179
Sweden, 31, 114, 115
Switzerland, 42, 47, 137
Syria (*and see under* Aleppo), 13, 17-18, 193

Tobago, 45
Trinidad, 112, 174
Turkey, 13-14, 17, 19-20, 28, 49, 51, 98, 116-117, 239-240

U.S.A., 3-4, 12, 31, 52, 53, 79, 88, 90, 91, 93, 113, 139, 189, 207, 213, 215-216

Valencia, 49-50
Vendée, 125
Venice, 38, 200
Vienna, 5, 30, 201, 240
Voisin's Restaurant, Paris, 10

West Africa, 3, 83, 185
West Indies (*and see under* Barbados, British Guiana, British Honduras, Haiti, Jamaica, St. Kitts, St. Lucia, Tobago, Trinidad), 83, 234, 241

Yezidis (Devil-Worshippers) of Kurdistan, 18-19
Yugoslavia (*and see under* Dalmatia), 162